Competition
and Cooperation
in the Management
Theory
and Practice

Competition and Cooperation in the Management Theory and Practice

Edited by **Piotr Jedynak**

Jagiellonian University Press

REVIEWER
prof. dr hab. Janusz Teczke

COVER DESIGN
Pracownia Register

GRAPHICS ON THE COVER
ArtGraph/Fotolia

This publication was financed by the Faculty of Management and Social Communication of the Jagiellonian University and the Institute of Economics and Management of the Jagiellonian University

ISBN 978-83-233-3686-0

www.wuj.pl

Jagiellonian University Press
Office: ul. Michałowskiego 9/2, 31-126 Kraków
Phone: +48 12-663-23-80, Fax: +48 12-663-23-83
Distribution: Phone: +48 12-631-01-97, Fax: +48 12-631-01-98
Cell Phone: +48 506-006-674, e-mail: sprzedaz@wuj.pl
Bank: PEKAO SA, IBAN PL 80 1240 4722 1111 0000 4856 3325

TABLE OF CONTENTS

INTRODUCTION

Contemporary organizations (including in particular companies) in order to maintain market competitiveness have to take numerous actions which can be assigned to two categories: 1) competing and 2) cooperating. Parallel competition and cooperation can be regarded as an element of current paradigm in management sciences.

The present publication includes an analysis of selected activities of organizations oriented towards competition or cooperation.

The work starts with a paper on analysis of connections between implementation of CSR practices and competitiveness of an organization on the B2B market. The text illustrates CSR practices as a tool for managing relations between organizations and their suppliers. It also contains an exemplification of applying CSR practices by Arcelor Mittal in its relations with suppliers.

The next paper continues the theme of CSR. In this case, the focus is on the description of actions implemented in this area by companies of Polish energy sector. The text exposes the specifics of CSR in this sector with special regard to the stakeholders of energy enterprises.

The third text completes the preceding one discussed above. This time, description covers consumer opinions concerning CSR practices applied by companies of the energy sector. The authors verified the efficiency of these practices from the perspective of their social reception and provided utilitarian conclusions which allow to improve the mentioned practices in the future.

The fourth writing focuses on the subject of applying kaizen as a tool for improving competitiveness of suppliers. The text comprises both deliberations on the present status of kaizen in literature and an overview of current kaizen research streams with a case study of implementing kaizen as a tool for improving competitiveness of supplier in relation with recipient. Therefore, the paper presents a new application of the well-known management tool.

The fifth text deliberates on competitive and cooperative activities of companies online. On the basis of intentionally selected group of scientific articles the authors have indicated the leading research problems in the above stated field undertaken by Polish researchers.

The subsequent text defines brand and its competitiveness. Brand is here regarded as a tool for shaping company value, while its competitiveness is considered as a fundamental determinant of company competitiveness. The writing includes results of empirical studies of competitiveness of selected Polish jewellery brands.

The importance of packaging of confectionery products has been analysed in the seventh text. The role and the function of the packaging have been shown from the point of view of selected marketing concepts. Furthermore, results of research on Polish students' preferences of packaging used in chocolate production have been presented. Findings thus obtained may serve as feedback for managements of companies – chocolate producers.

The eighth text is dedicated to the very interesting issue of restructuring of organizations at risk of bankruptcy. From among the analyzed restructuring activities those of cooperational attitude towards stakeholders have been exposed. Consequentially, restructuring carried out in a crisis situation appears as a key factor of potential countermeasure of enterprise liquidation and creates a prospect for future consideration of its competitiveness.

The following text, the ninth, opens a collection dedicated to human factor in organization. It comprises reflection on competition and cooperation from the perspective of behavioural stream of management sciences. Discussion tackles among others mechanisms of competition and cooperation, relation between these two phenomena, organizational contexts and conditions for co-existence of competition and cooperation.

The tenth text introduces analysis of mutual dependencies between competition-oriented profile of an organizational culture and creating along with development of workaholism. In this article workaholism is regarded as pathology with numerous negative consequences, both organizational and individual. Yet, organizational culture oriented towards competition seems to favour the phenomenon of workaholism.

The eleventh text deals with the subject of presence and importance of competition and cooperation as individual and organizational elements of value systems. The article includes diagnosis of "stratification" of the indicated value systems which is based on studies of selected managers. Moreover, this part comprises also deliberations on relations between competition and cooperation in these systems.

Finally, the last, twelfth, text focuses on the absorbing phenomenon of glass ceilings which is presented as a significant competitiveness barrier for women in workplace. Empirical studies carried out in academic environment have supported this depressing thesis that unluckily women in their careers face glass ceiling which significantly impedes their promotion at universities.

The above short introduction to the content of individual parts of the book indicates that the subject of competitiveness and cooperation in present day management creates a very abundant and versatile space both from the perspective of real life and the subject along with methodology of scientific understanding.

Piotr Jedynak

Kraków 2013

PIOTR JEDYNAK
Jagiellonian University
Institute of Economics and Management
Chair of Standardized Management Systems

CSR PRACTICES AND COMPETETIVENESS OF THE COMPANY IN B2B MARKET

INTRODUCTION

Corporate Social Responsibility (CSR) is currently one of the key research areas of management. The status of CSR is proven not only by the impressive number of scientific publications in prestigious literature and magazines but also by general interest demonstrated by companies of various sizes. In the present paper the question of CSR is regarded in terms of possibilities of utilizing CSR practices in shaping relations between companies with status of client and supplier on the B2B market.

Among the fundamental goals of the paper the following ones can be distinguished:
- review of leading present theoretical stands regarding the stakeholder theory,
- identification of relations between the stakeholder theory and CSR,
- identification of relations between macro-level and micro-level of creating and undertaking CSR initiatives,
- review of the CSR standards,
- specification of possibilities of using CSR practices and tools in shaping company relations on the B2B market,
- exemplification of the CSR practices and tools in shaping relations between global smelting company (ArcelorMittal) and its suppliers including formulating requirements and adaptation practices.

1. MAIN ASPECTS OF STAKEHOLDERS THEORY

In opposition to an exclusive focus on a firm's stockholders, stakeholder theory makes serving the interests of those groups and individuals identified as "stakeholders" the primary purpose of an organization [Kaler 2003; Phillips 2003; Reed 1999]. Based on the assumption that all stakeholders have more or less legitimate interests in an organization, stakeholder theory is concerned with the nature of these relationships in terms of both processes and outcomes [Jones and Wicks 1999].

In the Donaldson and Preston's [1995] approach there are three key aspects of stakeholders theory: descriptive, normative and instrumental. Table 1 summarizes the main concern of these aspects.

Table 1. Main aspects of stakeholders theory

Aspect	Descriptive stakeholder theory	Instrumental stakeholder theory	Normative stakeholder theory
Concern	How do organizations take stakeholders interests into account?	Is it beneficial for organizations to take stakeholder interests into account?	By referring to different moral points of view, why should organizations take stakeholder interests into account?

Source: own elaboration.

The descriptive aspect of stakeholder theory explains how organizations actually take into account stakeholder interests. Accordingly, stakeholder theory is used to "describe, and sometimes to explain, specific corporate characteristics and behaviors" [Donaldson and Preston 1995, p. 70].

Another important stream of stakeholder theory tries to find out whether it is beneficial for an organization to engage with its stakeholders [Donaldson and Preston 1995, p. 71]. The goal is to identify connections, or a lack of connections, between the existence of stakeholder management and the achievement of corporate performance objectives.

Normative stakeholder theory discusses why organizations should take into account stakeholder interests [Donaldson and Preston 1995, p. 71]. This stream of stakeholder theory attempts to reach beyond instrumental arguments that base the question of "Why consider stakeholders?" on an exclusive discussion of performance. Normative stakeholder theory interprets the function of the corporation by referring to certain "moral guidelines."

2. STAKEHOLDER THEORY AND CSR INITIATIVES

In recent business ethics research Corporate Social Responsibility (CSR) has become one of the most prominent topics in business ethics discussion. Sukserm and Takahashi [2010] said that the most popular areas of CSR activities are: economy, society and environment.

There are three key perspectives of CSR interpretation [Aslander 2011]:

- *CSR as management requirement.* This perspective focuses on management procedures and governance structures; defines minimum ethical requirements and standards of behavior.
- *CSR as subsidiary co-responsibility.* This perspective describes subsidiary, non-voluntary responsibilities of corporations; corporations are defined as intermediate actors bearing specific duties in society.
- *CSR as voluntary contribution.* This perspective refers to the occasional philanthropic engagement of corporations; corporations voluntarily provide additional or alternative services.

Connections between stakeholders theory and CSR perspective are demonstrated in Figure 1.

Figure 1. CSR practices as a result of stakeholder theory and CSR perspective
Source: own elaboration.

Result of practical implementation of instrumental approach to stakeholder theory and CSR as management requirements is the building process of CSR practices, initiatives and standards.

3. MACRO- AND MICRO-LEVEL OF CSR INITIATIVES

CSR Initiatives are initiated on two levels [Gilbert and Rasche 2008]. As Donaldson and Preston [1995, p. 254] said:

> The macro-level contract is a normative and hypothetical contract among economic participants which defines the normative ground rules for creating the second kind of contract. The second is a micro-level contract that can occur among members of specific communities, including firms, departments within forms, national economic organizations and so on.

Connections between these levels are showed in Figure 2.

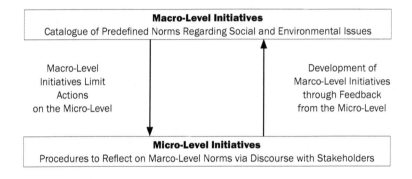

Figure 2. A framework to analyze standardized CSR initiatives
Source: adopted and modified from Gilbert and Rasche 2008.

The most widely used CSR initiatives were UN Global Compact, SA 8000, The Global Reporting Initiative and the Fair Labor Association.

On the macro-level:
- UN Global Compact defines ten principles on human rights, labor, the environment and corruption,
- SA 8000 defines eight central guidelines to audit ethical workplace conditions (e.g. child labor, forced labor, wages and health and safety),
- the Global Reporting Initiative provides predefined indicators in six central categories (e.g. environment and product responsibility),
- the Fair Labor Association defines nine key principles (e.g. on wages and benefits, hours of work, harassment and abuse, and non-discrimination).

On the micro-level the implementation of macro-level initiatives may relatively focus on:

- development of local level networks between participating firms and other stakeholders,
- implementation of a management system including procedures for stakeholder dialog,
- requirement of stakeholder dialog to identify relevant indicators from the overall list,
- development of relations with local labor, human rights, and religious organizations.

4. CSR STANDARDS

There are many CSR standards. Koerber [2010] classified corporate responsibility standards in three categories:
- *normative frameworks*, which provide guidance on acceptable performance and goals,
- *process guidelines*, which provide guidance on measurement, communication and assurance,
- *management systems*, which provide detailed and integrated guidance on how to integrate the management of social and environmental issues with firm operations.

The starting point for creating different CSR standards are 10 ethical principles of Global Compact (2008):
- principle 1: Businesses should support and respect the protection of internationally proclaimed human rights,
- principle 2: Businesses should make sure that they are not complicit in human rights abuses,
- principle 3: Businesses should uphold the freedom of association and the effective recognition of the right to collective bargaining,
- principle 4: Businesses should implement the elimination of all forms of forced and compulsory labor,
- principle 5: Businesses should implement the effective abolition of child labour,
- principle 6: Businesses should implement the elimination of discrimination in respect of employment and occupation,
- principle 7: Businesses should support a precautionary approach to environmental challenges,
- principle 8: Businesses should undertake initiatives to promote greater environmental responsibility,

- principle 9: Businesses should encourage the development and diffusion of environmentally friendly technologies,
- principle 10: Businesses should work against corruption in all its forms, including extortion and bribery.

In the Mueckenberger and Jastram's [2010] opinion the analysis of the implementation of the Global Compact is methodologically difficult and resource intensive, because the 10 principles potentially affect a number of activities within a multinational corporation in all its countries of operation. Currently the most popular CSR standard is ISO 26000. According to ISO 26000 [2010], the core CSR issues are as follows:

- organizational governance (including inclusiveness, ethical conduct, disclosure of information, respect for the rule of law, accountability),
- environment (including pollution prevention, prevention of global warming, sustainable consumption and land use, preservation and restoration of ecosystems and the natural environment, respect for future generations),
- human rights (civil and political rights; economics, cultural and social rights; fundamental labor rights; community rights),
- labor practices (occupational health and safety, dignified working conditions, human resources development, worker as a human being),
- fair operating practices (promotion of ethical and transparent activities; promotion of free competition, application of fair and ethical supply and after-supply practice, respect for intellectual and/or property rights and respect for users' interests, fight against corruption),
- consumer issues (providing consumers with accurate and adequate information; provision and development of socially-beneficial services and products; provision and development of safe and reliable products and services; protection of consumers' privacy),
- community involvement/society development.

5. CSR PRACTICES AS A TOOL FOR SUPPLIERS RELATIONSHIP MANAGEMENT IN B2B MARKET

CSR practices may be used in the suppliers relationship management in the firm.

5.1. VALUE CHAIN PERSPECTIVE

Figure 3 builds on Porter and Kramer's [2006] mapping of the social impact of the value chain.

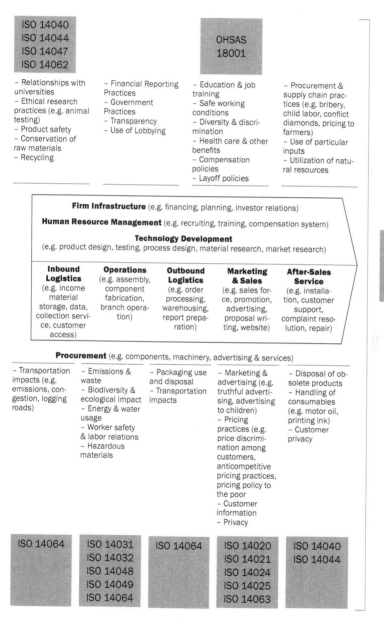

Figure 3. Value chain, ISO standards and CSR practices
Source: adopted and modified from Castka and Balzarova 2008.

Porter and Kramer [2006] argue that the value chain depicts all the activities a company engages in and can be identified with both positive and negative social impacts. In this point of view value chain is a specific platform where firm may use different CSR standards to manage own relationship with all interest parties, however especially with suppliers and customers.

5.2. SUPPLY CHAIN PERSPECTIVE

A corporation's supply chain may be generally defined as a series of companies, including suppliers, customers, and logistics providers that work together to deliver a value package of goods and services to the end customer. Despite the history of CSR, applications of CSR to the supply chain have only emerged in the last 15 years (Maloni and Brown 2006).

Carter and Jennings [2004] established the importance of CSR in supply chain decision-making with case study and survey research. Researchers have attempted to generalize the elements that characterize supply chain CSR in all industries, creating the concepts of Logistics Social Responsibility and Purchasing Social Responsibility. Framework for CSR application in the supply chain is illustrated with Figure 4.

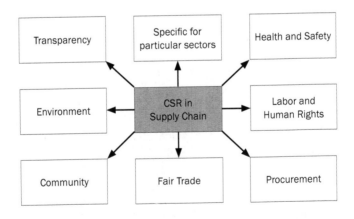

Figure 4. Dimensions of CSR in supply chain
Source: own elaboration.

6. CSR PRACTICES IN THE SUPPLIERS RELATIONSHIP MANAGEMENT – CASE STUDY OF ARCELORMITTAL

6.1. RESEARCH METHODOLOGY

Relations between ArcelorMittal and suppliers in the CSR perspective was the main subject of the research.

The author formulated the following research questions:
- *question 1 – Which macro-level CSR initiatives were reflected by ArcelorMital?*
- *question 2 – Which CSR practices must be fulfilled by ArcelorMital suppliers?*
- *question 3 – How ArcelorMittal suppliers may fulfil CSR requirements?*

Research techniques were: review of ArcelorMittal documents and records and action research connected with consulting carried out by the author for selected ArcelorMittal Suppliers.

6.2. ARCELORMITTAL CSR REQUIREMENTS FOR SUPPLIERS AND THEIR MEANING

ArcelorMital is the world's leading integrated steel and mining company, present in over 60 countries. CSR approach of ArcelorMital on strategic level is articulated by the following elements (ArcelorMittal 2011): investing in people, making steel more sustainable, enriching communities, transparent governance.

Table 2. CSR requirements for ArcelorMittal Suppliers

Requirement	Status	Reference
1. Health & Safety Policy implementation	obligatory	–
2. Occupational Health & Safety Management System implementation	recommended	OHSAS 18001
3. Occupational Health & Safety Management System certification	recommended	OHSAS 18001
4. Safety statistics of firm	recommended	–
5. Safety statistics of suppliers	recommended	–
6. Human Rights Policy implementation	obligatory	Arcelor Mittal Human Rights Policy
7. Membership of the Human Rights Societies	recommended	–

Requirement	Status	Reference
8. Code of Business Ethics Implementation	obligatory	–
9. Anticorruption Policy implementation	obligatory	–
10. Whistleblowing process or procedure implementation	obligatory	–
11. Environmental Policy implementation	obligatory	–
12. Environmental Management System implementation	recommended	ISO 14001
13. Environmental Management System certification	recommended	ISO 14001
14. GC emission measurement	obligatory	–
15. Water consumption measurement	obligatory	–

Source: own elaboration.

Table 2 demonstrates the key CSR practices which should be realized by ArcelorMittal suppliers. All of them are evaluated during periodic suppliers appraisal. Suppliers which do not meet a category must improve CSR practices. Otherwise ArcelorMittal removes them from list of qualified suppliers.

6.3. CASES OF CSR PRACTICES – ADAPTATIONS FOR ARCELORMITTAL REQUIREMENTS FOR SMALL SUPPLIERS OF MATERIALS

The main CSR practices of ArcelorMittal suppliers should include firstly these tools which are mandatorily required by ArcelorMittal. Their framework is showed below.

Code of Business Ethics
Code of business ethics of surveyed companies may consist of the following principles:

- *Principle 1 – observing law and principles of community life –* the company fully observes binding legal regulations and respects generally accepted principles of community life and good manners created in the venues of the company operations.
- *Principle 2 – respect –* everywhere and at all times the company follows the principle of respect to dignity of a man regardless of their education and position.
- *Principle 3 – satisfaction of all interested parties –* the company aspires towards sustained development which will deliver expected values to all parties interested in its activities.
- *Principle 4 – professionalism and high quality of products and services –* the company wishes to be regarded as professional and reliable. It adjusts its management processes, principles of employees evaluation and rules of co-operation with subcontractors to this philosophy.
- *Principle 5 – openness and communication –* management creates conditions for smooth and open exchange of opinions. It fosters fair

communication within the organization and in relations with clients and suppliers ensuring thus confidentiality of information they require.
- *Principle 6 – political neutrality* – the company declares that in its operations it fully shuns political context and does not involve in any political activities.

The principles are complemented with some practices of dealing with the environment (Table 3).

Table 3. Proposed stakeholders relationship practises for research firms

Party	Dominating attitude	Major activities
Clients	Client satisfaction is a priority. Clients have the right to expect highest quality products and services.	– meeting all obligations to clients – continuous improving implemented quality management system in conformity with the ISO 9001 standard – providing professional and friendly customer service – speedy reaction to potential complaints and analysis of their origin – maintaining relations based on respect and trust in relations with clients – reliable informing clients about offer and ensuring confidentiality of the data which require it
Subcontractors	Aspiring to develop and maintain continuous and mutually beneficial relations with subcontractors.	– following the free market rules when selecting subcontractors – meeting obligations to subcontractors on-time – aspiring to joint solving difficult problems in order to improve activity of the company and the subcontractors – conducting all transactions with subcontractors according to the principles of accounting
Owners	Aspiring to continuous growth of company value.	– owners' active participation in management processes and their full access to all data on the current situation – owners' decisions about directions and ways of development of the company
Employees	Employees are the key factor of the company success.	– creating dignified and friendly work conditions – providing all employees with equal chances of professional growth and self-development – protection of privacy of all employees – commitment of all employees to fully shun conflict of interests and not to conduct competitive activities – ban on employees' gathering information on competition from illegal sources – undertaking business commitments on behalf of the company only by entitled employees – employees' commitment to care for the possessions of the company without risking unnecessary costs – ban on offering and accepting financial benefits related with realizing tasks by the company employees – continuous aspiring to improve the work safety and protection of the health of the workers

Source: own elaboration.

Human Rights Policy

Human rights policy in the researched companies may consist of the following major principles:

- *Principle 1 – human rights awareness among employees* – assumes that all company employees should be fully aware of the rights they are entitled to. The company, as a part of following this principle, supports employees' right to free association.
- *Principle 2 – human dignity in the place of employment* – in the company human dignity is regarded as the greatest value which cannot be violated. As a part of following this principle the company commits to completely prevent compulsory work, child labour, to eradicate any manifestations of discrimination of employees in their workplace (e.g. due to their sex or age), to eradicate physical and psychological mobbing, violence or harassment of employees. Human dignity sensitivity is not limited to the employees of the enterprise but spreads to all business relations mostly in contacts with subcontractors from whom it is expected to follow similar standards.
- *Principle 3 – friendly work environment* – the company as an employer is interested in long-term employment. At the same time, it is aware of the need to provide the employees complete comfort in their workplace. In order to achieve this the following actions are undertaken: creating best possible ergonomic conditions in the place of employment, continuous investment in all employees' equipment, offering competitive salaries allowing to live with dignity, complete following committed terms and conditions of employment, promoting partner relations in the workplace based on co-operation and mutual trust.
- *Principle 4 – balance between private and professional life* – the company is fully aware of the fact that employees have their own private life interests, ambitions and needs which should be realized and developed. The company attempts to achieve an accepted by the employees' status of balance between private and professional life. In order to do that it undertakes a number of activities including complete observing employees' rights to holidays and days off, absolute ban to exceed working hours, individual treatment of each employee and adjusting organization policy to their needs and expectations, introducing flexible working hours adjusted to situations of individual employees.

Whistleblowing Procedure

Procedure of reporting suspicion of alleged abuse and unethical behaviour is one of the tools of the policy preventing corruption risk of the researched companies. All the employees are obliged to use the procedure while optionally any person not being an employee can report it. The management of the company undertakes to analyse all reported suspicions of alleged abuse and unethical behaviors regardless of who reports them. The course of the process is presented in Table 4.

Table 4. Proposed framework of Whistleblowing Procedure for research firms

Who					Activity	Records		
Employees	Others	Members of the Board	Managing Director	Person responsible for HR		Report	Background papers	Personnel documentation
×	×	×	×		Disclosing instances of suspicions of alleged abuse and unethical behaviours	×		
		×			Urgent passing a resolution on investigating and explaining authenticity of the suspicion of alleged abuse and unethical behaviours		×	
		×	×		Decision on the mode of conducting initial regulatory contacts		×	
		×	×	×	Conducting initial regulatory contacts		×	
		×	×	×	Discussion of the results of initial regulatory contacts		×	
		×			Decision on finalizing the proceedings (should the suspicion prove unjustified)		×	
		×	×		Decision on the mode of conducting intensified regulatory contacts		×	
		×	×	×	Conducting intensified regulatory contacts		×	
×		×	×	×	Giving explanation by the employee suspected of the alleged abuse and unethical behaviour		×	
		×			Decision on finalizing the proceedings (should the suspicion prove unjustified)		×	
		×	×		Decision on the mode of conducting finalizing regulatory contacts		×	
		×	×	×	Conducting finalizing regulatory contacts		×	
		×			Decision on the type of o sanction against the employee whose abuse and unethical behaviour have been proven		×	×
		×	×	×	Enforcing sanctions against the employee whose abuse and unethical behaviour have been proven			×

Source: own elaboration.

Procedure schedules three stages of explaining each of the instances:

- in the first stage the regulatory contact proceeds within top management without the employee's involvement. Should the suspicion prove unjustified the case is dismissed.
- in the second stage the suspected employee gives explanations. It is also in this stage that the case can be dismissed should the suspicion be unjustified.
- in the third stage the case is ultimately resolved and sanctions against the employee who proved guilty of the suspicion are defined.

The major principle of preliminary investigation in companies is presumption of innocence of an employee (stages 1 and 2) until the suspicion of alleged abuse and unethical behaviour is proven.

Environmental Policy

Approach towards environmental management implemented in the researched companies is determined by the following principles:

- *Principle 1 – environmental awareness* – all employees should be fully aware of their co-responsibility for the state of natural environment.
- *Principle 2 – environmental competencies* – all employees should have indispensable knowledge and qualifications for responsible and efficient actions related with protection of natural environment.
- *Principle 3 – full responsibility* – employees should know they are responsible for the influence of the company and its subcontractors on the environment.

The specified and fundamental directions of realization of the policy are as follows:

- continuous identification of environmental aspects concerning our activity,
- introducing environmental programmes directed at improvement of our environmental accomplishments,
- taking environmental criteria into account in our business decisions including those in relations with our subcontractors,
- restricting the level of pollution emissions and the amount of used water and disposed sewage,
- sorting waste we generate,
- continuous improvement of our practices of proceeding in terms of environmental management, in particular: specifying and monitoring of measurable environmental targets, training employees and increasing their competencies in terms of environment protection,
- communicating principles of environmental policy to all employees and subcontractors of the companies.

In its literal meaning environmental policy also respects ISO 14001 requirements. Environmental policy is communicated to the employees of the companies:

- during all introductory and periodic trainings,
- by placing its content in all workplaces in the seats of the companies,
- at monthly meetings of the board with the employees dedicated to the management issues,
- always whenever the resolutions of the policy are amended.

Environmental policy is communicated to the representative of suppliers (the entire substance of the policy of the organization is passed immediately after issuing new edition of the policy, while informing about its resolutions takes place during on-going business contacts).

Health and Safety Policy

Approach towards health and safety issues used in the companies is determined by the following principles:

- *Principle 1 – health and safety awareness* – all employees should be fully aware of the risks related with their work.
- *Principle 2 – health and safety competencies* – all employees should have knowledge and qualifications indispensable for responsible and efficient actions related with health and safety.
- *Principle 3 – locations* – employees of the companies should act safely in all locations related with performing work duties.

The specified and fundamental directions of implementation of the present policy are as follows:

- identifying, obtaining and following currently binding requirements in terms of health and safety, including legal requirements, requirements specified by our clients and other interested parties, guidelines and good practices of international and domestic organizations;
- maintaining continuous professional risk assessment conducted holistically, i.e. including the following places of risk resulting from the type of work: seat of the organization, way from home to work and back, business trips, seats of clients;
- continuous improvement of our practices of conduct in terms of health and safety, in particular: specifying and monitoring of implementation of measurable targets, motivating employees to report suggestions for improvement, training employees and increasing their competencies in terms of health and safety, conducting benchmark activities and following model practices in terms of health and safety, shaping organizational atmosphere favourable to developing safety culture and providing indispensable means for following health and safety principles;
- communicating principles of health and safety policy to all employees and other persons temporarily being under supervision of the organization as well as to all suppliers of the organization.

In its literal meaning health and safety policy also respects OHSAS 18001 requirements. Environmental policy is communicated to the employees of the companies:
- during all introductory and periodic health and safety trainings,
- by placing its content in all workplaces in the seat of the company,
- at monthly meetings of the board with the employees dedicated to the management issues,
- always whenever the resolutions of the policy are amended.

Health and safety policy is communicated to other persons:
- at each visit to the seat of the company (employee responsible for co-operation with the visitor is responsible for presentation of the health and safety policy),
- representative of suppliers (the entire substance of the policy of the organization is passed immediately after issuing new edition of the policy, while informing about its resolutions takes place during on-going business contacts).

CONCLUSION

The text analyses conditions and possibilities of using CSR practices in shaping relations between companies on the B2B market. Conducted literature studies and empirical research allow forming the following conclusions:
- Stakeholder theory demonstrates close relation with the CSR trend. Particular influence on creating CSR initiatives, practices and standards results from including instrumental aspect of the stakeholders theory and regarding CSR as requirement for the management system.
- CSR initiatives originate on macro and micro levels, while from the first one their meaning is normative and from the latter one operational.
- On the macro-level the major collection of guidelines of conduct are Gobal Compact principles, in turn among the CSR standards of management ISO 26000 appears to be the most significant.
- Using CSR practices in managing relations between companies as interpreted with the help of value chain and supply chain demonstrates the effect of growth of competitiveness of recipient and supplier due to following the given practices.

- The researched global company ArcelorMittal is an example of an organization in which case diversified CSR initiatives spread to the management level. The company makes use of the CSR principles in shaping its relations with suppliers.
- Researched organizations being suppliers of ArcelorMittal must introduce at least the obligatory CSR tools; otherwise they lose their status of approved supplier.
- Significant part of the introduced CSR solutions should include internal requirements of ArcelorMittal along with requirements of international management standards ISO 14001 and OHSAS 18001.

REFERENCES

ArcelorMittal Corporate Responsibility (2011), http://www.arcelormittal.com/corporate/cr.html [access: 2011].

Aslander M.S. (2011). Corporate social responsibility as subsidiary co-responsibility: A macroeconomic perspective. *Journal of Business Ethics*, No. 99.

Carter C.R., Jennings M.M. (2004). The role of purchasing in corporate social responsibility: A structural equation analysis. *Journal of Business Logistic*, No. 25.

Castka P., Balzarova M.A. (2008). Social responsibility standardization: Guidance or reinforcement through certification? *Human Systems Management*, No. 27.

Donaldson T., Preston L.E. (1995). The stakeholder theory of the corporation – concepts, evidence, and implications. *Academy of Management Review*, No. 20.

Gilbert D.U., Rasche A. (2008). Opportunities and problems of standardized ethics initiatives – A stakeholder theory perspective. *Journal of Business Ethics*, No. 82.

Global Compact. The Ten Principles (2008), http://www.unglobalcompact.org/aboutthegc/TheTenPrinciples/index.html [access: 2011].

ISO 26000. Social responsibility (2010). International Organization for Standardization.

Jones T.M., Wicks A.C. (1999). Convergent stakeholder theory. *Academy of Management Review*, No. 24.

Kaler J. (2003). Differentiating stakeholder theories. *Journal of Business Ethics*, No. 23.

Koerber Ch.P. (2010). Corporate responsibility standards: Current implications and future possibilities for peace through commerce. *Journal of Business Ethics*, No. 89.

Maloni M.J., Brown M.E. (2006). Corporate social responsibility in supply chain: An application in the food industry. *Journal of Business Ethics*, No. 68.

Mueckenberger U., Jatram S. (2010). Transnational norm-building networks and the legitimacy of corporate social responsibility standards, *Journal of Business Ethics*, No. 97.

Phillips R. (2003). *Stakeholder Theory and Organizational Ethics*, Berrett-Koehler, San Francisco.

Porter M.E., Kramer M.R. (2006). Strategy & Society. The link between competitive advantage and corporate social responsibility. *Harvard Business Review*, No. 12.

Reed D. (1999). Stakeholder management theory – a critical theory perspective. *Business Ethics Quarterly*, No. 9.

Sukserm T., Takahashi Y. (2010). A prospective process for implementing human resource development for corporate social responsibility. *Interdisciplinary Journal of Contemporary Research in Business*, No. 5.

NATALIA DUDZIŃSKA-KORCZAK

Jagiellonian University
Institute of Economics and Management
Chair of Organization and Management

ANETA LIPIŃSKA

Jagiellonian University
Institute of Economics and Management
Chair of Standardized Management Systems

MAŁGORZATA BUDZANOWSKA-DRZEWIECKA

Jagiellonian University
Institute of Economics and Management
Chair of Organizational Behaviour

THE SPECIFICITY OF CORPORATE SOCIAL RESPONSIBILITY ACTIVITIES IN THE POWER SECTOR – THE REVIEW OF THE IMPLEMENTED ACTIVITIES

INTRODUCTION

The energy industry is considered to be the world leader in implementation of the corporate social responsibility (CSR) strategy. Recently, the development of CSR activities by Polish companies in the power engineering sector has been visible. Power engineering, as a part of the energy industry next to gas and fuel – oil sector, faced dynamic changes in the business and social sphere which necessitated the companies to adapt to the expectations of their stakeholders. There appeared the need to consider the idea of responsible business and initiatives for the sake of sustainable development. Polish energy companies, including power companies, attempt to take this tendency into account in their strategies.

The purpose of the article is to present and systematize selected aspects of CSR activities implemented by power companies in Poland. The emphasis was put on identifying these activities and the tools used in their implementation.[1] The realization of the purpose was possible as part of the review of

---

[1] The presented analyses are part of the research project entitled *Identification and assessment of CSR in the power sector in Poland* developed at the Institute of Economics and Management at the

selected CSR programs implemented by power companies and the studies conducted by the Energy Regulatory Office (ERO).

1. THE CONCEPT OF CORPORATE SOCIAL RESPONSIBILITY

Corporate social responsibility comes from the concept of sustainable development which is understood as inevitable and desirable economic development which does not irreversibly disturb the human environment, does not lead to degradation of the biosphere and which reconciles the laws of nature, economy and culture [PricewaterhouseCoopers 2010]. According to this approach, companies implementing the CSR concept in practice take into account, predict and maximize economic, environmental and social value to the benefit of all stakeholders.[2]

The CSR concept is implemented thanks to international regulations. The most important of these relate to sustainable development, for instance the European Community Fifth Environmental Action Programme defining a new EU approach to sustainable development (1993) and to business activity e.g. Business Charter for Sustainable Development (1991), Guidelines for Multinational Enterprises OECD (1976) or Caux Principles for Business (1994). The last of the mentioned documents self-regulate the sphere of business [Rok 2004, pp. 1–74].

Apart from legal actions implemented at an international level, the factor which has an influence on popularizing the concept of sustainable development is the intensification of civil movements connected with defence of human rights, the natural environment and protection of consumer rights. Public opinion has become a major force in democratic societies.

In the literature of the subject, there are several ways of defining CSR. The collation of classical concepts of Corporate Social Responsibility is presented in Table 1.

Jagiellonian University in Cracow as part of the article's authors' own research conducted at the turn of June and July 2011.

  [2] Stakeholders are individuals or groups which may influence or are influenced by companies' actions through their products, strategies and manufacturing processes, management systems and procedures [Rok 2004, p. 19].

Table 1. The selected concepts of Corporate Social Responsibility

The key aspects of the CSR concept	The way of defining CSR	The authors of the concept
Objective approach	CSR initiatives defined as social, economic, legal or discretionary (connected with additional activities of the company for the society) commitments	A.B. Caroll
Subjective approach	CSR defined as companies' responsibility to stakeholders	M.B.E. Clarkson

Source: own elaboration on the basis of Dąbrowski 2011, pp. 2–9.

The majority of CSR definitions cited in scientific and business publications can be attributed to one of these two approaches. For example, the definition of the CSR Centre in Poland represents an objective approach. CSR is here understood as companies' obligation to contribute to sustainable socio-economic development, particularly through voluntary ethical, social and environmental commitments going beyond the minimum set by the applicable legal standards implemented in cooperation with civil society [CSR Centre 2010]. The Institute for Responsible Business combines CSR with the assumption that organization is a part of the society and cannot be accounted for its actions by it, which is characteristic of the subjective approach [Institute for Responsible Business 2010].

In other approaches, CSR is defined as actions motivated by ethical reasons or a management process [Dąbrowski 2011, pp. 2–9].

In EU documents, such as, the *Lisbon Strategy* and the *Strategy for Permanent Development*, the concept of CSR is regarded as one of the important tools to promote the competitiveness of companies and increase economic and social cohesion of the EU [ERO 2008].

2. THE DESCRIPTION OF THE POLISH POWER SYSTEMS ENGINEERING SECTOR – THE SELECTED INFORMATION

Power engineering, the essential part of the power industry, is a separate part of the economy and is crucial for its economic potential and the standard of living of citizens. Power engineering consists of three sub-sectors: *generating* (created by professional power stations, also known as system stations, and heat and power plants supplying electricity to industrial and distribution networks), *transmission* (the network of high voltage lines 750 kV, 400 kV and 220 kV along with stations and substations) and *distribution* (the system of distribution networks of high, medium and low voltage of 100 kV and less [Energy Market Information Centre 2007].

Under the influence of gradually increasing widely understood costs of energy supply, many countries decided to implement reforms of the power industry (privatization, liberalization, competition), including power engineering and the shaping of the modern electricity market. The consolidation of state companies from the Polish power sector, carried out in the years 2006–2007 in accordance with the guidelines of the government's *Power Engineering Program* [Ministry of Economy 2006], led to the creation of four new groups (with different contribution to the generation and distribution sub-sectors) out of many energy companies. At the same time, PSE Operator SA, serving as the Transmission System Operator in the Polish power industry, was isolated and equipped with high voltage networks.

The current structure of the power sector includes energy companies conducting business activity within generation, trade, transmission and distribution of electric energy, such as (Figure 1):

– power stations (generating companies),
– a transmission-network company – responsible for the functioning of a transmission network and control of the whole power engineering system as well as purchase of energy in the amount necessary to close the energy balance in the National Power System (PSE Operator SA),
– distribution-network companies – responsible for the functioning of distribution networks and purchase of energy in the amount equal to the difference in the amount of energy flowing into the distribution network and energy taken by recipients (distribution companies),
– companies engaged in energy trading (trading companies).

The Energy Law does not limit the forms of energy trading in Poland which resulted in there being three basic ways of marketing it: contract, balance and the stock market (Polish Power Exchange SA) and Electric Energy Trading Platform (Internet platform). As organized part of the market, Polish Power Exchange SA provides open, transparent and equal principles for all commercial transactions and the obtaining of market information, reduces the costs of a negotiation process and allows for flexibility in the process of concluding transactions [Energy Market Information Centre 2007].

Distribution system operators and trading companies, created as a result of the separation of commercial and distribution activity of existing power companies, conduct two independent kinds of business activity: energy trade and its transport through distribution networks (Table 2; Figure 2).

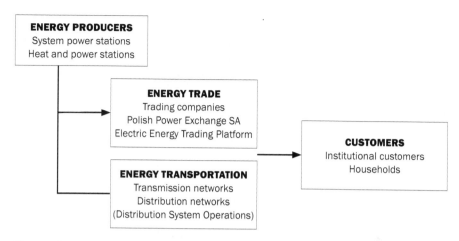

Figure 1. The structure of the Polish power engineering sector

Source: own elaboration on the basis of Energy Market Information Centre 2007.

Table 2. Distribution System Operators and Trading Companies in Poland (in 2011)

Distribution System Operators	Trading Companies
OSD included in Tauron Polska Energia S.A.: – EnergiaPro S.A. (headquarters: Wrocław, Branches: Jelenia Góra, Legnica, Opole, Wałbrzych, Wrocław) – ENION S.A. (headquarters: Kraków, Branches: Bielsko Biała, Będzin, Częstochowa, Kraków, Tarnów)	Trading companies included in Tauron Polska Energia S.A.: – EnergiaPro Gigawat Sp. z o.o. (Branches: Legnica, Jelenia Góra, Walbrzych, Opole) – ENION Energia Sp. z o.o. (headquarters: Kraków)
OSD included in the Polish Energy Group: – PGE Dystrybucja SA Branch Łódź-Miasto – PGE Dystrybucja SA Branch Łódź-Teren – PGE Dystrybucja SA Branch Lublin – PGE Dystrybucja SA Branch Rzeszów PGE Dystrybucja SA Branch Skarżysko-Kamienna – PGE Dystrybucja SA Branch Zamość – PGE Dystrybucja SA Branch Białystok – PGE Dystrybucja SA Branch Warszawa	Trading companies included in the Polish Energy Group S.A.: – PGE Łódzki Zakład Energetyczny S.A. – PGE ZEŁT Obrót Sp. z o.o. – PGE Lubelskie Zakłady Energetyczne S.A. PGE Rzeszowski Zakład Energetyczny S.A. – Zakłady Energetyczne Okręgu Radomsko--Kieleckiego S.A. – PGE Zamojska Korporacja Energetyczna S.A. – PGE Zakład Energetyczny Białystok S.A. – PGE Zakład Energetyczny Warszawa – Teren S.A.
ENEA Operator (Branches: Zielona Góra, Gorzów Wielkopolski, Szczecin, Bydgoszcz)	ENEA SA (Branches: Zielona Góra, Gorzów Wielkopolski, Szczecin, Bydgoszcz)
ENERGA–OPERATOR SA (Branches: Koszalin, Słupsk, Elbląg, Olsztyn, Toruń, Płock, Kalisz)	ENERGA-OBRÓT SA (Branches Koszalin, Słupsk, Elbląg, Olsztyn, Toruń, Płock, Kalisz)
Vattenfall Distribution Poland S.A. (headquarters: Gliwice)	Vattenfall Sales Poland Sp. z o.o. (headquarters: Gliwice)
RWE Stoen Operator Sp. z o.o. (headquarters: Warszawa)	RWE Polska S.A. (headquarters: Warszawa)
PKP Energetyka S.A. (headquarters: Warszawa)	PKP Energetyka S.A. (headquarters: Warszawa)

Source: own elaboration on the basis of the data from Energy Market Information Centre 2007.

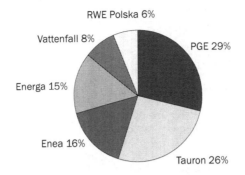

RWE Polska 6%

Vattenfall 8%

PGE 29%

Energa 15%

Enea 16%

Tauron 26%

Figure 2. The structure of the biggest Polish energy suppliers' shares of the market (as of 2009)

Source: own elaboration on the basis of the data from Energy Market Information Centre 2007.

It should be emphasised that Polish energy companies (with Polish capital and Polish engineering solutions) gained a significant position in a relatively short time. There are more and more energy consumers who change the supplier and the amount of energy introduced on the market through the power exchange and most energy companies are listed on the stock exchange [Chojnacki 2011, pp. 60–62].

In 2010, the privatization of Energa Group and the next stage of privatization of Enea Group began, as of today none of these processes has been finalized.

The necessity to adjust strategies to the EU environmental requirements forces power companies to reduce electricity production from coal and to invest in renewable energy and gas [Ciepiela 2011, pp. 48–50; 52–54]. These facts indicate the appropriate direction of changes in the Polish energy market. These are not, however, sufficient changes and their pace does not enable Polish power companies to create global corporations with a recognizable brand in the world and compete on the global market.

3. ENERGY COMPANY AS AN IMPLEMENTER OF CORPORATE SOCIAL RESPONSIBILITY ACTIVITIES

The definition of the concept of a socially responsible energy business accepted by the Chairman of ERO underlines the contribution of these industries to the implementation of the country's energy policy and company management which does not abuse its advantage over consumers of electricity, gas or heat [ERO 2008]:

> this is a strategy which harmoniously combines ethical and ecological aspects of business activity with its dominant attribute, that is, efficiency exposing openness, transparency of action, fairness to customers (calculation of prices, quality of supplies and service) and in contacts with other stakeholders (including employees, shareholders, suppliers, a local community), self-limitation of monopolistic advantage [ERO 2010].

In the light of the accepted definition, the social responsibility of a power company can be implemented at different levels of social involvement in various forms and ranges (Figure 3).

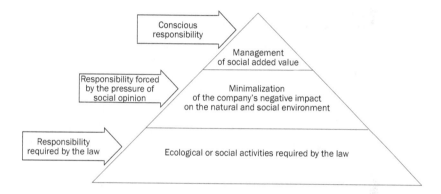

Figure 3. The levels of social responsibility of power companies
Source: own elaboration on the basis of Rok 2004, p. 52.

Challenges which stimulate energy companies to implement CSR enterprises are the growing demands for energy, the planned release of energy prices and the need to reduce greenhouse gas emissions. The observed change of behaviour of the energy industry companies in this field is caused by external stakeholders' rising expectations in relation to these issues and also the companies' desire to build further elements of competitive advantage, gain easier access to qualified staff and build the system of effective risk management in business activity. These reasons, which affect the financial position of energy companies and the possibilities of their development, have an influence on the acquisition of social acceptance, trust and access to new markets.

The stakeholders' increased attention to power companies results from new problems and customers, citizens, public authorities and investors' expectations in the context of globalization and industrial change on a large scale. There are more and more demands for transparency of business activity which is facilitated by the media and ICT. Aspects and social criteria determine investment decisions of consumers and investors to a greater and greater extent. Due to growing environmental awareness of society, the concern about environmental damage caused by energy companies has greater presence. Below, there is a list of stakeholders who are potential recipients of activities implemented by power companies (Table 3).

Table 3. The list of stakeholders in Polish power engineering[3]

Energy companies[3]	The environment of energy companies
• boards of power companies and energy companies – CEOs of the company – Members of the boards of the company • Supervisory Boards – The Chairman of the Supervisory Boards of the company – Members of the Supervisory Boards of the company • Employees of energy companies • Spółka Giełda Energii S.A. • Trade unions	• centres of central and local government – ownership authorities (the Ministry of Economy, the ministry of the Treasury) and the government – members of the authorities in the voivodeships connected with the power industry – members of the Sejm in the voivodeships connected with the power industry • local government institutions, industrial chambers (Polish Chamber of Power Industry and Environment, Polish Chamber of Industrial Energy and Energy Consumers) • banks, insurance companies, financial institutions • debtors and creditors • domestic and foreign competitors • suppliers – hard coal mines and brown coal mines, – producers of machinery and equipment for energy and protection of the environment – suppliers of computer systems, – suppliers of digital automation systems, – medium and small companies providing design, construction, installation services and cooperating with professional and industrial energetics. • electricity customers (private and institutional customers, forum of Electricity and Gas Customers) • Energy Regulatory Office • The Office of Competition and Consumer Protection • National Atomic Energy Agency • industry associations, supporting institutions • Polish Power Exchange SA • journalists dealing with electric power engineering issues • research and design base: e.g. The Energy Committee affiliated with the PAN Presidium, the Institute of Energetic.

Source: own elaboration.

---

[3] Energy companies – local power stations, thermal power engineering companies, distribution companies, system power stations, trading companies, a transmission system operator.

4. CORPORATE SOCIAL RESPONSIBILITY ACTIVITIES CARRIED OUT BY COMPANIES IN THE POWER SECTOR – IN THE LIGHT OF THE RESEARCH OF ENERGY REGULATORY OFFICE (ERO)

The monitoring of CSR activities in the power sector is one of the tasks which have regularly been implemented since 2009 by ERO as part of the questionnaire survey.[4]

In the light of these findings, it can be stated that a large group of companies does not have a formal CSR strategy but, to a great extent, behaves according to the ideas of the CSR concept. Power companies implement many activities from the field of CSR but they do not have formal documentation for this. CSR principles are usually a part of the overall strategy of the company [ERO 2010]. What should be emphasized is an increasing number of entities which decide not to accept voluntary initiatives and self-regulations referring to social responsibility of power companies (in 2009 – 37% of companies in 2010 – 52% of companies which decided not to adopt any self-regulations referring to CSR) [ERO 2010]. Companies most often indicated the following regulations: Codes of Ethics, Manager's Principles of Good Practices, Procurement Regulations, the Integrated Management System, the Code of Conduct for Suppliers, Regulations for conducting charitable activity and sponsorship or the signing of "the Declaration on Sustainable Development in the energy sector in Poland" from 17th June 2009 [ERO 2010].

ERO studies are conducted with consideration of four categories: the employee environment, relations with the market, the natural environment and the local community.

As part of social responsibility of power companies in relation to the employee environment, the implemented activities are typical employee programs. They most often aim at increasing competence, motivation and professional potential of employees, development of career paths and creating conditions for the staff to have a real impact on working conditions which would provide benefits for the company and raise the level of workers' satisfaction.

The research shows that the degree of the power companies' involvement in changing relations with the market (relations with suppliers and electricity customers) does not change significantly. 68% of companies in 2009

---

[4] The conclusions included in the article refer mainly to the survey conducted in 2009 and 2010 because the overall research results for the year 2011 are not published in a widely available form.

reported their activity on the market, while in 2010 – 66% of the surveyed entities [ERO 2010]. The examples of activities in relation to the market, in particular to the so-called socially sensitive recipient include: the drawing up of personalized customer service procedures, classification of suppliers of products and services, continuity of communication with customers, the conducting of marketing activities, improvement of websites in order to establish communication with the environment, network status monitoring, constant modernization of equipment, investments which use optimal technologies, sponsorship activities, the reliability of the supply of the media, information about current changes in rates [ERO 2010].

Not all companies are engaged in CSR activities oriented towards the natural environment. The companies enumerated activities aimed at protection of the environment, such as: reduction of the negative impact on the environment, protection against contamination and elimination of pollution of the ground – water environment, improvement of energy efficiency and promotion, use of safe and environmentally friendly technological solutions [ERO 2010].

What should be taken into account is the growing popularity of renewable energy sources, which is the result of increasingly stringent regulations at the European Union level, including the Europe 2020 strategy [European Commission 2010]. This solution is essential because of the necessity to diversify fuel mix by using renewable sources. Nevertheless, this is very often the companies' reaction to customers looking for environmentally friendly solutions in this field. Thus, the majority of energy companies included in their offer "green rates," for example the Eko Premium rate introduced by Tauron. As a result of the power companies' initiatives, the consumer is not only the recipient of a service or product but also the producer of energy from renewable sources, for instance the Energia company introduced the project "SmartEco" which allows for connecting home wind turbines to the distribution network.

Power companies reported their activity for the local community in the vast majority of the surveyed entities (68% of the surveyed companies in 2009 introduced programs for the local community, in 2010 it was as many as 83% of the surveyed companies) [ERO 2010]. The companies claimed they were engaged in the following types of activities: charitable activities, sponsorship, supporting initiatives and events important to local communities, educational activities (through websites, calculators of energy consumption), contests for children and young people, development of principles of cooperation with NGOs and local partners, involvement in philanthropic activities in health care, education, culture, employment policy adjusted to the specifics of the local labour market, cooperation of public institutions (self-government), patronage, development of relationships with trade unions and inclusion of customers in environmental protection activities, e.g. common tree planting campaigns [ERO 2010].

The overall collation of the implementation of selected activities in the field of corporate social responsibility by power companies according to the data for the year 2010 is shown in Figure 4.

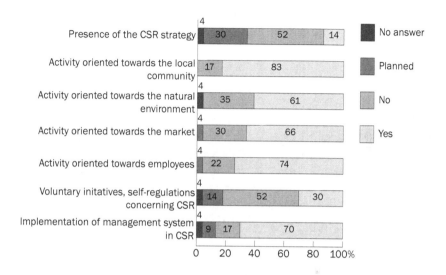

Figure 4. The selected aspects of social responsibility of power companies in the questionnaire survey by Energy Regulatory Office 2010

Source: own elaboration on the basis of the data from ERO 2010.

5. THE SELECTED EXAMPLES OF CORPORATE SOCIAL RESPONSIBILITY PRACTICES IMPLEMENTED BY POWER COMPANIES IN POLAND

The selected good practices of corporate social responsibility implemented in Polish power engineering sector were systematized with regard to basic areas, such as the impact on the environment, the local community, the employee environment, and the market. Additional areas included in the analysis are management and social reporting. The review was based on the available secondary data [Responsible Business Forum 2009; 2010; 2011; ERO 2010; PGNiG/PricewaterhouseCoopers 2011].

All of the presented cases are currently implemented on the market. The selection of the cases was deliberate. It aimed to determine whether and what activities are conducted in the-above-mentioned areas in the power engineering sector.

In part, the selected examples of good practices are implemented by the signatories of the "Declaration on sustainable development of power companies in Poland".[5] This additional criterion was deliberately used in the assumption that it is impossible to analyse strategies, tools and activities undertaken by power companies without referring to the initiative which is the platform for establishing cooperation in the field of social responsibility, exchange of experiences, dissemination of good practices and popularization of inter-sectorial dialogue. The Declaration is a set of commitments which the company, the signatory, voluntarily makes in order to operate in a sustainable way. These commitments include eight activities: occupational safety and health, respect for the rights of consumers, cooperation with local governments and the non-governmental sector, transparency of action and effective management, stakeholders' involvement and concern for the environment, equal treatment of customers, suppliers and subcontractors, promotion of energy efficient measures and clean technologies, ecological energy sources, industrial cooperation, knowledge sharing, transparency, credibility, public access to reports. In 2009 the Declaration was signed by: PGNiG S.A., EDF Polska, Gaz – System S.A., GDF Suez Energia Polska, Tauron S.A., ENEA S.A. and Vattenfall Poland Sp. z o.o. A year later this group was also joined by: Fortum Power and Heat Polska, Lotos and Polskie Sieci Elektroenergetyczne Operator, PKN Orlen, Dalkia Polska.

The first area in which it was decided to identify the implemented activities is the environment. The review of the implemented programs allowed for distinguishing three basic types of implemented practices concerning protection of the environment, technological innovations aimed at sustainable development and environmental education of energy consumers (Table 4).

---

[5] „The Declaration…" was established on 17th June 2009 as a result of cooperation and inter-sectorial dialogue during the First National Conference on Sustainable Development in the Energy Sector organized by PGNiG along with the consultancy company PricewaterhouseCoopers. As the first of the kind enterprise, the conference provided an opportunity to initiate a nationwide discussion on social responsibility in the energy sector (more information about the conference can be found on the website: www.odpowiedzialna-energia.pl).

Table 4. The selected examples of good CSR practices implemented in Polish power engineering sector in relation to the natural environment

Name of the power company	Start date and type of practice	Description of the good practice implemented by the power company
Vattenfall Poland Sp. z o.o.	2008 Environmental education	– the "Climate for the Earth, heat for Warsaw" program – competitions "School with a climate" and "Teacher with a climate" – a series of seminars on climate change
RWE Polska S.A.	2007–2008 Environmental education	– the program "Conscious Energy"
Tauron Polska Energia S.A. (Group)	2009–2010 Protection of the environment	– the project "Offset with Tauron": cooperation of Tauron group with the foundation Aeris Futuro for the sake of protection of the climate and sustainable development – the program "Time for the forest" implemented by the foundation Aeris Futuro. In this program, the companies' activities for the sake of the environment and the climate involve neutralization of carbon dioxide emissions by planting trees
RWE Polska S.A.	2009–2010 Innovation of sustainable development	– energy from windmills in West Pomerania and the Warmian-Masurian region (production of 125 MWh, which together allows for powering 62,000 households and will allow for reducing CO_2 emissions by 125 tons) – adopting a sustainable development strategy, in which RWE Poland committed to continuing investment in renewable energy sources and introducing innovative products for customers (2010)

Source: own elaboration on the basis of Responsible Business Forum 2009–2011.

When talking about environmental education, one should refer to the program "Climate for the Earth, heat for Warsaw," which promotes the idea of heat and electricity conservation. It was started in 2008 by Vattenfall Poland Sp. z o.o. under the patronage of the Embassy of Sweden, the Masovian Board of Education and the President of Warsaw. The program is based on emphasizing the benefits not only to the environment but also to the program's recipients who were given an opportunity to pay lower bills thanks to the appropriate patterns of energy use.

The program includes trainings on climate for policy-makers: MPs, senators and councillors of Warsaw and Pruszków, competitions "School with a climate" and "Teacher with a climate" and grants worth PLN 5,000 each for 5 educational institutions and environmental organizations as well as 30 teachers for their year-round work for the sake of the environment (grants worth PLN 500 each), seminars on climate change for more than 120 teachers and trainings for journalists and local governments.

The activities are supported with campaigns in the media and the distribution of educational leaflets among the residents of Warsaw and Pruszków. The website www.klimatdlaziemi.pl containing information on climate changes was created.

Different forms of activities were used in the "Conscious Energy" program which took the form of public campaign sponsored by RWE Poland S.A. conducted in 2007. The program aims to change behaviours concerning energy efficiency. The project focused on informational activities and consultancy on the conscious energy use oriented towards households, initiatives addressed to business customers, such as, *Business Guide* which contains information on the potential and benefits of reducing energy consumption in the company and the presentation of specific solutions for individual companies.

What is worth noting in the next category of activities for the sake of the environment is the project "Offset with Tauron" which is a part of the program "Time for the forest,"[6] implemented by the foundation Aeris Futuro in cooperation with Poland Tauron Energia S.A. (Group). In the years 2009 and 2010, thanks to the cooperation with Tauron, 20 thousand trees were planted in three places of southern Poland (the Tatra National Park and the town of Zakopane, the Karkonosze National Park and Ojców National Park). Experts from the foundation visited three orphanages where they promoted pro-ecological activities and donated the so-called eco-packages which consisted of energy-efficient computer equipment and white goods.

In reply to the increased needs of Polish customers, for whom it is important that the energy they use comes from renewable sources, RWE Poland S.A. in 2009 as one of the first power companies in Poland offered their business customers the ecological product "Energy from windmills." The initiative helps protect the environment but also promotes environmentally-friendly attitudes. Windmill companies in West Pomerania and the Warmian-Masurian region will annually produce 125 MWh, which together allows for powering 62,000 households and will reduce CO_2 emissions by 125 tons. Customers can decide what percentage of their annual volume is to be produced in wind farms. In return, they receive the certificate confirming that the energy purchased by them comes from renewable sources. It is worth noting that in the first year of its operation, the company sold almost

---

[6] As part of the program "Time for the forest," companies include activities for the sake of protection of the environment and climate, such as, neutralization of carbon dioxide emissions through planting trees.

the entire volume intended for the market. In 2010, RWE Poland adopted a strategy of sustainable development and undertook to continue invest-ment in renewable energy sources and introduction of innovative products for customers.

The second area, in which the implemented activities were identified, is engagement in activities for the sake of the local community (Table 5).

Table 5. The selected examples of good CSR practices implemented in the Polish power engineering sector in relation to the local community

Name of the power company	Start date and type of practice	Description of the good practice implemented by the power company
PKP Energetyka S.A.	2010 Education	the program "The Academy of Little Ampere"
Tauron Polska Energia S.A. (Group)	2009 Health and safety	the support of Mountain Volunteer Rescue Service

Source: own elaboration on the basis of Responsible Business Forum 2011.

Programs in this area can be aimed at solving various important prob-lems of the local community, including those concerning education and health care. The example of such a program is "The Academy of Little Am-pere" started in 2010 by PKP Energetyka S.A. It focuses on raising aware-ness among children from 3 to 6 years old in the field of safe use of electri-cal appliances and electric energy. The idea for the program resulted from the initiatives of employees of PKP Energetyka – Zakład Północny. They prepared the presentation for pre-school pupils on the principles of safe use of electrical appliances. The level of interest was so great that "The Acad-emy of Little Ampere" involved all plants of the company PKP Energetyka in Poland.

Another example is support for the Mountain Volunteer Rescue Ser-vice which, as part of CSR activities, is provided by Tauron. The coopera-tion of Tauron and MVRS was established in 2009. MVRS rescuers, under the contract with Tauron, receive funds for the purchase of means of trans-port, equipment and rescue equipment. The company is also the strategic sponsor of the Internet training program "Safer in the mountains. Higher Mountains".

Among the programs implemented on the Polish market, there are prac-tices addressed to the employees (Table 6).

Table 6. The selected examples of good CSR practices implemented in the Polish power engineering sector in relation to the employees

Name of the power company	Start date and type of practice	Description of the good practice implemented by the power company
Zespół Elektrociepłowni Wrocławskich KOGENERACJA S.A.	2009 Business ethics	– adjustment of corporate ethical project of the EDF Group to its own needs – activity of the Council of Ethics
RWE Polska S.A.	2010 Equal chances and diversity	– adoption of the strategy of sustainable development – The program "Women with energy"
PGE Polska Grupa Energetyczna – Polish Energy Group	2000 Participation of employees in management	– Human Oriented Productivity Improvement Programme (HOPP)

Source: own elaboration on the basis of Responsible Business Forum 2011.

The group of the Wrocław power stations KOGENERACJA SA adjusted the corporate ethics project to its own needs which can be regarded as a strategy for sustainable development of the whole EDF Group. The company appointed the Council of Ethics which operates socially outside of the company structure, which allows for maintaining its impartiality and independence. The mission of the Council of Ethics is promotion of ethical principles among employees as well as identification of ethical problems. Employees have direct access to the members of the Council of Ethics which guarantees confidentiality, discretion and systematic feedback which is supposed to help build trust between the parties. The Board of Ethics, on the company level, reports its activities once every two months to the Managing Director and an Annual Report is published in the Internet. As part of the Annual Report on Social Responsibility, employees are informed of the achievements of the EDF Group France.

In 2010, RWE Poland SA adopted a sustainable development strategy the purpose of which is to promote diversity within the company in terms of culture, gender and age. As a result, the initiative "Women with energy" came into being. It aims to build relationships with female representatives of companies and institutions from Polish energy sector, to promote women's management and leadership style and involvement in the nationwide women's initiatives.

The following demands were formulated:
- greater transparency and openness during the recruitment process,
- inclusion of women and foreigners in the "short list" of recommended candidates for employment,
- support for working mothers,

– inclusion of the Diversity purposes to the Core Business Card of managers and board members,
– 2 × 10 until 2012: until 2012 ten more women holding senior manager positions at the headquarters of RWE AG and 10 more women in the boards of the concern.

Polish Energy Group developed the Human-Oriented Productivity Improvement Programme (HOPP). Its main principle is to create conditions for continuous innovation of employees and use of grassroots ideas which can contribute to improvement of the company operations. Employee participation in management is possible through tabling individual or group motions containing the proposal for changes and improvements in the company. Trainings, financial rewards and material prizes are a form of incentive to participate in the program. In addition, the program allows for implementation of restructuring-modernising processes in the manner most beneficial to employees. This is also a source of savings in the production process and allows for increased efficiency, occupational health and safety and higher qualifications.

Apart from the described practices, power companies also operate in two remaining areas included in the analysis – in relation to the market and management and social reporting.

The example of good practices aimed at consumers (in this case the socially sensitive recipient) is the program "Safer with electricity" initiated in 2002 by the Polish Society of Transmission and Distribution of Electricity (PST&DE) and companies supplying electricity. Its aim is to increase the safety of use of electrical devices, reduce the number of accidents with electric current among children and young people and to promote rational use of electric energy. During the implementation of the program, there are presentations of educational films and special lectures and, thanks to the cooperation with the Fire Service, trainings for teachers involved in the program. Each subsequent year of the program shows its growing popularity among schools and local communities (fire brigades, the police, educational centres, television rooms, community centres, cultural centres, etc.) [Responsible Business Forum 2010].

In the case of good practices in management and social reporting, it is worth to mention the activities of ENEA SA Capital Group [Responsible Business Forum 2011]. Since 2010, the process of organizing the existing enterprises from the field of social responsibility and development of a comprehensive strategy in this area has been taking place. An element of this process was the review of initiatives in the area of the company's social involvement which resulted in the report "'ENEA Close to community.' The review of social involvement of ENEA SA in the years 2007–2009," prepared in accordance with the principles of Global Reporting Initiative.

The Work Group for the Formulation of Strategy and Implementation of CSR was appointed to implement the process of developing the CSR strategy in the company. The work focused on four elements: the diagnosis of the current state, design of strategies, development of operational plans and implementation of the strategy. What is important is that apart from the representatives from specific company groups and employees of all key departments, the Group also included the representatives of the stakeholders of the company. The CSR Strategy of GK ENEA, integrated with the corporate strategy, focuses on issues connected with management of human capital, promotion of environmentally friendly initiatives and contacts with the local community.

The presented examples prove the involvement of power companies in CSR activities. They are often conducted in cooperation with various groups of stakeholders. Their recipients are frequently individual consumers encouraged to change habits and the way of thinking. The activities are very often multi-faceted and they do not refer to the narrow sense of the area of activity (for example they refer to the actions for the sake of the local community and the environment at the same time). They also require the use of different tools.

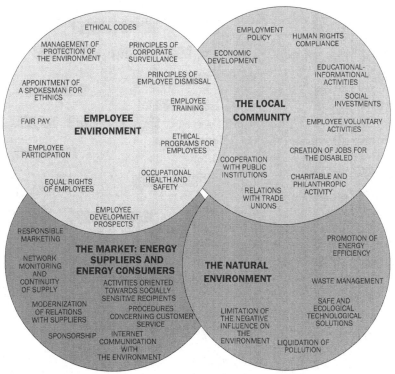

Figure 5. The map of the areas connected with social responsibility of power companies in Poland

Source: own elaboration.

On the basis of the authors' own analysis of the cases of good practices implemented in the sector and the research results of the Energy Regulatory Office in the years 2008–2010 [ERO 2008, 2009, 2010] and the previously accepted definition of CSR in the power engineering sector, the map of possible areas of activities connected with social responsibility of power companies was created (Figure 5).

SUMMARY AND CONCLUSIONS

Stakeholders' increased awareness and liberalization of energy markets emphasize the need to increase efficiency and care for the reputation of companies in the power engineering sector. The current activity of power companies in CSR (e.g. investments in the protection of the environment, fulfilment of requirements of occupational health and safety, social issues) should evolve towards the focus on measurable long-term aspects of ecological, economic and social activities. The benefit will take the form of loyalty of consumers as well as strengthening of relations with local communities and increased effectiveness of crisis prevention on the power market.

The key issues seem to be the research – development area and cooperation with academic institutions, exchange of experiences (the search for inspiration and benchmarking), the development of intra-sector system of communication and education for sustainable development.

Against a background of these challenges, there appears the regulator's special role in the dissemination of solutions, models, strategies and CSR tools.[7] Hence, the primary task of the Energy Regulatory Office in this context is the support of development of competition in the sector and maintenance of balance between the interests of companies and consumers, particularly for the sensitive customer who is at risk of energy poverty.[8]

---

[7] The President of the ERO, recognizing the importance of CSR and willing to arouse interest in the problem of the company, established in April 2008 The Group for Research on Problems of Corporate Social Responsibility of Energy Companies (which deals with projects on development and promotion of sustainable development among companies in the energy industry) and in 2009 The Team for Conducting and Designing Surveys Concerning The Problems of Corporate Social Responsibility of Energy Companies.

[8] see more: [ERO 2006].

BIBLIOGRAPHY

Caroll A.B. (1991). The pyramid of Corporate Social Responsibility: Toward the moral management of organizational stakeholders. *Business Horizons*, No. 34(4), pp. 39–48.

Carroll A.B. (1979). A three-dimensional conceptual model of Corporate Social Performance. *Academy of Management Review*, No. 4, pp. 497–505.

Centrum CSR w Polsce, 2010, http:///www.centrumcsr.pl [accessed: 21st June 2010].

Centrum Informacji o Rynku Energii (2007). *Uczestnicy rynku i formy handlu energią*, http://www.rynek-energii-elektrycznej.cire.pl [accessed: 10th March 2009].

Chodyński A. (2007). Kompetencje i reputacja w budowie zaufania między organizacjami odpowiedzialnymi społecznie. *Przegląd Organizacji*, No. 4, pp. 21–23.

Chojnacki I. (2011). Odbiorca wybiera sprzedawcę. *Nowy Przemysł*, No. 4, pp. 60–62.

Ciepiela D. (2011). Strategiczne miksowanie. *Nowy Przemysł*, No. 4, pp. 48–50.

Ciepiela D. (2011). Zyski pod napięciem. *Nowy Przemysł*, No. 4, pp. 52–54.

Clarkson M.B.E. (1995). Stakeholder framework for analyzing and evaluation corporate social performance. *Academy of Management Review*, No. 1, pp. 92–106.

Dąbrowski T.J. (2011). Polityka CSR jako element umacniania reputacji. Przykład banków. *Marketing i Rynek*, No. 2, pp. 2–9.

Dąbrowski T.J. (2011). Cause-related marketing w kreowaniu i komunikowaniu polityki społecznej odpowiedzialności biznesu. *Marketing i Rynek*, No. 3, pp. 2–8.

Ellen S.P., Webb D.J., Mohr L.A. (2006). Consumer attributions for corporate socially responsible programs. *Journal of the Academy of Marketing Science*, No. 34(2), pp. 147–157.

ERO (2006). *Dobre praktyki sprzedawców energii elektrycznej i Operatorów Systemów Przesyłowych*, http://www.ure.gov.pl [accessed: 13th July 2011].

ERO (2008). *Prezes Urzędu Regulacji Energetyki a społeczna odpowiedzialność przedsiębiorstw energetycznych*, http://www.ure.gov.pl/portal/pl [accessed: 15th June 2011].

ERO (2009). *Społeczna odpowiedzialność przedsiębiorstw energetycznych w świetle badań ankietowych – Raport*, http:// www.ure.gov.pl [accessed: 14th June 2009].

ERO (2010). *Społeczna odpowiedzialność przedsiębiorstw energetycznych w świetle drugich badań ankietowych – Raport*, http:// www.ure.gov.pl [accessed: 18th July 2010].

Forum Odpowiedzialnego Biznesu (2009). *Odpowiedzialny biznes w Polsce 2008. Dobre praktyki*, http://odpowiedzialnybiznes.pl/ [accessed: 13th October 2009].

Forum Odpowiedzialnego Biznesu (2010). *Odpowiedzialny biznes w Polsce 2009. Dobre praktyki*, http://odpowiedzialnybiznes.pl/ [accessed: 21st November 2010].

Forum Odpowiedzialnego Biznesu (2011). *Odpowiedzialny biznes w Polsce 2010. Dobre praktyki*, http://odpowiedzialnybiznes.pl/ [accessed: 12th June 2011].

Gajdzik B. (2007). Biznes odpowiedzialny społecznie. *Przegląd Organizacji*, No. 7–8, pp. 17–20.

Hąbek P., Pawłowska E. (2009). Społeczna odpowiedzialność Organizacji a kompetencje menedżerów. *Przegląd Organizacji*, No. 2, pp. 17–20.

Instytut Odpowiedzialnego Biznesu (2010), http://www.iob.org.pl [accessed: 20th June 2010].

Komisja Europejska (2010). *Europa 2020 – strategia na rzecz inteligentnego i zrównoważonego rozwoju sprzyjającego włączeniu społecznemu*, http://ec.europa.eu/eu2020/pdf/1_PL_ACT_part1_v1.pdf [accessed: 18th July 2011].

Kozłowski W. (2008). Cause-related marketing w badaniach naukowych i praktyce biznesowej. *Marketing i Rynek*, No. 6, pp. 9–14.

Maignan I., Ferrell O.C. (2004). Corporate social responsibility and marketing: An integrative framework. *Journal of the Academy of Marketing Science*, No. 32(1), pp. 3–19.

Marcinkowska M. (2010). Społeczna odpowiedzialność przedsiębiorstw a ich wyniki ekonomiczne – aspekty teoretyczne. *Przegląd Organizacji*, No. 10, pp. 7–10.

Marcinkowska M. (2010). Społeczna odpowiedzialność przedsiębiorstw a ich wyniki ekonomiczne – przegląd badań. *Przegląd Organizacji*, No. 12, pp. 3–5.

Ministerstwo Gospodarki (2006). *Program dla elektroenergetyki*, http://www.cire.pl/pliki/2/Program_dla_elektroenergetyki.pdf [accessed: 2nd March 2010].

Ministerstwo Gospodarki (2009). *Polityka energetyczna Polski do 2030 roku*, http://www.mg.gov.pl/Gospodarka/Energetyka/Polityka+energetyczna, [accessed 20th June 2009].

PGNiG/PricewaterhouseCoopers (2011). *Deklaracja w sprawie zrównoważonego rozwoju branży energetycznej w Polsce*, http://www.odpowiedzialna-energia.pl [accessed: 18th July 2011].

PricewaterhouseCoopers (2010). *Strategiczne myślenie o CSR w branży energetycznej*, http://www.pgnig.dk/oenergia/konferencja/9532 [accessed: 20th June 2011].

Rok B. (2004). *Odpowiedzialny biznes w nieodpowiedzialnym świecie*. Akademia Rozwoju Filantropii w Polsce, Forum Odpowiedzialnego Biznesu, Warszawa, http://www.konkurencyjnafirma.pl/dokumenty/odpowiedzialny_biznes_w_nieodpowiedzialnym_swiecie.pdf [accessed: 16th March 2010].

Vlachos P.A., Tsamakos A., Vrechopoulos A.P., Avramidis P.K. (2009). Corporate social responsibility: attributions, loyalty, and the mediating role of trust. *Journal of the Academy of Marketing Science*, No. 37, pp. 170–180.

MAŁGORZATA BUDZANOWSKA-DRZEWIECKA

Jagiellonian University
Institute of Economics and Management
Chair of Organizational Behaviour

NATALIA DUDZIŃSKA-KORCZAK

Jagiellonian University
Institute of Economics and Management
Department of Organization and Management

ANETA LIPIŃSKA

Jagiellonian University
Institute of Economics and Management
Chair of Standardized Management Systems

CORPORATE SOCIAL RESPONSIBILITY ACTIVITIES IMPLEMENTED BY COMPANIES IN THE POWER SECTOR IN THE OPINION OF INDIVIDUAL CUSTOMERS

INTRODUCTION

In recent years, the interest in the concept of corporate social responsibility (CSR) has grown among both researchers and entrepreneurs. These activities are often carried out to improve the competitive position. However, it is impossible to make use of the concept of CSR without being involved in cooperation with entities present on the market. The cooperation of stakeholders[1] takes place, for example, through self-regulatory initiatives, such as, the Codes of Good Practice or the Codes of Ethics and as part of the companies' cooperation and dialogue with local environment and customers. Thanks to CSR, companies can, while working with stakeholders, contribute to the reconciliation of economic, social and environmental goals [Energy Regulatory Office 2008]. More often Polish companies from the energy sector engage in CSR activities. Therefore, it seems relevant to look for the answer

---

[1] Stakeholders are individuals or groups which may influence or are influenced by companies' actions through their products, strategies and manufacturing processes, management systems and procedures [Rok 2004, p. 19].

to the question about the perception of these activities among the entities to which they are addressed, both for pragmatic and cognitive reasons. The study focuses on one of the major groups of recipients – consumers. The aim of this paper is to describe individual consumers' (representatives of households – consumers of electric energy) perception of CSR activities in the power sector in Poland. The realization of the goal was possible thanks to the systematization of CSR activities on the basis of scientific and trade publications and empirical verification of the reception of these activities.

1. THE CONCEPT OF CORPORATE SOCIAL RESPONSIBILITY

In the literature of the subject, one can find references to different ways of defining the concept of CSR. The transition from its objective presentation to a subjective one can be noted. In the first case, theories and research focus on defining the area and the way of implementing CSR activities, in the second – the focus is on the recipients of these activities. In early scientific concepts, the emphasis was put on objective understanding of corporate social responsibility. CSR initiatives were defined, as part of these concepts, as social, economic, legal or discretionary[2] commitments [Maignan, Ferrell 2004, pp. 3–19; Caroll 1979, pp. 497–505]. In other research currents, CSR was understood as actions taken as a result of ethical reasons or as a management process [Dąbrowski 2011a, pp. 2–9]. The subjective approach to CSR provides answers to the question of to whom companies are socially responsible, most often taking into account the perspective of stakeholders [Maignan, Ferrell 2004, pp. 3–19; Dąbrowski 2011a, pp. 2–9].

The references to the concept of corporate social responsibility can also be found in the studies on the issues of individual industries and sectors. In the documents from the Energy Regulatory Office (ERO), CSR is characterized as a strategy which harmoniously combines ethical and ecological aspects of business activity with its dominant attribute, that is, effectiveness, great openness, transparency of action, fairness to customers (the calculation of prices, quality of supply and service) and in contacts with other stakeholders (including employees, shareholders, suppliers, local community), self-limitation of monopolistic advantage [*Społeczna odpowiedzialność przedsiębiorstw energetycznych w świetle III badań ankietowych* 2011].

---

[2] Discretionary activities are connected with the companies' voluntary activity oriented to the society. These activities go beyond the binding norms and values in this society [Dąbrowski 2011, p. 3].

In the literature of the subject, one can observe the researchers' interest in the perception of CSR among individual consumers [Brown, Dacin 1997, pp 68–84; Sen, Bhattacharya 2001, pp. 225–243] and marketing practitioners [Singhapakdi, Vitell, Rallapalli, Kraft 1996, pp. 1131–1140 cited in Maignan, Ferrell 2004, pp. 3–19]. The research on specific dimensions of CSR is also undertaken. It includes, for instance, supporting charity actions [Barone, Miyazaki, Taylor 2000, pp. 248–262] or the environmental protection [Drum-wright 1994, pp. 1–19].

On the basis of the analysis of the mentioned concepts, it was assumed that CSR activities will be regarded as part of the four areas of responsibility, that is the market, employees, the environment and local communities. These areas can be related to the so-called levels of social involvement of companies which was shown schematically in Figure 1.

Figure 1. The levels of social involvement of the company
Source: own elaboration based on Rok 2004, p. 46.

The basic level of involvement relates to the main activity of the company and includes the effects of this activity on all interested parties. The activities at the basic level are an element of business activity regulated by the law and, therefore, are of an obligatory nature. The remaining levels include voluntary activity which covers commercial undertakings in the social environment (e.g. sponsorship of culture, education or sports), investments in the local community (e.g. cooperation with social organizations, corporate volunteering) and philanthropic activity (such as grants for philanthropic projects [Rok 2004, pp. 1–74].

When engaging in CSR activities, companies expect the effects in the form of improvement of the image and reputation and an increase in profitability and value [Marcinkowska 2010, pp. 7–10; Chodyński 2007, pp. 21–23; Dąbrowski 2011a, pp. 2–9].

2. CORPORATE SOCIAL RESPONSIBILITY ACTIVITIES WITHIN THE POWER SECTOR IN POLAND

As already mentioned, in recent years there has been a significant increase in CSR activities implemented by power companies in Poland. The research of the Energy Regulatory Office[3] shows that companies from this sector successively develop their own strategies for CSR. In 2010, more than a half of the companies (52%) did not have their own developed formal CSR strategy and only 14% of them claimed they had it. A year later, these proportions were reversed and they were 42% and 16%, respectively. Even more power companies claimed they had included CSR principles in their business strategies (42% in 2009, 65% in 2010 and 84% in 2011).

An equally significant increase appeared in the case of adoption of voluntary initiatives and self-regulations referring to CSR. In 2010, only 30% of power companies claimed they adopted self-regulation and in the next year – more than twice as many (75%) [*Społeczna odpowiedzialność przedsiębiorstw energetycznych w świetle III badań ankietowych* 2011].

Actions promoting CSR in the power sector are, to a great extent, stimulated by the Energy Regulatory Office thanks to the initiatives, such as, regulations, spread of knowledge about the energy market as part of informational and educational activities or the establishment of *the Team for the Coordination of Works on the Issues of Corporate Social Responsibility of Power Companies in ERO* named *The recipient zone in the power industry*. The enumerated actions have been carried out by the Energy Regulatory Office from 2007 to the present and are aimed at end consumers [Energy Regulatory Office 2009].

The benefits of the introduction of CSR strategies include: increasing consumer and stakeholder loyalty, improvement of relations with the local community, raising the level of organizational culture of companies and ensuring permanent development and growth of the value of companies [Energy Regulatory Office 2008].

The examples of the tools by the use of which power industry companies engage in CSR activities in specific areas were shown in Figure 2 as a reference to the previously discussed concept of CSR.

---

[3] The study *Społeczna odpowiedzialność przedsiębiorstw energetycznych w świetle III badań ankietowych* was conducted by the Energy Regulatory Office (ERO) in Poland in the years 2009–2011. The study included from 61% (in 2009) to 90% (in 2011) of the power companies on the base of ERO granted concessions. They represented the energy industry sectors, such as, electric power, gas industry, heat engineering. The results of the studies concerning the energy sector were used in this article.

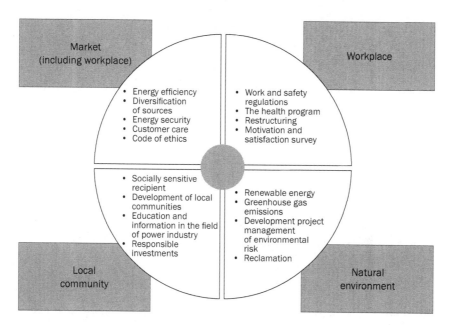

Figure 2. The areas of the implementation of CSR activities by power companies
Source: own elaboration on the basis of PricewaterhouseCoopers 2010.

3. CONCEPTUAL BACKGROUND AND SAMPLE

The results of the studies involving individual consumers [Sen, Bhattacharya 2001, pp. 225–243] suggest that the awareness of the company's CSR activities among consumers is a key factor limiting the process of gaining benefits from them. The consumers' skills concerning correct identification of CSR activities of the companies the products of which they consume are actually insignificant.

As part of the presented studies, the focus was primarily on establishing the level of awareness of the implementation of CSR activities by power companies and their assessment among individual electricity users (household representatives of both sexes).

The study was completed in July 2011.[4] The sample was purposely selected. It was decided to analyse the opinions of consumers of electric en-

[4] The presented studies are part of the research project entitled *Identification and assessment of CSR in the power sector in Poland* developed at the Institute of Economics and Management at the Jagiellonian University in Kraków as part of the article's authors' own research conducted at the turn of June and July 2011.

ergy in Malopolskie Voivodeship. 140 respondents took part in the study. 136 correctly completed questionnaires were classified for further analysis (Table 1 includes research sample characteristics).

Table 1. The distributions of the most important metrical variables

Variable	Values	Frequency	Percentage
Sex	Female	66	48
	Male	70	51
Place of residence	Countryside	56	41
	City up to 100 thousand residents	29	21
	City above 100 thousand up to 500 thousand residents	9	7
	City above 500 thousand residents	42	31
Per capita net income	Below PLN 1000 / person	32	24
	PLN 1001–2000 / person	51	37
	PLN 2001–3000 / person	30	22
	Above PLN 3000 / person	17	12
	No data	6	5
Professional links with the sector	Current professional work	3	2
	Previous professional work	10	7
	No professional links	107	79
	No data	16	12

N = 136

Source: own elaboration.

Most respondents identify the companies from the power sector only as suppliers of electricity. Their contacts with energy companies are limited to paying bills (79% of respondents), contacts with Customer Service (14%) and completing the formalities of connecting to the electricity supply (7%). 3% of respondents indicated that there is no direct contact with the companies from the examined sector.

4. THE RESPONDENTS' EXPECTATIONS OF THE COMPANIES' CSR ACTIVITIES IN THE POWER SECTOR

CSR activities are, among other things, to increase the competitiveness of companies which engage in them, provided that the recipients are able to identify these activities and assess the involvement in them as a valuable attribute matching their expectations.

The results of the conducted studies indicated that in the range of opinions concerning basic objectives realized by the entities of the analysed sector, the respondents notice, above all, the efforts to make and keep a stable profit (Figure 3).

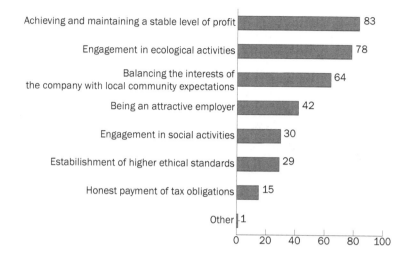

Figure 3. The main objectives of the companies in the power sector in the opinion of responders

N = 342 (dichotomous question)

Source: own elaboration.

More than a half of the respondents (78 people, 57%) believes that companies should engage in ecological activities. What is important is that respondents do not combine the objectives of the companies with ethical actions – these categories received the smallest number of indications.

Most respondents, in their assessment of power companies, did not take into account the activities carried out for the sake of corporate social responsibility. Respondents point mainly to typical market criteria referring to the price (66 cases, 49%) and the service provided (Figure 4).

CSR activity factor which received the greatest number of indications as one of the evaluation criteria of power companies was the contribution to the environmental protection (45 people, 33%) which confirms earlier observations. Expectations concerning the involvement in activities aimed at the widely understood environmental protection are consistent with the answers to the question about the type of actions which should be taken into account by companies from the power sector. Care for the environment and the resulting development and implementation of new technologies were the most often chosen categories connected with CSR (Figure 5). More-

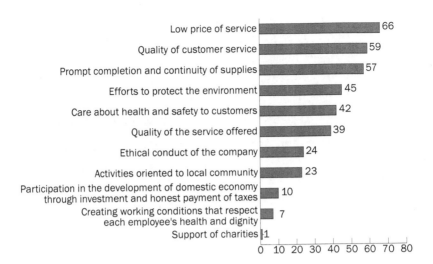

Figure 4. The criteria of the assessment of companies from the power sector used by the responders

N = 373 (multiple choice question)

Source: own elaboration.

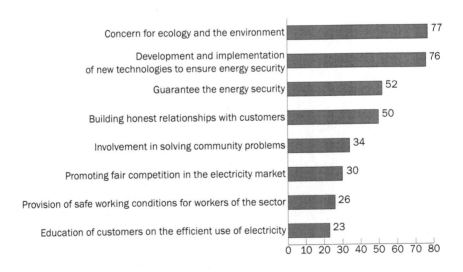

Figure 5. The responders' expectations of CSR activities in the power sector

N = 368 (multiple choice question)

Source: own elaboration.

over, respondents emphasized the importance of commitments made by the companies to individual consumers, expecting to build honest relationships with customers and ensuring energy security. Interestingly enough, respondents expect activities concerning solving problems connected with environmental protection believing at the same time that the activities in the field of environmental education are unnecessary among recipients (the lowest number of indications – 23 persons, 17%).

5. THE FAMILIARITY WITH CSR ACTIVITIES CARRIED OUT BY POWER COMPANIES AMONG RESPONDERS

Individual customers are one of the groups of stakeholders for which companies engage in CSR activities using various tools. The results demonstrated very low awareness of this type of activities at the cognitive level. The familiarity with the concept of CSR among respondents in the case of theoretical knowledge and the skills of identifying actual activities of the company are extremely low. Only 26 respondents (19%) made an attempt to define what corporate social responsibility is by combining it with activities aimed at protecting the environment and stakeholders (employees, co-workers and customers). A significant part of respondents (43 people, 32%) had difficulty determining whether the entities in the examined sector engage in CSR activities. Among those who undertook to determine their frequency, only 45 (33%) respondents stated that such activities are frequently carried out (including 7 answers *very often*). Such a low level of awareness of these activities probably explains why they are not used as a basis for the assessment of the companies in the power sector.

As mentioned earlier, CSR actions are often classified as part of the four areas, namely work environment, a local community, the market and the natural environment. In the case of the presented studies, this typology was used in order to determine the level of respondents' knowledge about each category of these activities.

The greatest difficulty for the respondents was the group of activities concerning relations between companies and workers. Respondents are not aware of the implementation of activities aimed at improving working conditions and protecting workers and do not connect them with CSR activities. In the case of all specific categories which were examined, the responses *I don't know* were dominant (Figure 6). On average, 88 (65%) respondents reported the lack of knowledge about the activities in this area and 10% were quite convinced that such activities are not carried out. Only in the case of the assessment of the care of industrial safety, 50 (37%) respondents claimed that companies in the sector carry out such activities.

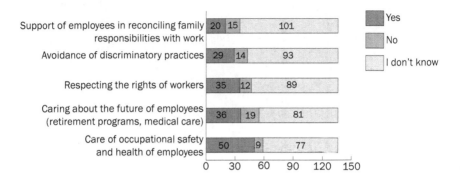

Figure 6. Familiarity with CSR activities in the work environment from the point of view of responders

Source: own elaboration.

The inability to indicate whether a given CSR activity from the field of the relations with workers is carried out by power companies is clearly evident in the case of category of supporting workers in their attempt to reconcile family responsibilities with work. It was decided to determine whether these doubts concern both sexes to the same extent (Figure 7).

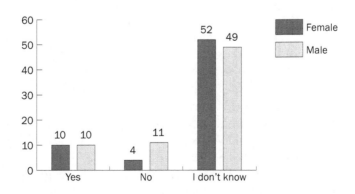

Figure 7. The support of workers in reconciling family responsibilities with work in the opinion of responders

Source: own elaboration.

There appeared little variation in the assessments of the presence of the discussed activity depending on sex. Males showed greater scepticism about the companies' support of employees in reconciling work with family responsibilities; at the same time much fewer females think that such actions are not implemented. The possible interpretation of this observation may be the stereotypical division of gender roles in Polish society, in which, males pay no attention to such practices.

In the case of the remaining specific categories of activities, no significant variation of the responses depending on sex was observed except for men's characteristic tendency to express their opinion. They more often opted for the presence or absence of a given activity in comparison to females whose responses were dominant in the category indicating the lack of sufficient knowledge or the urge to avoid responding (most answers – *I don't know*).

The second analysed area focused on determining the level of knowledge about customer service (the supplier and customer market). In this category of activities respondents showed greater ease of identifying CSR activities probably due to the fact that they themselves were their recipients (Figure 8).

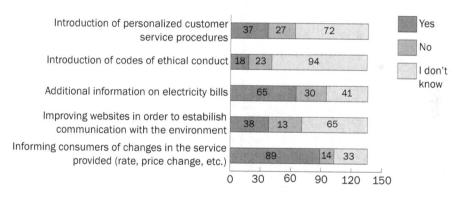

Figure 8. The familiarity with CRS activities within customer service among respondents
Source: own elaboration.

Respondents agreed that power companies carry out activities connected with informing them of the changes in the service provided, including those placed on bills for their services. However, they had huge doubts about the existence of the codes of ethical conduct which regulate the principles of customer service (69% of respondents were unable to clarify their views on this subject).

The tested connections between the variation in awareness of the specific activities in the area of customer service and sex revealed trends similar to those from the previously analysed area (the activities in the work environment). Females and males similarly assess individual activities. However, women are more equivocal and more often choose the answer *I don't know*. It is worth noting that in the case of the assessment of current informing about the changes in the service provided only 2 women (1%) claimed that these actions do not occur (Figure 9). This may be due to the fact that women are more often burdened with the necessity to pay bills and hence their slightly greater certainty of the presence of this category of activities in comparison to men (12 – 9% responses *The activity does not occur*).

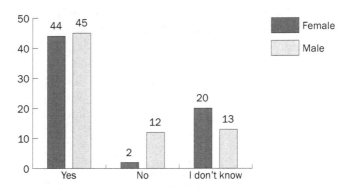

Figure 9. Informing customers about changes in the service provided from the point of view of respondents

Source: own elaboration.

Another analysed area referred to different activities for the sake of the widely understood welfare of the local community. Although the respondents are indirectly the recipients of these activities (especially those with commercial overtones, such as, sponsorship), they had difficulty in identifying their presence (Figure 10). It is interesting that as many as 29 people (21%) believe that companies do not engage in charitable activities.

The greatest number of doubts in the opinion of the responders was raised by the cooperation with public (self-governmental) institutions (72% of the responses *I don't know*) and corporate volunteering (70% of the responses *I don't know*). According to the research results, both men and women were hesitant about the implementation of this kind of activities. However, here (similarly to the previously discussed trend in the distribution of variables depending on sex), women's indications were dominant. Men more often pointed to the presence or non-presence of the activities (Figure 11).

The last area of activities referred to the environmental protection initiatives. Only two categories of activities in this area were examined (Figure 12). It turned out that, despite the previously identified expectations of the implementation of measures to protect the environment, the respondents

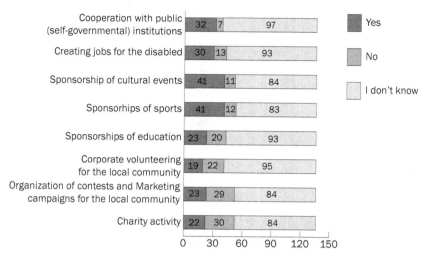

Figure 10. The familiarity with CSR activities as part of the activities for the sake of the local community among responders

Source: own elaboration.

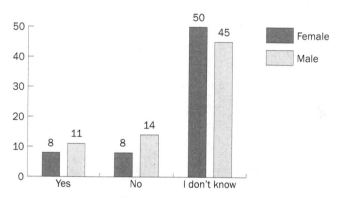

Figure 11. Corporate volunteering for the sake of the local community in the opinion of the respondents with the division into sex

Source: own elaboration.

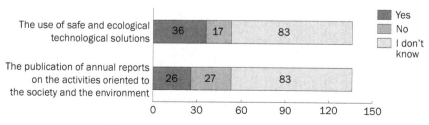

Figure 12. The familiarity with CSR activities oriented to environmental protection among respondents

Source: own elaboration.

are unable to name any of them. They only took a position on the categories presented in the research tool and, thus, demonstrated that they are not aware of their implementation (83 people, 61%).

6. THE ASSESSMENT OF CSR ACTIVITIES CARRIED OUT BY THE COMPANIES FROM THE POWER SECTOR

As part of the conducted studies, respondents were asked to assess CSR activities carried out by the companies from the power sector. The respondents assessed them as average (the average of the indications 3.15), which may be connected with low awareness of the activities carried out by the companies in this sector. No significant differences were noticed between women's (3.15) and men's (3.16) evaluations.

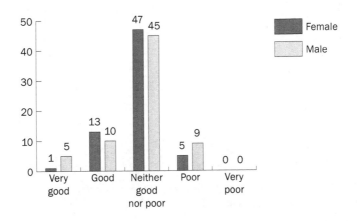

Figure 13. The assessment of CSR activities carried out by the companies from the power sector in the opinion of respondents

N = 135

Source: own elaboration.

Only in the case of positive assessments, the distributions indicate that sex diversifies assessments (Figure 13). Males chose an extremely positive assessment while females on the contrary. None of the respondents assessed the level of the service very negatively. In comparison to this, positive assessments appeared more often.

Similar results were obtained by asking respondents to assess the companies' involvement in CSR activities. In both cases, the respondents assessed these activities as being at a moderate level (average 3.3), males –3.2, females –3.35 (Figure 14).

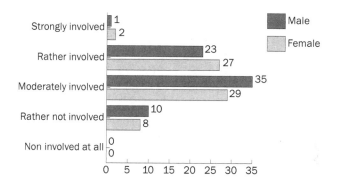

Figure 14. The assessment of involvement in CSR activities carried out by the companies from the power sector in the opinion of respondents

N = 135

Source: own elaboration.

The results show that females evaluate the companies' involvement in CSR as better. Importantly, neither males nor females pointed to the total lack of involvement in this sphere of activity.

It was assumed that the assessment of CSR activities can correlate with the assessment of the quality of the service provided, which would be consistent with the results of earlier research on the basis of which the creation and implementation of CSR activities were recommended to those who offer a high standard of service [Vlachos et al. 2009, pp. 170–180]. The results confirmed this correlation (Figure 15).

Respondents who assessed the level of service quality as low also negatively assessed CSR activities carried out by the companies from the sector. However, in the case of the respondents satisfied with the purchased service, there appeared a trend towards a higher assessment of CSR activities. This can be explained by the *halo effect* in which a positive evaluation of the purchased service translates into a favourable attitude towards other activities carried out by the company.

The intentions ascribed to the activities carried out by companies were also examined. For this reason, respondents were asked to assess the activities using a semantic scale (Figure 16). The average assessment rate was most often chosen which may result from a small amount of knowledge about the activities, as shown above.

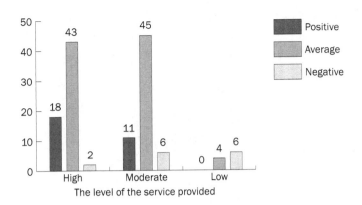

Figure 15. The assessment of CSR activities of power companies vs. the level of satisfaction with the service

The average assessment ratio of the service provided by companies – 3.45

Source: own elaboration.

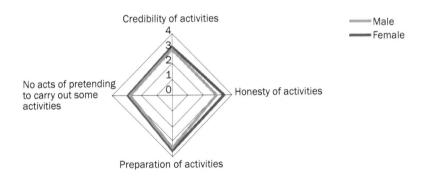

Figure 16. The assessment of CSR activities carried out by companies in the power sector with the division into sex

Source: own elaboration.

There appeared small differences in assessing the fairness of the activities depending on sex. Males showed greater scepticism by more often ascribing dishonest intentions to CSR activities. Males also provided lower assessments of the credibility of the implemented activities.

Despite a large percentage of people who could not identify CSR activities in the four areas (work environment, the local community, supplier and customer markets and the natural environment), the level of assessment of these activities was determined with taking into account the responses of people who pointed to such activities.

In the case of the assessment of the activities aimed at individual service recipients, the similar level of assessment of individual types of activities was observed. Average assessment rates ranged from 3.3 to 4.0 on a five-point scale (Figure 17).

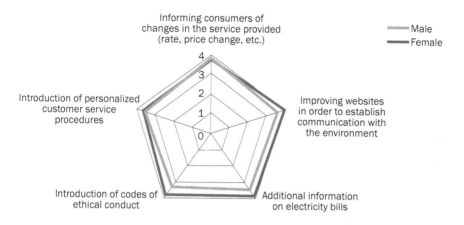

Figure 17. The assessment of CSR activities in customer service with the division into sex
Source: own elaboration.

There appeared differences in assessments depending on sex. In all cases, women provided higher assessments of the implementation of the activities than men. This result is consistent with the distribution of assessments of involvement in CSR activities in which women provided higher evaluations of the variable.

As part of this category, the greatest variation in the assessment appeared in relation to the codes of ethics. Out of 18 respondents who assessed the activities, men (13 people) were the majority. Despite greater ease of identifying the activities, they assessed them more negatively (3.31) than women (3.8).

The assessments of CSR activities aimed at employees were also analysed. As previously noted, in this case due to the activities' being aimed at stakeholders, respondents had a problem with identifying the activities. However, those who indicated that the actions are implemented made relatively high assessments (the average close to 4) (Figure 18).

As it appears from the data analysis that the assessments of the activities depend on sex. However, in this case, men made higher assessments of individual activities. The largest variation can be seen in the case of the evaluation of avoidance of discriminatory practices. Men positively assess these activities (4.25), while women evaluate them as average (3.4). This result can be explained by a different professional situation of men and women and unequal treatment of employees because of sex.

<figure>Figure 18. The assessment of CSR activities in relations with employees with the division into sex

Source: own elaboration.</figure>

Differences in assessments were also observed in relation to specific activities for the sake of the local community. In most cases, in this category men evaluated the implemented activites higher (Figure 19).

Figure 19. The assessment of CSR activities oriented to the local community
Source: own elaboration.

The differences are especially evident in the assessment of corporate volunteering and sponsorship of education. Women proved to be more sceptical. In the case of the assessment of corporate volunteering, there appeared a difference in one assessment (women 3.37 – *average*; men 4.2 – *good*). Larger differences appeared in relation to the assessment of the sponsorship of education. In this case, men assessed the activities as *very good* (4.58) and women as *average* (3.33).

The activities oriented to the environmental protection were the last analyzed area. In this case, there appear differences in the evaluation of the activities depending on sex (Figure 20).

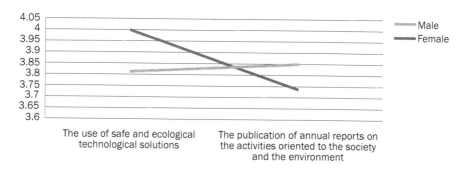

Figure 20. The assessment of CSR activities oriented at the environmental protection with the division into sex

Source: own elaboration.

Women assessed the efforts to implement safe and ecological technological solutions higher. Men, on the other hand, made higher assessments of the reports of the activities oriented at the environmental protection. Men's lower evaluation of the implementation of proecological technologies may be linked to their greater knowledge of the functioning of the sector.

CONCLUSIONS

Companies implementing CSR activities should pay more attention to informing and educating the recipients of these activities. The analysis showed that a great number of CSR activities in the power sector does not go along with raising the awareness of these activities in the opinion of individual consumers. The results showed differences in assessments at the cognitive and affective level. In the case of little familiarity with the activities, the assessments are comparatively high. However, women are more equivocal in their answers concerning their familiarity and they more often chose the answer *I have no opinion*. There is no reason to interpret the result as a manifestation of a smaller amount of knowledge. The reason being that men more often answered that the activities do not exist, although they are actually implemented by the companies of the analysed sector.

It seems a valuable conclusion seems that the assessment of CSR activities depends on the quality of the service provided. It appears that only in the case of positive assessment of the quality of service, consumers value the company on the basis of other attributes.

What is important is that sex modifies the assessment of the implemented CSR activities. Women have a tendency to make higher assessments of them. The exception included the activities from the area of the work environment and local community, in which men evaluated the implemented initiatives higher.

The obtained results are not fully consistent with other studies on this subject according to which consumers have higher and higher expectations of a corporation and are becoming more demanding and aware of its behaviours [EURO RSCG Poland 2008]. Low awareness of the implemented CSR activities may be connected with the specificity of the analysed sector.

BIBLIOGRAPHY

Barone M.J., Miyazaki A.D., Taylor K.A. (2000). The influence of cause-related marketing on consumer choice: Does one good turn deserve another? *Journal of the Academy of Marketing Science*, Vol. 28, No. 2, pp. 248–262.

Brown T.J., Dacin P.A. (1997). The company and the product: Corporate associations and consumer product responses. *Journal of Marketing*, No. 61, pp. 68–84.

Caroll A.B. (1991). The pyramid of corporate social responsibility: Toward the moral management of organizational stakeholders. *Business Horizons*, Vol. 34, No. 4, pp. 39–48.

Carroll A.B. (1979). A three-dimensional conceptual model of corporate social performance. *Academy of Management Review*, No. 4, pp. 497–505.

Chodyński A. (2007). Kompetencje i reputacja w budowie zaufania między organizacjami odpowiedzialnymi społecznie. *Przegląd Organizacji*, No. 6, pp. 21–23.

Dąbrowski T.J. (2011a). Polityka CSR jako element umacniania reputacji. Przykład banków. *Marketing i Rynek*, No. 2, pp. 2–9.

Dąbrowski T.J. (2011b). Cause-related marketing w kreowaniu i komunikowaniu polityki społecznej odpowiedzialności biznesu. *Marketing i Rynek*, No. 3, pp. 2–8.

Drumwright M.E. (1994). Socially responsible organizational buying: Environmental concern as a noneconomic buying criterion. *Journal of Marketing*, No. 58, pp. 1–19.

EURO RSCG Poland (2008). *Przyszłość marki korporacyjnej*, http://media.sensors.pl/pr/110310/euro-rscg-poland-prezentuje-wyniki-badania-przyszlosc-marki-korporacyjnej [accessed: 21st August 2010].

Gajdzik B. (2007). Biznes odpowiedzialny społecznie. *Przegląd Organizacji*, No. 7–8, pp. 17–20.

Hąbek P., Pawłowska E. (2009). Społeczna odpowiedzialność organizacji a kompetencje menedżerów. *Przegląd Organizacji*, No. 2, pp. 17–20.

Kozłowski W. (2008). Cause-related marketing w badaniach naukowych i praktyce biznesowej. *Marketing i Rynek*, No. 6, pp. 9–14.

Maignan I., Ferrell O.C. (2004). Corporate social responsibility and marketing: An integrative framework. *Journal of the Academy of Marketing Science*, Vol. 32, No. 1, pp. 3–19.

Marcinkowska M. (2010). Społeczna odpowiedzialność przedsiębiorstw a ich wyniki ekonomiczne – przegląd badań. *Przegląd Organizacji*, No. 12, pp. 3–5.

Marcinkowska M. (2010). Społeczna odpowiedzialność przedsiębiorstw a ich wyniki ekonomiczne – aspekty teoretyczne. *Przegląd Organizacji*, No. 10, pp. 7–10.

PricewaterhouseCoopers (2010). *Strategiczne myślenie o CSR w branży energetycznej*, http://www.pgnig.dk/oenergia/konferencja/9532 [accessed: 20th June 2011].

Rok B. (2004). *Odpowiedzialny biznes w nieodpowiedzialnym świecie*. Akademia Rozwoju Filantropii w Polsce, Forum Odpowiedzialnego Biznesu, http://www.konkurencyjnafirma.pl/dokumenty/odpowiedzialny_biznes_w_nieodpowiedzialnym_swiecie. pdf [accessed: 16th March 2010].

Scholder E.P., Webb D.J., Mohr L.A. (2006). Consumer attributions for corporate socially responsible programs. *Journal of the Academy of Marketing Science*, Vol. 34, No. 2, pp. 147–157.

Sen S., Bhattacharya C.B. (2001). Does doing good always lead to doing better? Consumer reactions to corporate social responsibility. *Journal of Marketing Research*, No. 38, pp. 225–243.

Społeczna odpowiedzialność przedsiębiorstw energetycznych w świetle III badań ankietowych (2011). III Ogólnopolska Konferencja Odpowiedzialność sektora energetycznego a wyzwania społeczno-gospodarcze Polski i świata, http://www.pgnig.pl/oenergia/24092/24801 [accessed: 10th June 2011].

Urząd Regulacji Energetyki (2008). *Prezes Urzędu Regulacji Energetyki a społeczna odpowiedzialność przedsiębiorstw energetycznych*, http://www.ure.gov.pl/portal/pl [accessed: 15th June 2011].

Urząd Regulacji Energetyki (2009). *Społeczna odpowiedzialność przedsiębiorstw energetycznych w świetle badań ankietowych*, http://www.cire.pl/pliki/2/spolodpowprzed.pdf, [accessed: 30th June 2010].

Vlachos P.A., Tsamakos A., Vrechopoulos A.P., Avramidis P.K. (2009). Corporate social responsibility: attributions, loyalty, and the mediating role of trust. *Journal of the Academy of Marketing Science*, No. 37, pp. 170–180.

MONIKA JEDYNAK

Jagiellonian University
Institute of Economics and Management
Chair of Marketing and Operational Management

USING KAIZEN TO IMPROVE COMPETITIVENESS OF SUPPLIERS

INTRODUCTION

The need to maintain competitiveness of a company, region, city or a country is becoming a prerequisite from the management sciences perspective. Nevertheless, in order to achieve the required level of competitiveness it is necessary to reach for various management tool. M. Imai [1986] in his paper under the highly expressive title of *Kaizen: The Key to Japan's Competitive Success* indicates the groundbreaking significance of applying kaizen from the point of view of Japanese economy. In this philosophy M. Imai seeks the key success factor both for individual Japanese companies and the Japanese economy as a whole. From the date of publication of the famous above mentioned work we have been dealing with a certain kind of phenomenon of a difficult to quantify kaizen diffusion. The diffusion is manifested among others in:

- immense popularisation of applying kaizen principles in numerous countries and organizations,
- continuous enhancement of kaizen methodology,
- dynamic rise in the number and diversity of kaizen applications,
- stimulating with the use of kaizen creation and development of other management concepts, methods and tools,
- growth and professionalization of consulting and training services in the kaizen area.

The above outlined global kaizen tendencies, occurring in practice in operations of organizations of various sectors, do not remain neutral against management sciences both in cognitive and pragmatic dimension. For, if a research subject of a science field or discipline (management in this case) undergoes some changes, it requires some reflection from the researchers representing this field. The above premise justifies the kaizen studies started

by the author of the present paper. Among the fundamental objectives of the publication there are:
- – attempt to determine the formal status of kaizen,
- – identification and arrangement of current directions and research problems concerning kaizen,
- – specification of possibilities to use kaizen in a new manner in order to increase competitiveness of suppliers in their relations with client.

1. FORMAL STATUS OF KAIZEN
– REVIEW OF LITERATURE

The above mentioned study of M. Imai [1986] triggered an "cascade" of scientific research dedicated to kaizen. In majority of the scientific publications their authors formulate views on formal status of kaizen. It is worth to start deliberations on the subject from revising terminological issue. The term of kaizen was coined as a combination of two components [Suarez-Barraza, Lingham 2008, p. 3]: *kai* (change) and *zen* (to become good).

In the first stage of its development kaizen was an offer to complete, or at times to replace, change management theories and models worked out and used in the West [Pettigrew 1990; Mintzberg, Westley 1992]. Thanks to kaizen, processes of transformation of solutions applied in organizations became oriented towards continuous improvement. The last term is sometimes regarded synonymous to kaizen and very well clarifies the essence of approach towards organization improvement as understood in kaizen. Therefore, change and improvement are inseparable conceptual correlates of kaizen. The third complementary element of kaizen results from the main objective of its application which originally is elimination of muda [Suarez Barraza, Smith, Dahlgaard-Park Su Mi 2009, p. 146], that is waste.

From the point of view of selected management concepts and some solutions used in business practice, kaizen functions as principles creating them, usually of fundamental character. Such perception of kaizen concerns, among others, such management concepts as: Total Quality Management [Imai 2006; Doolen, Van Aken, Farris, Worley, Huwe 2008, p. 640], Lean Management [Emiliani 2005, p. 39], Six Sigma [Doolen, Van Aken, Farris, Worley, Huwe 2008, p. 639], as well as Toyota Production System [Suarez Barraza, Smith, Dahlgaard-Park Su Mi 2009, p. 144]. Understanding of kaizen as a principle gives it solely a status of a component of the listed concepts.

In the literature of the subject [Suarez-Barraza, Lingham 2008, p. 3] one can also find definition of kaizen as a procedure methodology. In this respect kaizen methodology can be explained either with the use of its key principles or by the set of detailed methods and techniques comprised and used by this methodology.

It is not infrequently that kaizen is regarded as philosophy. According to M.F. Suarez-Barraza and T. Lingham [2008, p. 3], kaizen as a philosophy consists of two concepts, i.e. Kaizen (Continuous Improvement) and Kairyo (Process Improvement). Defining kaizen as a philosophy is the highest status in the hierarchy and refers to fundamental assumptions of organization functioning and views of the top management. Nevertheless, such a definition indicates general and relatively abstract nature of kaizen which can be questioned.

Assigning kaizen the status of management concept does not raise this sort of doubts. With respect to its conceptual meaning kaizen is described by the set of key rules of conduct, implementation of which will be possible by way of operationalization with the use of selected models and methods. In the classical proposal of M. Imai [1986] the key kaizen principles are as follows:

- Kaizen is process-oriented;
- Improving and maintaining standard;
- People orientation.

When deliberating on kaizen as a management concept two approaches can be noticed. The first one, as above, treats kaizen as an autonomous management concept. Doolen, Van Aken, Farris, Worley, Huwe [2008, p. 639] rightly point that kaizen may concern all areas of company operations. Lack of functional or hierarchical restrictions indicates multithreaded and very universal character of kaizen.

Simultaneously, it can be observed that kaizen is treated as a management concept with its own character complementary to other management concepts, e.g. Lean management [Suarez Barraza, Smith, Dahlgaard-Park Su Mi 2009]. This type of perspective results in attempts to integrate kaizen with other management concepts with the intention to achieve the synergy effect. The recalled integration activities lead to coining new terms, e.g. Lean-kaizen. In such case, kaizen becomes the subject of integration.

Highly important cognitive findings can be reached by including the time factor in deliberations on kaizen. Traditional view [Sawada 1995] commonly shared is that kaizen is a process of activities that are implemented continuously. In line with this interpretation time span of implementing kaizen is unlimited. At the same time however, M.F. Suarez Barraza, T. Smith, Su Mi Dahlgaard-Park [2009] note that currently two approaches can co-exist:

- the first one, long-term, based on traditional Japanese quality management system;

– the second one, short-term (one or two weeks) based on projects where implementation of kaizen is restricted to a selected area.

With reference to the latter, treating kaizen as a programme or project can be found every now and then [Van Aken, Farris, Glover, Letens 2010; Doolen, Van Aken, Farris, Worley, Huwe 2008]. Introduction of this sort of formal status draws attention towards organizational conditions and instruments used in case of project and programme management – kaizen events management.

Kaizen can also be attributed with a process status [Emiliani 2005, p. 39]. Perceiving kaizen as a process directs attention particularly towards the sequence of activities taking place as part of improvement. The sequence has been presented in a series of framework reference models the most popular of which being the PDCA model which forms the basis for constructing a series of modern management standards, e.g. quality, environment, occupational health and safety, risk management, etc.

Similarly to the above, kaizen also happens to be regarded as a management technique [Suarez Barraza, Smith, Dahlgaard-Park Su Mi 2009, p. 147]. Such an understanding of kaizen refers to its operational character. In this case the above given models of procedure gain the status of management technique by specifying them and multiple verification in practice.

Summary of the above deliberations on the formal status of kaizen are included in Table 1.

Table 1. Main interpretations of kaizen's status

Author	Status	Description
Imai 2006 Doolen, Van Aken, Farris, Worley, Huwe 2008 Emiliani 2005 Suarez Barraza, Smith, Dahlgaard-Park Su Mi 2009	Kaizen as a principle	Kaizen as a principle co-creates the conceptual foundation of superior management concepts or practical solutions. Degree of implementation of kaizen as a principle partly determines the success of implementation of a management concept or practical solutions.
Suarez-Barraza, Lingham 2008	Kaizen as a methodology	Kaizen integrates and uses detailed methods and techniques which are applied in specific configuration. It is possible to characterize kaizen as a methodology with the use of framework principles and management guidelines.
Suarez-Barraza, Lingham 2008	Kaizen as a philosophy	Understanding kaizen as a philosophy refers to the general collection of assumptions which result from beliefs of top management in an organization.

Author	Status	Description
Doolen, Van Aken, Farris, Worley, Huwe 2008 Suarez Barraza, Smith, Dahlgaard-Park Su Mi 2009	Kaizen as a management concept	Kaizen as a management concept, with the use of a set of principles it outlines formal framework for management models and methods. Kaizen can be regarded as an independent or complementary management concept.
Van Aken, Farris, Glover, Letens 2010 Doolen, Van Aken, Farris, Worley, Huwe 2008	Kaizen as a program	Implementation of kaizen is embedded in time and concerns a selected area. In kaizen implementation methodology adequate for project management is used.
Emiliani 2005	Kaizen as a process	Proceeding as part of kaizen follows in a specified sequence. There are reference kaizen models.
Suarez Barraza, Smith, Dahlgaard-Park Su Mi 2009	Kaizen as a technique	Verified in previous implementations proceeding as part of kaizen is regarded as a routine tool for solving management problems.

Source: own elaboration.

2. EXISTING RESEARCH

Scientific studies of kaizen can be categorized within four dominating streams outlined below. Interpretative stream covers meditations on ontology and origin of kaizen. Furthermore, it determines the status and qualities of kaizen with particular attention paid to other management concepts, such as [Doolen, Van Aken, Farris, Worley, Huwe 2008; Suarez-Barraza, Lingham 2008]: TQM, Six Sigma, business process reengineering, continuous process improvement, just in time and others. The nature of research results of this stream have above all cognitive and systematizing nature. Scientific knowledge of current relations between kaizen and other management concepts is being completed along with quantification of changes occurring within the formal status of kaizen.

The second but nonetheless important and vast scientific stream is methodological. The stream embraces a series of detailed research problems connected with development of kaizen instruments. Exemplary, the more momentous research issues of the methodological current concern:

- Kaizen events programme; modelling and verification of organizational solutions for designing, management and improvement of kaizen programmes [Doolen, Van Aken, Farris, Worley, Huwe 2008; Van Aken, Farris, Glover, Letens 2010].

- Integration of kaizen with other management concepts. For instance integration of kaizen with lean management [Suarez Barraza, Smith, Dahlgaard-Park Su Mi 2009]. The integration attempts are accompanied with the care for efficiency of applying kaizen. Integration from the perspective of its subject usually tackles general concepts, dominating principles and management techniques.
- Application of detailed techniques allowing to implement kaizen in operations of an organization. Among these techniques there are among others [Suarez Barraza, Smith, Dahlgaard-Park Su Mi 2009]: the kanban method, TPM, 5S method, SMED, process mapping, supplier development and many others.

The discussed methodological stream forms a strong part of implementation of projective function of management sciences.

The third research stream in order is the efficiency one. As part of this stream efficiency of implementation of kaizen is studied. In detail, it concerns evaluation of kaizen programme results as well as creating measures of this evaluation [Doolen, Van Aken, Farris, Worley, Huwe 2008; Suarez-Barraza, Lingham 2008]. What is more, efficiency of functioning of kaizen teams can also be a specific research issue. Formulation of the efficiency stream results from a fundamental change in perception of kaizen. Namely, with time the traditional view that continuous improvement is an aim in itself has given way to the belief that improvement process should periodically end with measurable results. These results are nowadays the measure of success or failure of kaizen programmes.

The presented research streams are complemented with the exemplification current. As its part kaizen instruments are tested in organizations of various sectors. As much as traditionally kaizen was applied in industry now it can be implemented in organizations of various sectors, including for instance the public one [Emiliani 2005; Suarez-Barraza, Lingham 2008; Suarez Barraza, Smith, Dahlgaard-Park Su Mi 2009]. It needs to be added that scientific research conducted within the exemplification stream play, at the same time, a significant popularizing role by strengthening the phenomenon of kaizen diffusion.

It should be emphasized that the above discussed streams are tightly connected what is represented on Figure 1.

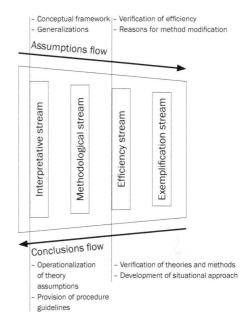

Figure 1. Relations between kaizen research streams

Source: own elaboration.

3. RESEARCH METHODOLOGY

The research covered relations between two organizations one of which, Toyota Tsusho Europe (TTE), functions as the supplier while the other one Toyota Motor Manufacturing (TMM) acts as the client. The research scope has been limited exclusively to the relations which concern one of the services, i.e. waste management, provided by TTE to the benefit of TMM. The key qualities of the studied service have been included in Table 2.

Table 2. Key qualities of the studied service, waste management, provided by TTE to TMM

Service qualities	Description
Foundation for providing the service	The service is provided on the basis of framework agreement concluded between the parties. TTE has been selected as the service provider by way of beauty contest.
Scope of the service	The service covers collection, sorting, temporary storage, transport and sale of selected production waste generated in the TMM plants. The service scope, initially specified by the agreement, can be and is modified depending on the needs what is legitimized with annexes. Both parties can initiate change of the scope of the agreement.

Service qualities	Description
Method of service performance	The service in terms of collection, sorting, temporary storage of waste is executed on the site of TMM production plants, in designated areas, by employees delegated by TTE at all production shifts. In the process of waste transport and sale TTE uses providers' services.
Payment terms for the service	TTE as the service provider is entitled to lump sum remuneration and shares in profit from waste sale. The amount of the remuneration changes together with the scope of the service.

Source: own elaboration.

3.1. ASSUMPTIONS, OBJECTIVES AND RESEARCH QUESTIONS

Empirical research refer partly to each of the above outlined research streams. The following key assumptions have been adopted:
- Assumption 1. Competitiveness of the supplier, TTE, is understood as the ability to maintain long-term, mutually beneficial relations with TMM.
- Assumption 2. Kaizen is regarded as a potential tool for increasing the above defined competitiveness of TTE.

The fundamental objectives of empirical research include:
- Objective 1. Identifying the possibility to apply kaizen in the provision of the studied service of waste management.
- Objective 2. Specifying the mechanisms of potential influence of kaizen on increasing competitiveness of TTE as the supplier of TMM.

In relation to the above objectives the following research questions have been formulated:
- Q 1. How can kaizen be applied to improving provided service of waste management?
- Q 2. How can implementation of kaizen contribute to increasing competitiveness of TTE as the supplier of TMM?

3.2. RESEARCH PROCEDURE AND METHODS

Empirical researches have been carried out in several stages with the use of numerous research methods. The key research methods were case study and Action Research method, completed with a series of detailed methods.

First stage of research
The basic objective of the first stage of research was identification of the existing state of formal and organizational conditioning of execution

of the studied service of waste management provided by TTE. As part of this stage the following research activities took place: 1) analysis of the content of agreements concluded between the parties, 2) analysis of the content of agreements between TTE and providers of services of collecting and transporting waste, 3) analysis of the process of provision of the studied service on the basis of written procedure P09 – Waste management TMM, 4) analysis of adopted measurements and results of implementation of the process, 5) interviews with employees engaged in performance of the service in the TMM plant in Wałbrzych, Poland, 6) interviews with management of Waste Management Department and TTE plenipotentiary for quality management, 7) observation of the process of providing the service of waste management in the TMM plant in Wałbrzych, Poland.

Second stage of research

The second stage involved an attempt to develop an example of a kaizen program which would obtain approval of TMM. As a superior assumption it was adopted that the program as a tool for shaping client relations would realize the win-win strategy, i.e. it would generate measurable benefits for both parties. The author of the present paper played the role of a coordinator of a working team which was appointed for the purpose and consisted of individuals listed in Table 3.

Table 3. Members of the working group developing kaizen program at TTE

Participant	Key functions in the working group
Author	Coordination of team works Supervision over work methodology of the team
Waste Management Department Manager	Quantification of kaizen results for TTE and TMM Developing improved solution
TMM Customer Service Leader	Identification of the area for improvement of the service of waste management Designing an improved solution
Representative of employees delivering the service	Identification of the area for improvement of the service of waste management Designing an improved solution
TTE Plenipotentiary for quality management	Codification of the kaizen program from the perspective of the requirements of Quality Management System
Lawyer	Evaluation of compliance of kaizen with formal conditions

Source: own elaboration.

Third stage of research

In the third research stage efforts were made to conceptualize directions and mechanisms of using the kaizen programme as a tool for increasing competitiveness of TTE as a TMM supplier. The nature of this stage was of strategic reflection. Apart from the author, representatives of TTE top level management took part in this process. Participants of several sessions implemented, among others, assumptions of M. Porter's 5 forces analysis.

Fourth stage of research

In the final, fourth, stage an attempt was made to develop a solution connected with continuous application of kaizen programmes as a tool for shaping client relations of TMM which would allow for long-term improvement of competitiveness of TTE. The discussed solution referred to existing in TTE guidelines as part of implemented quality management system compliant with ISO 9001. As a result, representative of TTE for quality management was a leader in this research section apart from the author.

4. RESULTS

4.1. EXEMPLIFICATION OF USING KAIZEN FOR IMPROVEMENT OF THE STUDIED SERVICE OF WASTE MANAGEMENT

As a result of research works carried out as part of the second stage of research a kaizen programme proposal addressed for organization – client (TMM) was formulated. The proposal was prepared in such a graphic form (Figure 2) which can at the same time be presented for approval of TMM.

The subject of the proposed kaizen programme is improvement of existing practices of plastic and cardboard waste management. Firstly, the weak points of the current solution were identified which included lack of full segregation of the mentioned waste already on the TMM site. They concerned mostly:
   - financial issues related to high costs of waste transport relatively low prices obtained for not segregated waste,
   - issues related to the risk of lack of total control over the generated waste and becoming dependent from one sub-contractor which segregates waste outside the TMM area,

- organizational issues connected to being forced to expand the scope of control over the process and coordination requirements related to substantial participation of sub-contractors in implementation of the process.

In the proposed kaizen programme it was suggested to introduce changes of organizational nature which involved:

- restriction of the role of TMM production employees in the process exclusively to storing waste in designated areas,
- taking over by TTE the function of in-plant waste transportation,
- introduction of internal waste segregation,
- resignation from the sub-contractor's services who segregated waste outside the TMM plant.

Introduction of the suggested modifications would require finance expences connected with: 1) purchase of pressing machines, 2) purchase of several trolleys, 3) changes in power supply installation, 4) modifications of work environment. In relation to the fact that in case of approval of the kaizen program TMM would be its fundamental beneficiary, it was assumed in the program that this organization would cover the costs of the above mentioned investments.

In the kaizen program (see Figure 2) costs and benefits of the current and modified solutions were estimated. The modified solution proved to be far more financially profitable. Taking into consideration the amount of finance expenses related to introducing the changes which would equal PLN 176 962 the payback period amounted to 1.8 year. Therefore applying the modified solution after this period would mean continuous generating financial profits in relation to:

- lowering the costs of waste transport,
- obtaining higher prices for segregated and pressed waste,
- entering the competitive waste market thanks to the segregation and pressing.

Simultaneously for the organization – the client, there will be other benefits, such as:

- improvement of waste control,
- lowering the probability of errors in waste management,
- improvement of occupational health and safety in the areas of waste storage.

Table 4. Exemplification of using kaizen for improvement of the studied service of waste management

PLASTIC AND CARBOARD WASTE (P&CW) RESOURCES

1. Clarify Target

Decreasing logistic costs by Plastic and Carboard Waste (P&CW) by new management solution: segregation/ logistic costs reduction

Visualisation of PCW management process

Problems

1. High transportation costs

2. Risk situations (safety) - FACTORY members have to enter waste storage area.

3. segregation quite complicated (risk of mistakes)

4. Prices of resources decrease (not pressed material means cost)

5. Scalling outside factory - not controlled

6. Low competition - only one subcontractor company can provide such service

Layout of current situation and possibilities

MANAGEMENT IMPROVEMENTS PROPOSAL FOR ONE-SHIFT PERIOD (KAIZEN)

3. Kaizen proposal

Advantages of kaizen proposal

1. Transportation cost decrease
2. Better price for materials due to segregation and pressing.
3. Competetive prices for materials (possibility of using different receivers)
4. Better control of wastes management - scalling inside factory
5. Decreasing mistakes of segregation in wastes area
6. Safety at waste storage area improvement (FACTORY members will not have to enter during container loading/unloading)

4. Kaizen investment and profit calculation

Investment cost

Investment cost	PLN		
1 Pressing machines	150 720		
2 Trolley for wastes from resting area	3 016	Total PLN	176 962
3 Trolleys for packages (4 units)	5 976		
4 Trolleys for packages transport	7 296	Non-investment equipment:
5 Power supply installation	1 750	– ERKA,
6 Weight	5 000	– forklift
7 Window and antileakage protection	3 204	(taken unused from FACTORY)

Estimation of costs and profits for current situation

Current yearly amount (calculation for decreased production)	Waste/Service	Recycling/disposal wastes [PLN]			Transport/Service [PLN]			GRAND TOTAL
		Quantity [Mg]	Purchase / Cost	Total	Unit	Cost	Total	
	Cardboard/Paper	200.000	0	0	500	-80	-40000	-40 000.00
	Plastic	90.000	0	0	300	-80	-24000	-24 000.00
	Oiled foil	40.000	-1200	-48 000	134	-80	-10720	-58 720.00
								-122 720.00

Estimation of costs and profits after kaizen

Estimated yearly amount (calculation for decreased production)	Waste/Service	Recycling/disposal wastes [PLN]			Transport/Service [PLN]			GRAND TOTAL
		Quantity [Mg/Unit]	Purchase / Cost	Total	Unit	Cost	Total	
	Cardboard/Paper	61.530	+100	+6 153	22	-290	-6380	-227.00
	Foil	30.660	+200	+6 132	17	-290	-4930	1 202.00
	Oiled foil	13.560	-1200	-16 272	20	-290	-5800	-22 072.00
	Maintenance	12	-410	-4 920			0	-4 920.00
								-26 017.00

Summary

Yearly costs saving	96 703.00	PLN	
Investment reimbursement	1.8	years	(remark - for higher production like in 2007 and normal market of resources: **1 year**)

Source: own elaboration.

4.2. APPLICATION OF KAIZEN FOR IMPROVEMENT OF COMPETITIVENESS OF TTE AS A SERVICE SUPPLIER

The search for mechanism for increasing competitiveness of TTE as a supplier of waste management services for TMM, thanks to applying kaizen, was based on the M. Porter's analysis of 5 forces. Model of this methodology adjusted to the studied situation is presented on Figure 3.

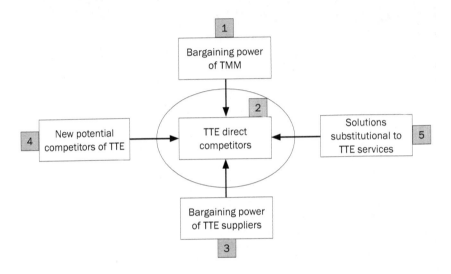

1 – meeting and exceeding of requirements and expectations of TMM thanks to kaizen
2 – quality leadership and generating value for TMM to a greater extent than competitors thanks to kaizen
3 – restriction, thanks to kaizen, of participation of suppliers of great bargaining power, shift to competitive supplier markets
4 – creating, thanks to kaizen, entry barriers for new, potential suppliers for TMM
5 – continuous improvement, thanks to kaizen, of provided service of waste management, preventing substitution

Figure 3. Impact of kaizen on improvement of competitive situation of TTE according to M. Porter's analysis of 5 forces
Source: own elaboration.

Impact of kaizen on the client's bargaining power TMM (1), may concern:
- Exceeding by TTE, thanks to kaizen, the requirements of TMM; in particular obtaining the effect of very high client satisfaction which is according to Kano's proposal [Lee, Lin, Wang 2011].
- It may result from exceeding functional requirements in terms of expected quality level. Usually, high satisfaction level is closely followed by loyalty.
- Active participation of TTE in the processes of creating value by TMM [Ippolito 2009]. The role of TTE will be to provide TMM with relational capital and to remain in interaction allowing to co-par-

ticipate in implementation of TMM development strategy. While kaizen will be here a tool for realization of policy of co-creating of value.

• Thanks to kaizen practical and active use of Customer Relationship Management. Kaizen may be helpful in achieving such CRM objectives as [CRM Kotorov 2003; Nguyen, Mutum 2012] conceptualization of benefits expected by TMM, gaining trust of TMM, commitment of TMM to improve the quality of services provided to it, etc.

With reference to direct competitors (2) application of kaizen should support the following competitive actions of TTE:

• Continuous improvement of services provided to TMM, especially in terms of their comprehensiveness. Kaizen should support TTE implementation of quality leadership strategy. Thanks to its differentiation TTE may gain the status of unique supplier.

• Providing TMM with a greater "dose" of relational capital than other competitors [Castro, Lopez Saez, Navas Lopez 2004; Delerue-Vidot 2006]. Providing by TTE relational capital will become the source of additional benefits for TMM, at least in the form of structure externalization. Kaizen, as a supporting tool, may serve e.g. current determination of the value of relational capital.

In the context of competitive advantage of TTE suppliers (3) using kaizen heads towards [Lasch, Janker 2005]:

• Current analysis of suppliers market, in particular due to its structure and competitiveness.

• Reaching decisions of potential internalization of these functions performed by suppliers in the case of which their policies or restrictions hindered relation policy of TTE towards TMM.

• Reduction of TTE risk in its relations with suppliers, e.g. by the back-up suppliers policy.

When it comes to the new potential competitors (4), application of kaizen by TTE should lead to creating specific, endogenous entry barriers [Pehrsson 2009]. At the same time, these barriers should not be standard solutions (e.g. promotion, trade war, advertising) but should co-create high level of expectations of TMM reaching of which would not be possible for competitors.

Finally, with regard to the substitutes of services provided by TTE (5) applying kaizen should lead to such a continuous maintenance of these services which would be greater than analogous attractiveness of alternative solutions.

5. CONCLUSION

In the present paper a new application of kaizen has been presented which increases supplier's competitiveness.

Since current policy of clients addressed to suppliers usually leads towards continuous rise of requirements, the suppliers, if they intend to maintain their competitiveness, should undertake actions allowing to successfully solicit clients' satisfaction and loyalty.

The paper presents several possibilities of perceiving kaizen status, next key kaizen research streams are identified and analyzed, finally in order to move on to empirical studies involving exemplification of using kaizen in the above mentioned application.

Based on the carried out literature and empirical studies it is possible to formulate the following conclusions:

- In case of kaizen, similar to other "beings" of management sciences, it is possible to ascertain complexity of its formal status. Kaizen may be treated among others as: a principle, methodology, philosophy, management concept, programme, process, technique. As it can be noticed, concept quantificators of kaizen are substantially different and its selection is not neutral for further interpretation. To date multiplication of meanings of kaizen does not need to be the source of conflicts according to the author. In her opinion, several interpretations of kaizen can be used parallel what only proves the wealth of the research subject.
- The indicated significance dilemmas of kaizen are confirmed in the great number of research streams as part of which attempts are made to clarify and solve various research problems. The author has identified four main kaizen research streams: interpretative, methodological, effectiveness and exemplification.
- Kaizen may be used as a holistic tool for increasing supplier's competitiveness in its relation with client. Application of kaizen allows to operationalize organization strategy and policy towards its clients, including application of assumptions of many contemporary management concepts and models (e.g. co-creation of value, building relational capital, customer relationship management, outsourcing).
- Thanks to application of kaizen suppliers can increase their competitiveness in their relations with clients impacting at the same time all leading competition forces in the sector. As understood by Porter, these forces are: bargaining power of clients, intensity of competitive rivalry, bargaining power of suppliers, threat of new entrants and substitutes.

- Applying kaizen, under assumption, should lead to supplier's creating long-term mutually beneficial client relations. In the analyzed hereby case of relations on B2B market such supplier policy may lead to making efforts to create, thanks to kaizen, entry barriers for other potential suppliers in the sector, what is usually a very difficult task due to the rising competitiveness on the market of waste management services providers. Nevertheless, compared to traditional competing tools, kaizen may prove to be difficult to imitate and allowing the supplier to maintain its competitive advantage.

REFERENCES

Castro G., Lopez Saez P., Navas Lopez J. (2004). The role of corporate reputation in developing relational capital. *Journal of Intellectual Capital*, No. 5.

Delerue-Vidot H. (2006). Opportunism and unilateral commitment: the moderating effect of relational capital. *Management Decision*, No. 44.

Doolen T.L., Van Aken E., Farris J., Worley J.M., Huwe J. (2008). Kaizen events and organizational performance: a field study. *International Journal of Productivity and Performance Management*, No. 8.

Emiliani M.L. (2005). Using kaizen to improve graduate business school degree programs. *Quality Assurance in Education*, No. 1.

Imai M. (1986). *Kaizen: The Key to Japan's Competitive Success*. New York: Random House.

Imai M. (2006). *What is total flow management under kaizen focus?* Three days Conference Lecture in Barcelona.

Ippolito A. (2009). Creating value in multiple cooperative relationships. *International Journal of Quality and Service Sciences*, No. 1.

Kotorov R. (2003). Customer relationship management: strategic lessons and future directions. *Business Process Management Journal*, No. 9.

Lasch R., Janker C. (2005). Supplier selection and controlling using multivariate analysis. *International Journal of Physical Distribution & Logistics Management*, No. 35.

Lee Y., Lin P., Wang Y. (2011). A new Kano's evaluation sheet. *The TQM Journal*, No. 23.

Mintzberg H., Westley F. (1992). Cycles of organizational change. *Strategic Management Journal*, No. 13.

Nguyen B., Mutum D. (2012). A review of customer relationship management: successes, advances, pitfalls and futures. *Business Process Management Journal*, No. 18.

Pehrsson A. (2009). Barriers to entry and market strategy: A literature review and a proposed model. *European Business Review*, No. 21.

Pettigrew A.M. (1990). Longitudinal field research: theory and practice. *Organization Science*, No. 3.

Sawada N. (1995). *The Kaizen in Toyota Production System*, Nagoya: Quality Control.

Suarez-Barraza M.F., Lingham T. (2008). Kaizen within kaizen teams: Continous and process improvements in Spanish municipality. *The Asian Journal of Quality*, No. 1.

Suarez-Barraza M.F., Smith T., Dahlgaard-Park Su Mi (2009). Lean-kaizen public service: an empirical approach in Spanish local governments. *The TQM Journal*, No. 2.

Van Aken E., Farris J., Glover W., Letens G. (2010). A framework for designing, managing and improving kaizen event programs. *International Journal of Productivity and Performance Management*, No. 7.

MAŁGORZATA BUDZANOWSKA-DRZEWIECKA

Jagiellonian University
Institute of Economics and Management
Chair of Organizational Behaviour

ANETA LIPIŃSKA

Jagiellonian University
Institute of Economics and Management
Chair of Standardized Management Systems

THE COMPETITIVE AND COOPERATIONAL ACTIVITIES OF COMPANIES ON THE INTERNET IN THE LIGHT OF POLISH RESEARCHERS' STUDIES – AN ASSESSMENT OF METHODOLOGIES

INTRODUCTION

The dynamic development of information and communications technology (ICT) and the constant increase in the availability and usability of the Internet affect the functioning of individuals and social groups, public institutions, markets, business entities and others. Therefore, the researchers' interest in examining this field seems justified.

The Internet in research studies is most often defined at three mutually conditioning levels of analysis – as a medium of communication, a technological tool (network of networks) and a place of realization of social and economic interaction. [Markham 2004, p. 96]. The last area is the basis for analyses in this study.

The purpose of the study is to analyse research methodology used by Polish academics in their studies of the activities of companies on the Internet. The purpose is twofold. Firstly, the study is supposed to show typical principles of research methodology. Secondly, thanks to the review, it allows to create recommendations for future research. Thus, the analysis refers to the systematization and identification of the type of research which is of interest to Polish academics.

From this purpose, there appear two basic directions of the analysis:
- the establishment of subject areas of research of the Internet conducted by Polish academics,
- the identification of the principles of research methodology used by Polish researchers.

1. THE AREAS OF RESEARCH ON THE USE OF THE INTERNET IN BUSINESS ACTIVITIES

The development of information technologies, including the Internet, is one of the factors influencing the intensification of competition and the reduction of permanence of competitive advantage on the market which is defined in the literature as hyper-competition [D'Aveni 1994, pp. 217–218; Polowczyk 2011, pp. 6–10]. This is also influenced by the phenomena, such as globalization, an increasing number of substitutes, an increase in consumer awareness and the ease of obtaining information about products and services. Enterprises operate in the information society because information has become a crucial resource which often determines the degree of competitiveness of companies on the market [Grudzewski, Hejduk 2002, p. 58; Mroczko, Stańkowska 2010, p. 144].

The Internet has an influence on, among other things, increasing the possibility of sharing and obtaining information about products, services and the market (promotional activities and marketing research); establishing relations, exchanging opinions and ideas (negotiations, lobbying), conducting business transactions (payments, e-commerce) and the creation of new distribution channels (e-services) [Szapiro, Ciemniak 1999, p. 63]. These factors play a significant role in forming competitive advantage of companies.

In business activities on the Web, in addition to the activities resulting in increased competitiveness, one can distinguish a different plane of actions aiming to expand cooperation. These activities are realized mainly through the processes of knowledge sharing on the Internet with the use of social media[1] [Internet Trends 2010].

---

[1] Social media represented by portals, such as Facebook, MySpace, or NK (Nasza Klasa) are Internet services which enable their users to create individual profiles, communicate and share information with other users as well as undertake other activities using available tools, such as blogs, messengers and others [Boyd, Ellison 2008, pp. 210–230; Trusov, Bodapati, Bucklin 2010, pp. 643–658].

The changes which occurred as a result of the development of the Internet and the technologies spreading its use, such as those in mobile devices, caused a significant increase in organizational – informational potential of the Web through the development of the concept of Web 2.0. The Internet in the new edition provides its users not only with opportunities to receive information but also to create and publish content. Moreover, it allows to participate in the existing activities of a social or economic nature or creating new ones. These opportunities are increasingly used in business activity, especially in the field of cooperation between enterprises and customers. Don Tapscott defined partnership which used the Internet as wikinomics. [Tapscott, Williams 2006], while Jeff Howe is the author of the term crowdsourcing which means gaining knowledge from inspiring a crowd [Howe 2006]. In recent years, crowdsourcing has become almost synonymous with the word cooperation and stands for both collective sharing of various types of information, experience, ideas and – in a narrower sense – sharing professional knowledge. Companies using the idea of crowdsourcing in their activities benefit from the exchange of ideas and innovations proposed and assessed by consumers themselves. This is a qualitative change in comparison to conventional solutions solely based on expert knowledge.

Along with the development of the Internet, the area of Web usability in business activities has also become of interest to researchers. The research includes different threads, including economic, social, cultural and technological issues connected with the functioning of the Internet [Castells 2007, 2008, 2009; Wrycza 2010] and those of a managerial nature, such as, the analysis of models and actions taken in the Internet environment [Afuah, Tucci 2003; Tapscott 2007; Warner, Witzel 2005]. The issues connected with business strategy on the Internet can be found in the studies by Michael E. Porter [Porter 2001, pp. 63–78] and Rajan Varadarajan et al. [Varadarajan, Yadav, Shankar 2008, pp. 293–308; Varadarajan, Yadav 2002, pp. 296–312].

A significant part of the research connected with the activities of companies on the Internet covers two areas: electronic commerce and activities of selected marketing mixed instruments.

Researchers who analyse the issues of electronic commerce (e-commerce) mainly focus on the strategies of competition in this area [Nikolaeva 2007, pp. 560–571] and the possibilities of lowering prices by offering online products [Zettelmeyer, Morton, Silva-Risso 2006, pp. 168–181].

Another thread present in the research is the analysis of the possibility of shaping the product on the Internet. The possibility of positioning brands thanks to the development of open space is also an interesting topic apart from referring to the development of e-services [Pitt et al. 2006, pp. 115–127].

One of the better represented research threads is the promotion policy. This trend focuses primarily on issues connected with online advertising [Zhang, Wedel 2009, pp. 190–206]. It is worth noting that some of them focus on mutual interactions between online and offline advertising as part of integration of promotional activities [Goldfarb, Tucker 2011, pp. 207–227]. Significant part of the studies is devoted to the promotion and other instruments used on the Internet, such as Word of Mouth online (WOM). One can distinguish the studies examining not only the functioning of WOM [Moe, Trusov 2011, pp. 444–456] but also the impact of this form of Internet promotion on the sale of products [Chen, Wang, Xie 2011; Chevalier, Mayzlin 2006, pp. 345–354]. Interest in this research area may result from the development and importance of social media. The use of social media in business is one of the most current research topics of contemporary international and Polish literature. For example, Michael Trusov et al., tried to identify these social media users whose activities affect the decisions made by other Internet users, which at the same time is the foundation of the effectiveness of WOM and viral marketing as well [Trusov, Bodapati, Bucklin 2010, pp. 643–658]. Other studies in this area focused on blogs which are one of the main determinants of the Web 2.0 trend [e.g. Liu et al. 2007, pp. 232–237]. Furthermore, the subject of the research in the field of possible use of knowledge sharing on the Internet is Internet communities, including the motives of Internet users for participating in crowdsourcing activities undertaken by business entities [Brabham 2008, pp. 75–90; Lakhani et al. 2007; Lietsala, Joutsen 2007].

2. CONCEPTUAL BACKGROUND AND METHODOLOGY

The review of the studies published in recent years in western literature allowed to define the general scope of research topics connected with the activities of companies on the Internet (Table 1). Within the scope of subjects raised by Polish academics, two important areas were emphasized – defining basic research questions and identifying them as part of activities of the companies on the Web (cooperation or competition). The review was also supposed to present basic analytical categories used for the review of Polish academics' studies within the area of the research into the Internet. The conceptualization of the analysis of methodology for examining the Internet was the result of important elements of a research process, including, above all, the applied method and the principles of sampling.

Table 1. The detailed scope of the analysis

The subject matter of the research into the Internet	The methodology of the research into the Internet
1. What issues concerning the activities of companies on the Internet are addressed by Polish researchers? 2. Which of the activities concern cooperation and which competition on the Internet?	3. What kind of research is conducted by Polish researchers? 4. What research methods are used by Polish researchers? 5. What sampling criteria are used by Polish researchers? 6. What data analysis methods are used by Polish researchers?

Source: own elaboration.

The realization of the objectives of the study was possible thanks to the use of the content analysis method for the articles published in selected magazines. The selection of research material was two-stage. At the first stage, the available databases were analyzed through specifying the titles of Polish-language journals. It was assumed that research results published in scientific magazines would be analysed and popular scientific journals would not be taken into account.

The following criteria were used:

– the presence on the current list of scored journals of the Ministry of Science and Higher Education (the criterion of value on the basis of merit of the conducted research),

– the business subject matter of the journal – specialization in management and marketing,

– the availability of annual bound volumes for the years 2006–2011.

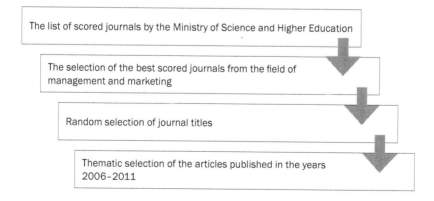

Figure 1. The selection of research material
Source: own elaboration.

It was decided to analyse articles from the last 5 years (2006–2011). One of the reasons was the fact that during these years the Internet underwent a transformation. This change, known as Web 2.0, has brought about the development of social media and led to qualitative changes in the ways of using of the Web, including business and promotional activities [Krain 2007, pp. 28–31]. The focus on the analysis of research material from this period allowed to identify new and significant research threads.

Next, out of the created database, two titles of journals were purposely selected. The review of the collected material allowed to select the final list of 35 articles included in further analysis.

Table 2. The list of journals chosen for analysis

Subject matter	Analysed Polish-language journals	The number of analysed articles	The number of articles concerning the Internet
Business	Marketing i Rynek	515	19
Business	Przegląd Organizacji	747	16

Source: own elaboration.

It should be emphasized that in the case of the two analysed titles, the number of studies devoted to the companies' activities on the Internet was only a small percentage.

3. THE ISSUES CONCERNING THE ACTIVITIES OF COMPANIES ON THE INTERNET ADDRESSED BY POLISH RESEARCHERS

Quantitative and qualitative analyses had to be carried out in order to determine the regularities concerning the subject matter of studies conducted by Polish researchers. The following table provides the review of basic information about the analysed studies.

Table 3. Review Summary

Authors	Year	Journal	Subject matter	Detailed scope	Type of research
Bartmańska. M.	2009	MR pp. 7-14	Methodology of research on the Internet	Characteristics and possibilities of using the ethnographic method in online research	TA
Brzozowski M.	2007	PO pp. 7-11	Model and organization of activity on the Internet	Attempt to define the concept and typology of virtual organization	TA
Chodak G.	2010	PO pp. 40-43	E-commerce	The importance of electronic commerce, the possibilities of using the Internet to sell on a global scale	RR TA
Fedorowicz E.	2009	MR pp. 30-37	Promotional activities	The analysis of possibilities of development of online advertising in comparison to its other forms (offline) during crisis	RR
Fedorowicz E.	2009	MR pp. 35-41	Promotional activities	The specificity of blogs as an online advertising medium.	RR
Frąckiewicz E.	2007	MR pp. 31-33	E-consumer	The characteristics of Internet users over 60 years old	OR
Frąckiewicz E.	2007	PO pp. 43-45	E-consumer	The characteristics of consumers of services based on the use of ICT	TA
Frąckiewicz E.,	2009	PO pp. 41-43	E-consumer	New technologies as a source of value or market discrimination of the customer	TA
Grzegorczyk W., Sibińska A., Krawiec W.	2010	MR pp. 35-39	Functionality of web pages	Polish customers' expectations of the functionality of websites on the financial services market	OR
Grzegorczyk W., Sibińska A., Krawiec W.	2008	MR pp. 29-35	Functionality of web pages	The analysis of the functionalities provided by websites on the financial services market in 1998-2006	OR
Grzegorczyk W., Sibińska A., Krawiec W.	2007	MR pp. 23-29	Functionality of web pages	The identification of functionalities of websites on the financial services market	TA
Jaciow M.	2011	MR pp. 27-34	E-consumer	Purchasing behaviour of an e-consumer – research methodology	OR
Jelonek D.	2006	PO pp. 68-72	E-commerce	Theoretical and practical aspects of risk in electronic commerce	TA

Authors	Year	Journal	Subject matter	Detailed scope	Type of research
Kaczmar I.	2010	MR pp. 25–30	Promotional activities	The principles of SEO on the Internet in the opinion of practitioners	OR
Kaczmar I.	2009	MR pp. 30–31	Promotional activities	The functioning of Internet services which cause certain actions supporting the promotion (redirection, click)	OR
Kaczmarek-Śliwińska M.	2006	MR pp. 31–35	Promotional activities	The use of Public Relations by public universities in Poland	OR
Kelm M.,	2008	PO pp. 65–69	E-commerce	Comparative analysis of e-commerce in Poland and in the European Union	OR
Komańda M.	2011	PO pp. 31–34	Methodology of research on the Internet	Ethical standards in qualitative research and problems in the context of their implementation on the Internet	TA
Komańda M.	2010	PO pp. 36–39	Methodology of research on the Internet	The discussion of the selected problems of qualitative research on the Internet	TA
Krain K.	2007	MR pp. 28–31	Promotional activities	The overview of the basic forms of promotional activities on the Internet	RR
Łazowska-Widz K.	2008	MR pp. 25–29	Creating content / knowledge sharing	The possibilities of using the phenomenon of content creation on the Internet from the perspective of marketing	TA
Mróz M.	2008	PO pp. 42–45	Model and organization of activity on the Internet	Characteristics of e-business in virtual space	TA
Najda M.	2007	PO pp. 24–28	Model and organization of activity on the Internet	The definition of virtualization of organization in the categories of the process. The formulation and verification of the method for measuring virtualization	OR
Pizło W.	2008	MR pp. 11–21	Marketing mix on the Internet	The theoretical basics of marketing activities on the Internet	TA
Polasik M., Wiśniewska A.	2007	MR pp. 20–27	E-services	The motives and aims of using electronic services by commercial banks in Poland	OR
Polowczyk J.	2007	PO pp. 37–40	Creating content / knowledge sharing	The overview of the book by D. Tapscott and A.D. Williams on Wikonomics	RR

Authors	Year	Journal	Subject matter	Detailed scope	Type of research
Romaniuk K., Kosmalski G.	2009	MR pp. 23–28	E-commerce	The description of online auctions – an element of e-commerce in Poland on the example of Allegro	OR
Rudawska I.	2010	MR pp. 8–15	E-services	E-health, the possibilities of providing e-services on medical services market	OR
Sanowska A., Wańtuchowicz M.	2007	PO pp. 35–37	Model and organization of activity on the Internet	The study of virtual organization as a separate configuration of other management concepts	OR
Tomaszewski A.	2009	PO pp. 19–22	Model and organization of activity on the Internet	The genesis, characteristics and business inspirations with the open source model	TA
Unold J.	2010	PO pp. 41–44	Methodology of research on the Internet	The outline of the concept of Web 2.0 with an indication of the key social aspects and organizational – informational potential	TA
Wirkus M., Wilczewski S.	2006	PO pp. 39–42	Functionality of web pages	The description of horizontal information portals	RR TA
Wojciechowski T.	2009	MR pp. 3–6	E-commerce	The description of the potential of the Internet as a distribution channel	TA
Zarębska A., Sobka M.	2006	PO pp. 24–27	Model and organization of activity on the Internet	The intangible assets of a company (including identity) as a source of competitive advantage	TA
Zdonek I.	2007	MR pp. 8–13	Promotional activities	The application of the hierarchy model of consumer's reaction to marketing message on websites	TA

Type of research: TA (theoretical analysis), OR (own research), RR (review of the results of collective research)
Journal: MR (*Marketing i Rynek*), PO (*Przegląd Organizacji*)

Source: own elaboration.

The review of the subject of the analysed articles allowed for selecting final analytical categories used in quantitative analysis (Figure 2).

The results of the analysis showed that most publications were devoted to the subject of *promotional activities*. The next subject area, which is very often presented in articles, is *the model and organization of activity on the Internet*. Even though the range of instruments used for promotional activities on the Internet is wide [Kaznowski 2008; Mazurek 2008; Maciejowski 2003],

Figure 2. The subject of studies conducted by Polish researchers in the analysed period (2006–2011)

Source: own elaboration.

in most cases the analysed articles on promotional activities referred to the issues connected with online advertising (its different forms and reactions to them). One study concerned PR activities on the Internet.

The analysis of the second most commonly present subject area i.e. *Model and organization of activity on the Internet* allowed to conclude that more than a half of (4 out of 6) the studies in this area is connected with the characterization of virtual organization or virtual space. The paper on the open source model refers to one of different business models which are implemented through the use of the Internet. The importance of intangible resources in the information society, which was mentioned in the theoretical part of this study, is reflected in raising this issue on the example of the identity of a company as a source of competitive advantage.

The diversity in subject matter depending on the title of the journal was noticed. Slightly more papers appeared in the *Marketing i Rynek* journal. All papers devoted to the development of promotional activities were published in this journal. In the *Przegląd Organizacji* journal however, *Model and organization of activity on the Internet* (6 cases out of 16) was the most often raised subject which was not present in *Marketing i Rynek*.

Most papers concerning the Internet were published in 2007 (10 cases out of 35), which may result from the visible growth of interest in the Internet of business and scientific environments (Figure 3). The second year in which a relatively large number of studies appeared was 2009 (8 articles out of 35). In both cases, the subject of articles was primarily devoted to *Promo-*

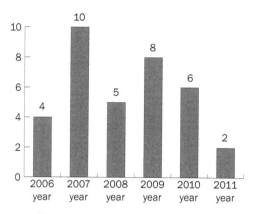

Figure 3. The number of studies conducted by Polish researchers in the analysed period (2006–2011) in an annual cross section
Source: own elaboration.

tional activities and *Model and organization of activities on the Internet.* The smallest number of articles on activities on the Internet was published in the examined sample in 2006 and 2011 (only the first 5 months of this year). It should be noted that it was observed that none of the subject areas was examined each year. Surprisingly, the subject of content creation / knowledge sharing was raised only in the years 2007–2008.

As part of the analysis, an attempt was made to identify and categorize the subject area of the studies published in the analysed journals. It was decided to determine whether these studies indicate the competitive aspect of the Internet or cooperation. After rejecting the content, in which it was not possible to identify the categories of activities, 27 papers were included for further analysis. The distribution of their categories is shown in the following figure (Figure 4).

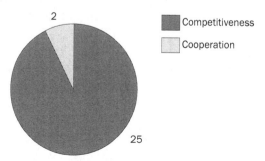

Figure 4. Type of strategy of operations examined by Polish researchers
Source: own elaboration.

The data analysis showed that Polish researchers most often raise issues which allow to compete effectively on the marked through operations on the Internet. Only in the case of two papers, the topic of cooperation among business entities on the Internet was emphasized.

4. THE RESEARCH METHODS CONCERNING THE ACTIVITIES OF COMPANIES ON THE INTERNET USED BY POLISH ACADEMICS

In characterizing the methodology of research on the activities of companies on the Internet, the attention was paid to the type of research, research methods and the principles of sample selection. This approach is the result of the stages of a research process in social sciences [Babbie 2005; Frankfort-Nachmias, Nachmias 2001].

There are many classifications of research in marketing research. Classifications used in the analysis were based on the type of sources (primary and secondary research), the type of data (qualitative and quantitative research) and geographical coverage (national / domestic and international research) [Kędzior, Karcz 2001].

From the conducted analyses, it appears that field research is dominant in the area of research into the Internet by Polish academics (Table 4). The articles which presented authors' own research were a minority in the examined sample (13 out of 35 cases). Among the articles based on the secondary data (22 cases), the majority of them was strictly theoretical. Part (3 – *Marketing i Rynek*, 3 – *Przegląd Organizacji*) included the review of the available research results from the Polish and English language reports.

An attempt was made to determine whether there is a connection between the subject area and the authors' tendency to conduct their own research more often. Two areas without any papers containing field research were distinguished. They include *Methods of research on the Internet*, and *Marketing mix on the Internet* and *Knowledge sharing on the Internet*. While in the first category it is in part connected with the specificity of the distinguished analytical category (recommendations how to examine), the analysis certainly indicates the need for research on knowledge sharing. Among the analysed articles, there was not any complete example of research

Table 4. The type of research presented in the articles vs. thematic categories with the division into journals

Thematic categories	Marketing i Rynek		Przegląd Organizacji	
	Field research	Desk research	Field research	Desk research
E-commerce	1	1	1	2
E-consumer	2			2
Functionality of web pages	2	1		1
Promotional activities	3	4		
Marketing mix on the Internet		1		
Creating content / knowledge sharing		1		1
Methods of research on the Internet		1		3
E-services	2			
Model and organization of activity on the Internet			2	4
Total	10	9	3	13

Source: own elaboration.

concerning the activities within all instruments of marketing mix. However, among the analysed articles, there were two containing raw data which related directly to the subject of e-services (i.e. one component of marketing mix).

Polish academics focus on quantitative research (100% of the presented results). Only one case of qualitative studies was reported but it was a complement to the quantitative research results.

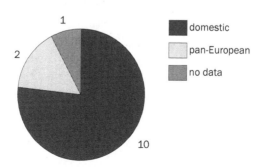

Figure 5. The structure of the research conducted in the analysed period – the geographic scope

Source: own elaboration.

From the analysis of the data, it appears that Polish researchers focus mainly on the domestic market (10 cases – 77%) (Figure 5). In the case of one article, it was not possible to identify the geographical coverage suggesting the research was not conducted abroad. In the case of two articles, the research was conducted in at least two European countries.

Another issue arising from research methodology is proper selection of the research method. It was decided to determine what methods / research techniques were used to conduct the published studies and whether or not they were carried out on the Internet.

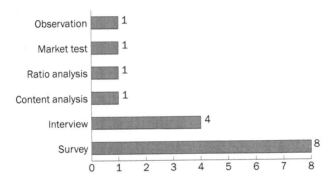

Figure 6. The applied research methods in the analysed articles from the years 2006–2011

N = 16, dichotomous question

Source: own elaboration.

The conducted research is mainly based on a survey (8 cases, which is 62% of the sample) (Figure 6). There were also attempts to use other research methods. One of the cases referred to the use of simulation (market test) concerning an imaginary portal. The content of websites was analysed by content analysis. The only qualitative method used was observation.

The Internet creates much greater opportunities to use research methods and techniques. None of the analysed cases used the experimental approach. Polish researchers did not pay attention to an increasing number of possibilities of conducting research with the help of qualitative methods (e-focus group or netography).

In one case, the research was of an econometric nature (it went beyond the methodology of marketing research). It referred to the analysis of statistical data.

In most cases, the analysed research did not include triangulation [Boksar 2009, p. 2]. Only in two cases, one could notice methodological triangulation between methods. The research combined a questionnaire and an interview. In one case, the mixed method was used, which means quantitative and qualitative methodology was applied in the research. Quantitative data were supplemented with qualitative research as part of the sequential design. The use of the mixed method approach seems to be correct because it allows to maximize the use of information and data as well as to ensure the accuracy of the research [Boksar 2009, pp. 2–6].

The majority of the studies was conducted outside the Internet. In 5 cases, online research was used. One case concerned the study of the content of web pages of a historical nature (thus, it was qualified for offline research). In 9 cases, the research was conducted outside the Internet (these were probably surveys or interviews).

The conducted online research referred to the data collection from individuals (Internet users – in 2 cases) and the conducted market test with the use of a web page. In the case of the research on institutional subjects, the research was conducted outside the Internet (5 cases). What is important is that individual respondents were surveyed outside the Internet and in each of the two reported cases it resulted from the age of the respondents (sample 60+ or defined as 15–80).

All surveys were carried out on the basis of the authors' own research questionnaire.

As part of defining the principles of research methodology, attention was paid to the principles of sample selection. The aim was to find out what principles were used when recruiting individuals for research, who the subject of the research was, how big the sample size was and what sample selection methods were applied.

From the conducted analyses it appears that in most cases the sampling was of a non-random nature (7 cases – 54%). It is important that in 5 cases it was impossible to identify the sampling selection method on the basis of the data included in the article. In one case, it was said that the sample was of a representative nature (estimations based on stratified sample selection) (Figure 7).

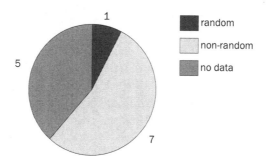

Figure 7. The research methods applied in the analysed articles from the years 2006-2011

Source: own elaboration.

The analyzed articles did not contain information about the databases which were used in the research. The basic parameters concerning the data confidence level and the acceptable statistical error were not estimated.

In the absence of the principles of sample representativeness, the sample size used by the Polish researchers was determined. Obviously, it depends on the research subject. In the case of the research on institutional subjects, the average sample size is 38 respondents. It should be noted that in the case of surveying this category of subjects, the researchers paid attention to the large percentage of refusals to participate in the study.

In the case of individual respondents, the average sample size for national surveys was 1298 people and it should be noted that this is due to the large diversity (the smallest sample – 168 respondents, the largest – 4314). The research of the pan-European scope included (1 case) 7934 respondents.

Among the analysed articles presenting primary research, 6 of them used the simple statistical analysis – percentages and frequencies – to present data. Similarly, six articles presented data which were analysed with the use of more advanced statistical methods (chi-square, Conjoint analysis, AHP method). The case of one article was specific – it presented research methodology by referring to the report which was not published in the study.

5. DISCUSSION, LIMITATIONS AND FURTHER RESEARCH

The results of the analyses indicated the advantage of theoretical studies. It therefore confirmed that there is not any issue (concerning companies' activities on the Internet) which is presented in Polish scientific literature which is mostly based on the results of primary research. It indicated the need to conduct the authors' own research. The presented results showed that the greatest interest among researchers was aroused by the subject of promotional activities. What is important is that most studies focused on advertising activities without including other instruments, especially those developing through social media. Thus, the possible area of research is, on the one hand, the focus on effectiveness of advertising but, above all, directing attention to the remaining possibilities, such as, viral marketing, SEO or online WOM.

The research thread which was represented only in the sphere of theoretical studies was the question of co-creating content on the Internet, that is to say, the dominant activity in Web 2.0. When referring to the analogical scope of research in western literature, it is important to focus the interests of Polish researchers on a widely understood concept of crowdsourcing and using the potential of subjects willing to share their knowledge.

An important aspect of any research is connected with appropriate methodological assumptions. In most cases, the analysed articles included descriptive research not designed to test the dependencies included in hypotheses. Moreover, the most frequently used methods were a survey and an interview. Probably, this is due to the nature of the research. However, what is disappointing is the lack of advanced research models that require a compilation of many methods and allow to arrive at more accurate and reliable conclusions.

One should remember, however, that the presented analysis does not show the whole research area of Polish academics. It concerned only a narrow sample. The conclusions are distorted by the selection of research material. They should be regarded only as an indication of certain tendencies. It is important to extend the analysis to the studies published in the journals of lower reliability (of lower scoring) which are available to the majority of Polish researchers.

It is also worth noting that a significant number of materials on the activities of the companies on the Internet, both in terms of competition and cooperation, are present in the form of popular science papers or practical analyses. These studies cannot be completely ignored in reflecting on research because they are often the first attempts to identify, describe and (unscientifically) analyse the phenomena which are at an early stage of development and, thus, are not subject to scientific (theoretical and empirical) verification. Instead, they can be scientists' inspiration to explore new and interesting research threads.

The limited advantages of the conducted analysis result from the presentation of fragmentary information on the methodology of the conducted research. This situation forces the demand for the introduction of some standard of the presentation of the principles of research methodology allowing for self assessment of research results and continuation of the research within a given subject area.

REFERENCES

Afuah A., Tucci C.L. (2003). *Biznes internetowy. Strategie i modele.* Kraków: Oficyna Ekonomiczna.

Babbie E. (2005). *Badania społeczne w praktyce.* Warszawa: Wydawnictwo Naukowe PWN.

Boksar T. (2009). Integrowanie badań ilościowych i jakościowych w rozwiązywaniu problemów marketingowych. *Marketing i Rynek*, No. 2, p. 2.

Boyd D.M., Ellison N.B. (2008). Social network sites: Definition, history, and scholarship. *Journal of Computer-Mediated Communication*, No 1, pp. 2–6.

Brabham D.C. (2008). Crowdsourcing as a model for problem solving: An introduction and cases. *Convergence: The International Journal of Research into New Media Technologies*, Vol. 14, No. 1, pp. 75–90.

Castells M. (2007). *Społeczeństwo sieci*. Warszawa: Wydawnictwo Naukowe PWN.

Castells M. (2008). *Siła tożsamości*. Warszawa: Wydawnictwo Naukowe PWN.

Castells M. (2009). *Koniec tysiąclecia*. Warszawa: Wydawnictwo Naukowe PWN.

Chen Y., Wang Q., Xie J. (2011). Online social interactions: A natural experiment on word of mouth versus observational learning. *Journal of Marketing Research*, April, pp. 345–354.

Chevalier J.A., Mayzlin D. (2006). The effect of word of mouth on sales: Online book reviews. *Journal of Marketing Research*, August, pp. 345–354.

Frankfort-Nachmias C., Nachmias D. (2001). *Metody badawcze w naukach społecznych*. Poznań: Zysk i S-ka.

Goldfarb A., Tucker C. (2011). Advertising bans and the substitutability of online and offline Advertising. *Journal of Marketing Research*, April, pp. 207–227.

Grudzewski W.M., Hejduk I.K. (2002). *Przedsiębiorstwo wirtualne*. Warszawa: Difin.

Howe J. (2006). The rise of crowdsourcing. *Wired*, June, http://www.wired.com/wired/archive/14.06/crowds.html [accessed: 31st March 2011].

Internet Trends (2010). *Morgan Stanley*, http://www.morganstanley.com/techresearch [accessed: 20st May 2011].

Kaznowski D. (2008). *Nowy Marketing*, http://kaznowski.blox.pl/2008/11/Ksiazka-Nowy-marketing-pobierz-pdf.html [accessed: 20th November 2010].

Kędzior Z., Karcz K. (2001). *Badania marketingowe w praktyce*. Warszawa: Polskie Wydawnictwo Ekonomiczne.

Krain K. (2007). *Czas reklamy internetowej*. Marketing i Rynek, No. 4, pp. 28–31.

Lakhani K.R., Jeppesen L.B., Lohse P.A., Panetta J.A. (2007). The value of openness in scientific problem solving. *Harvard Business School Working Paper*, No. 07-050, http://www.hbs.edu/research/pdf/07-050.pdf [accessed: 15th August 2010].

Lietsala K., Joutsen A. (2007). Hang-a-rounds and true believers: A case analysis of the roles and motivational factors of the star wreck fans. In: A. Lugmayr, K. Lietsala, J. Kallenbach (eds.). *MindTrek. Conference Proceedings*. Tampere University of Technology, pp. 25–30.

Liu S-H., Liao H-L., Zeng Y-T. (2007). Why people blog: An expectancy theory analysis. *Issues in Information Systems*, Vol. 8, No. 2, pp. 232–237.

Maciejowski T. (2003). *Narzędzia skutecznej promocji w Interencie*. Kraków: Oficyna Ekonomiczna.

Markham A.N. (2004). Internet communication as tool for qualitative research. In: D. Silverman (ed.). *Qualitative Research. Theory, Method and Practice*. London, Thousand Oaks, New Dehli: Sage Publications, p. 96.

Mazurek G. (2008). *Promocja w Internecie – narzędzia, zarządzanie, praktyka*. Gdańsk: ODDK – Ośrodek Doradztwa i Doskonalenia Kadr.

Moe W.W., Trusov M. (2011). The value of social dynamics in online product ratings forums. *Journal of Marketing Research*, June, pp. 444–456.

Mroczko F., Stańkowska M. (2010). Informacja jako kluczowy zasób współczesnych organizacji. In: R. Borowiecki, J. Czekaj (eds.). *Zarządzanie zasobami informacyjnymi w warunkach nowej gospodarki*, Warszawa: Difin, p. 144.

Nikolaeva R. (2007). The dynamic nature of survival determinants in e-commerce. *Journal of the Academy of Marketing Science*, pp. 560–571.

Pitt L.F., Watson R.T., Berthon P., Wynn D., Zinkhan G. (2006). The Penguin's window: Corporate brands from an open-source perspective. *Journal of the Academy of Marketing Science*, Vol. 34, No. 2, pp. 115–127.

Porter M.E. (2001). Strategy and the Internet. *Harvard Business Review*, No. 79, http://www.cis.gsu.edu/~emclean/R0103Dp2.pdf [accessed: 1st August 2010].

Szapiro T., Ciemniak R. (1999). *Internet – nowa strategia firmy*. Warszawa: Difin.

Tapscott D. (2007). Sieć biznesowa – bardziej dochodowa struktura. In: *Biznes. Zarządzanie firmą*. Warszawa: Wydawnictwo Naukowe PWN, pp. 149–152.

Tapscott D., Williams A.D. (2006). *Wikinomics. How Mass Collaboration Changes Everything*. London: Portfolio.

Trusov M., Bodapati A.V., Bucklin R.E. (2010). Determining influential users in Internet social networks. *Journal of Marketing Research*, August, pp. 444–456.

Unold J. (2010). Organizacyjno-informacyjny potencjał koncepcji Web 2.0. *Przegląd Organizacji*, No. 5, pp. 41–44.

Varadarajan R., Yadav M.S., Shankar V. (2008). First-mover advantage in an Internet – enabled market environment: Conceptual framework and propositions. *Journal of the Academy of Marketing Science*, pp. 293–308.

Varadarajan P.R., Yadav M.S. (2002). Marketing strategy and the Internet: An organizing framework. *Journal of the Academy of Marketing Science*, Vol. 30, No. 4, pp. 296–312.

Warner M., Witzel M. (2005). *Zarządzanie organizacją wirtualną*. Kraków: Oficyna Ekonomiczna.

Wrycza S. (2010). *Informatyka ekonomiczna*. Warszawa: Polskie Wydawnictwo Ekonomiczne.

Zettelmeyer F., Morton F.S., Silva-Risso J. (2006). How Internet Lowers Prices: Evudence form Matched Survey and Automobile Transaction Data. *Journal of Marketing Research*, May, pp. 168–181.

Zhang J., Wedel M. (2009). The effectiveness of customized promotions in online and offline stores. *Journal of Marketing Research*, April, pp. 190–206.

NATALIA LENIEC
Jagiellonian University
Institute of Economics and Management
Chair of Standardized Management Systems

BRAND AND ITS COMPETITIVE POTENTIAL IN THE POLISH JEWELRY MARKET

INTRODUCTION

Many phenomena which occur in the modern economy promote the growing importance of brand in creating the value of a company. Despite its intangible nature, brand is capable of generating up to 70% of company's profit. In the present paper the question of brand is regarded in terms of possibilities of utilizing brand's competitive potential in building company's competitiveness. The research endeavors to provide a clear and compelling empirical demonstration of brand's competitive potential creation based on the practices of Polish jewelry brands. Among the fundamental objectives of the study the following ones can be identified:

- presentation of brand's structure,
- identification of functions performed by brand,
- specification of the phenomena responsible for the increasing role of brand in building and sustaining company's competitive advantage,
- review of possibilities of using brand equity at the strategic level,
- introduction of the brand's competitive potential framework,
- measurement of competitive potential of Polish jewelry brands.

1. THE IMPORTANCE OF BRAND EQUITY IN CREATING THE VALUE OF A COMPANY

1.1. THE CONCEPT OF BRAND

A key premise behind the increasing role of intangible assets in creating value of a company is the difference between the market value of an organization and the book value of its net assets [Suszyński 2007, p. 323]. If managed effectively, intangible assets make up from 50% to 90% of the value of business depending on the profile of the industry [Dzinkowska 2000, p. 32]. For this reason, investments in tangible assets are increasingly being replaced by investments in intangible assets [Skrzypek 2003, p. 64]. Recent studies indicate that, among all off-balance sheet resources, it is the brand that needs to be given the most attention [Urbanek 2008, p. 45].

To provide a clear definition of what brand stands for, it is reasonable to make the distinction between two terms: 'product' and 'brand'. Product (including service) is a concept which relates to the physical form, physical parameters, characteristics, weight, performance, dimensions, color, composition of raw materials, technical parameters, technological standards [Altkorn 1996, p. 11]. Both products and services change over time as market conditions and customer preferences evolve. The concept of brand goes beyond the traditional meaning of the term 'product' [Table 1].

Generic products operate primarily on functional level whereas brands provide customers mostly with emotional benefits [Patkowski 2010, p. 15]. Hence, if regarded as a phenomenon, brand is characterized by significant durability and stability [Patkowski 2010, p. 12]. What makes it continuous is not only its inimitable identity but also the unique process of its creation. Indeed, researchers see brand as a result of an ongoing process of communication between an organization and its target group. They emphasize that the *current* view of the customers about a *brand* (*brand image*) is derived from company's long-term actions. This statement is of particular importance when it comes to products with short life cycles. Since technological superiority is lost rapidly, brands start to act as timeless symbols of companies.

Table 1. Semantic range of the term 'brand'

Author	Semantic range in ascending order	Concept of brand
Legal acts Kotler Ph.	I (trademark)	Any word, name, symbol, or design, or any combination thereof, used in commerce to identify and distinguish the goods of one manufacturer or seller from those of another and to indicate the source of the goods
Patkowski P.	II	I + brand is a mechanism which creates value for its owner by affecting the current and future sales and therefore has an impact on company's position in the market
Altkorn J.	III	II + brand is a main source of emotional value for which customers are willing to pay a premium price
Urbanek G.	IV	III + brand is a tool which, if managed efficiently, provides its users with economic benefits
Kall J.	V	IV + brand is a phenomenon which occurs on economic, social and cultural levels. For this reason strong brands enable companies to acquire groups of loyal customers and thus achieve a leading position in the market

Source: Kotler 1999, p. 410; Patkowski 2010, p. 18; Altkorn 1999, p. 12; Urbanek 2008, p. 46; Kall 2001, p. 12.

1.2. FOUR LEVELS OF BRAND

It is possible to present the structure of brand using Levitt's total product concept (Figure 1).

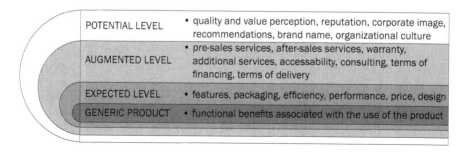

Figure 1. Four levels of brand

Source: De Chernatony et al. 2008, pp. 15–21; Patkowski 2010, pp. 23–28.

The first level of brand is constituted by the physical product. It acts as the core of brand and provides customers with functional benefits. Since competition between companies is increasing rapidly, it is difficult to identify brands which base their identity solely at generic level [Haig 2004, p. 245]. Examples include brands of unique products covered by legal protection, drugs without any counterparts and products in the early stages of life cycles. It should be noted that in the digital age it is no longer a problem to copy unique technology and imitate a product. Hence the authors of the model see generic product as a minor part of brand. The second level of brand is composed of elements that determine the way in which a brand is perceived by the environment. In most cases, these are important criteria used by customers while selecting brands [Batra, Ahuvia, Bagozzi 2012, p. 3]. Although at the expected level of brand focus is given mostly to rational characteristics, numbers of brands complement them with emotional benefits in order to create a unique identity (e.g. Alfa Romeo). Next level, known as augmented, consists of elements responsible for adding extra value to the offer. Increasingly now third level of brand becomes a real field of competition [Edwards 2006, p. 194]. For example, seven-year car warranty has successfully differentiated Kia from its competitors. Finally, brand's structure is completed by the potential level. It comprises of emotional components which are firmly rooted in the minds of consumers. According to the model, they are considered to be the only source of inimitable competitive advantage. It is worth mentioning that the perception of potential benefits depends strongly on the experience gained in previous layers. Unlike attributes that form lower levels, the fourth layer components are far less sensitive to short-term changes within the same brand.

1.3. FUNCTIONS PERFORMED BY BRAND

A broad understanding of the concept of brand makes it possible to understand the power of branding. There is no doubt that it has its origins in the variety of functions performed by brand [Taylor, Nichols 2010, pp. 112–114].

Since brand provides range of shareholders with various benefits, it is considered to be an important source of business value [Fehle, Fournier, Madden 2006, p. 224]. Without a doubt, strong brand contributes to the growth of operating revenues thus affecting organization's financial condition [Urbanek 2008, p. 156]. Benefits generated by brand appear to cause an increase in value and frequency of cash flows. Moreover, they tend to ensure the stability of financial streams which, in turn, translates into increased value for shareholders (Figure 2).

Table 2. Functions of branding

Identifying	highlighting features of the product (e.g. Volvo), exposing functional and emotional benefits provided by the product (e.g. BMW), distinguishing the value desired by a particular category of buyers (e.g. Ariel), suggesting personality of product's user (e.g. Marlboro), representing characteristics of organizational and/or national culture (e.g. Lindt)
Informing	providing direct or indirect information about the manufacturer, the distributor and the country or region of origin
Promoting	creating positive associations with the product and thus shaping company's image
Ensuring quality	guaranteeing constant level of expected performance

Source: Altkorn 1999, pp. 14–16; Kotler 1999, p. 413; Batra, Ahuvia, Bagozzi 2012, p. 4; Stahl et al. 2012, p. 49.

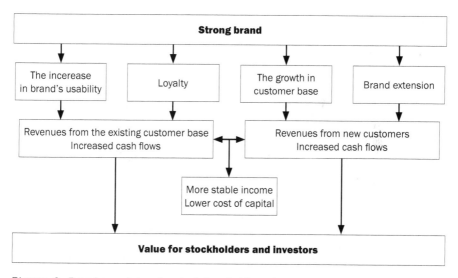

Figure 2. Brand as a determinant of shareholder value
Source: own elaboration.

In an effort to maximize shareholder value, special attention is given to these tasks of brand which are highly important in terms of industry profile [Stahl et al. 2012, pp. 49–50]. For example, identifying and promoting brand identity is seen to be a key to succeed in the consumer and luxury goods market whereas informing and ensuring quality is particularly important in the case of intermediate goods. Hence the specificity of the industry determines the extent to which one brand is capable of creating the market value of a business (Table 3).

Table 3. Brand's contribution to the market capitalization of a company

Brand	The share of brand's value (%) in company's market capitalization	The value of brand in 2002 ($ bn)
McDonald's	71	26.4
Disney	68	29.3
Coca-Cola	51	69.6
Nokia	51	30.0
Mercedes-Benz	47	21.0
IBM	39	51.2
Intel	22	30.9
Microsoft	21	64.1
Marlboro	20	24.2

Source: Interbrand 2012/JPMorgan 2002.

2. BRAND AS A SOURCE OF COMPETITIVE ADVANTAGE

2.1. DRIVING FORCES BEHIND STRATEGIC BRANDING

Modern economy is rich in phenomena that trigger the growing importance of brand in creating the competitiveness of business. These include [Patkowski 2010, pp. 7; Kall 2001, pp. 72–90, 258–290]:
- extremely intense competitive rivalry in the market, e.g. mobile network providers;
- mass customization, e.g. fashion;
- shortening product life cycles, e.g. mobile devices;
- changes in patterns of consumption and/or purchasing power, e.g. no-frills airlines;
- globalization, e.g. fast food chains.

As the business environment is becoming more and more diverse and unstable, brand is beginning to serve not only as a powerful marketing tool but also as a unique organizational resource.[1] Most importantly, it efficiently differentiates and positions company in the marketplace and thereby provides it with an inimitable competitive advantage [Clark 2004, p. 83]. This implies significant changes in the field of brand asset management. What the owners of the most powerful brands are experiencing now is the shift

---

[1] See: Value Based Management.

from operational to strategic brand asset management. Major changes concern the level of brand management (incl. time horizon, position of brand manager, objectives), its scope (incl. brand structure, numbers of brand) and the impact of external forces.

2.2. BRAND IN PORTER'S GENERIC STRATEGIES

According to M. Porter's theory, in order to gain the edge over competitors, companies need to choose one of the following strategies: cost leadership, differentiation, focus [Porter 2008, pp. 13–17]. Strategic implications of this choice are of huge importance for brand equity management.

Cost leadership

All activities here are aimed at increasing brand market share [Patkowski 2010, p. 79]. The reason for this is the fact that only if a particular brand is recognizable on a mass scale, a company can take advantage of economies of scale, learning curve effect and capital-labor substitution [Gierszewska, Romanowska 1994, pp. 104–105; Patkowski 2010, pp. 78–79]. Hence, when following cost leadership strategy, expanding brand awareness becomes a priority. At the same time expenses related to the creation of brand assets are reduced to a minimum [Domański 2005, p. 11]. In this case brand awareness is built mainly by ensuring brand availability in diverse distribution channels. Advertising is utilized to a lesser extent since emotional benefits are almost not present. It is worth mentioning that while offering a product at the lowest cost, the image of a brand is burdened with numbers of risks associated with the increase in the prices of materials, technological changes, the emergence of similar manufacturing methods or lower-priced substitutes [Patkowski 2010, p. 79]. Therefore cost leadership is achieved only when all elements of an organization and its environment are effectively coordinated.

Differentiation

In order to compete successfully, a company has to differentiate its offer in some way [Porter 2008, p. 14]. The most commonly utilzed points of differentiation are product quality, design or after-sale service. On the ground of brand theory, these are the substantial components of several brand's layers. Three major conditions must be met to achieve market leadership with differentiation strategy [Farhana 2012, pp. 225–230]. Firstly, customers need to be able to notice and appreciate the unique brand identity easily. It is a key to success for manufacturers or service providers whose products are so similar at the rational level to those offered by competitors that the emotions delivered by brand are the only source of differentiation. Secondly, the strategy has to provide a company with economic benefits. For example, differentiating products such as fruit or vegetables is going to be far less effective than in the case of luxury goods. Finally, a company must be protected from price and cost competition in the long run. If all of the above requirements are met, differentiation strategy seems to be highly profitable. However, it may be also exposed to several risks. First of all, it is not always possible to create unique brand identity and, at the same time, gain significant market share. It is also the case that the product differentiation may not be visible enough. What is more, customers might not be willing to pay extra money for the unique feature. In this situation they will probably go for private labels which imitate 'differentiated' products perfectly while keeping the manufacturing cost low.

Focus

The choice of focus strategy implies the fact that strategic operations are aimed at the specific group of buyers, the selected product segment or geographical area [Porter 2008, p. 15]. What makes this strategy different from the two mentioned earlier is its narrow scope. The objective is to offer brand that provide its customers with benefits that are fully tailored to their needs and expectations. Basically, it can be achieved in two ways. The first one relates to the cost leadership within a particular segment of the market whereas the second one – to the industry leadership achieved by product differentiation within a particular segment of the market. They are both aimed at positioning brands on the basis of differences that occur between the industry as a whole and the given segment of the market [Mallik 2009, p. 256]. In this case, the brand needs to be capable of meeting the needs and expectations of the target group with methods that are completely different from those used by competitors. It is also crucial to emphasize the unique nature of the relationship between the brand and the selected segment of the market [Gambetti, Graffigna, Biraghi 2012, pp. 668]. In terms of decision making, the level of profitability needs to be considered since the most effective uses of focus strategy tend to be associated with brands which are almost invulnerable to substitution [Porter 2008, p. 55]. Even though the strategy does not require actions on a mass scale, it is still risky. Firstly, it is almost impossible for a company to gain leadership in the whole industry. Secondly, the differences between market segments may be not that important for end users thus making it impossible to differentiate a brand within the industry. What is more, the differentiation might quickly become obsolete. One should not forget that brands which serve narrow segments of the market must 'work' much harder than those that operate on a larger scale in order to achieve competitive advantage [Meyers, Gerstman 2002, p. 45].

In short, the choice of competitive strategy has significant implications for brand management.

2.3. STRONG BRAND AS A BARRIER FOR COMPETITORS

In theory, brand strength represents the barriers that must be overcome by competitors in order to own a strong position in the market [Urbanek 2008, p. 48]. In practice it provides estimations of both the probability and the value of future cash flows. Systematic analysis of brand strength index results in [Urbanek 2008, p. 50]:
- – the assessment of the effectiveness of activities undertaken by the organization in the field of brand equity creation;
- – the comparison of brand strength index and its constituent elements within the industry, which, in turn, makes it possible to determine the relative competitive position of the brand;
- – the current valuation of the brand based on the income approach;
- – the increase in brand credibility since relevant information is revealed for external reporting.

It should be emphasized that brand strength index serves as the determinant of brand's competitive potential [Urbanek 2008, p. 48].

There is no agreement between researchers as to what elements make brand strong. However, the evaluation criteria shown in the Figure 3 are widely recognized.

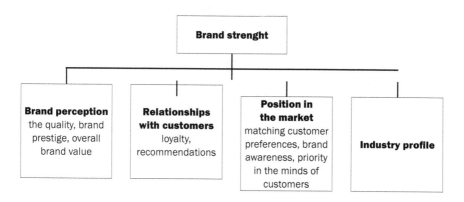

Figure 3. Brand strength dimensions
Source: Kall 2001, p. 200; Urbanek 2008, p. 48.

Brand perception is an indicator which informs how customers perceive a particular brand as opposed to other brands. Relationships with customers show users' behaviors towards brands. Consequently, market position gives an idea of the range of brand influence and its coverage. Finally, industry profile determines the relative role of brand in business operations. The relevance of brand strength varies across industries. For example, branding is an integral part of luxury goods but it is not essential when it comes to intermediate goods (Table 4).

Table 4. Industry profile and relative brand relevance

Type of industry	Relative brand relevance [%]
Luxury goods	100
Fashion	89
Food and beverages	79
Overall consumer products	53
Household appliances	53
Media, telecommunication and other services	32
Retail	21
Pharmaceuticals	15
Industrial goods	7

Source: Urbanek 2008, p. 49.

Regardless of industry profile, strong brands distinguish themselves by [Altkorn 1999, pp. 24–35]:
   – solving problems that are relevant to the target group;
   – offering high-quality products in terms of technical, functional and emotional characteristics;
   – sustaining leadership in the market;
   – reacting flexibly to changes occurring in the business environment;
   – keeping in touch with customers;
   – developing extra services that reflect the nature of brand identity.

3. BRAND'S COMPETITIVE POTENTIAL – FRAMEWORK

3.1. OVERVIEW OF THE MODEL

Conceptually, the competitive potential of brand is defined as a set of specific dimensions, which can be used to describe brand's capabilities to compete successfully in the market [Patkowski 2010, p. 105]. In other words, the concept refers to measurable outputs of the unique combination of functional and emotional values offered by a single brand. Hence only those brand assets which affect the way a customer perceives a particular brand are taken into account in the framework presented here.

It has been assumed that brand's competitive potential is composed of three inseparable parts (Figure 4). Each of them consists of two principal dimensions.

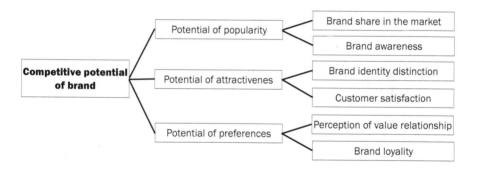

Figure 4. Competitive potential of brand – framework

3.2. REVIEW OF THE COMPONENTS OF BRAND'S COMPETITIVE POTENTIAL

Potential of popularity

It gives an idea of how well-known the brand is. Brand's market share relates to the physical presence of a particular brand in various distribution channels as well as brand share in the market total sales [Patkowski 2010, p. 125]. Hence numeric and weighted distribution are utilized here. The level of brand awareness shows how familiar customers are with the brand [Kall

2001, p. 47; Patkowski 2010, pp. 107–108]. Three types of brand awareness might be measured here: assisted, spontaneous and top-of-mind. Significant brand share has become the competitive advantage of Amazon whereas high level of brand awareness is perceived to be the key to the success of Microsoft Windows. Wikipedia is an example of a brand which has built its market dominance using both dimensions of potential of popularity.

Potential of attractiveness

If brand image is perceived by customers as attractive, the chances to gain the edge over competitors are getting higher. Unique brand identity serves as a basis of transferring brand values into the minds of brand users [Altkorn 1999a, p. 39]. It is composed of four elements: verbal identity, visual identity, brand positioning, customer experience. Next, the level of customer satisfaction shows how well one brand meets the needs and expectations of its target group. As a result, it affects the volume of sales. Moreover, customer satisfaction analysis helps to provide buyers with minimum value proposition (MVP) thus making them more willing to purchase another product of the same brand [De Chernatony et al. 2008, p. 78]. The Body Shop is a brand which has efficiently used its distinctive brand identity to gain market leadership. Customer satisfaction has, in turn, become Duracell's source of competitiveness. Heyah has focused on both dimensions of attractiveness in order to become successful in the Polish prepaid mobile market.

Potential of preferences

Its main objective is to make customers attached to a particular brand and thereby sustain competitive advantage. Price-value relationship is an indicator of how customers value the quality for the price they pay [Patkowski 2010, p. 116]. If one brand is referred to as good value for money, customers are far more willing to repurchase it. Moreover, high level of perceived quality makes it less risky to release new products. Consequently, the bargaining power of the brand towards its distributors is increased so the premium price may be charged. Brand loyalty is concerned with different stages of customer engagement with one brand [Patkowski 2010, p. 110]. It ranges from brand ignorance to brand religion [Aaker 1993, p. 40]. The level of loyalty can be determined with the use of behavioral and satisfaction measures, switching costs and brand associations [Patkowski 2010, s. 113–114]. Nivea has achieved its market dominance by offering goods that are good value for money whereas Apple has gained the edge over competitors by making its users extremely loyal. Burberry has acted tirelessly upon both dimensions and thereby sustained its competitive advantage.

Recent studies suggest that the most successful brands in the world score high in all three types of competitive potential shown here [Patkowski 2010,

p. 130]. However, the relative relevance of each component is determined by the profile of the target group. For example, brands which address their offers to teenagers see potential of attractiveness as a core source of competitive advantage. When it comes to FMCG brands, market superiority is achieved mainly due to the development of potential of popularity. At the same time, luxury brands get the edge over competitors with the use of potential of preferences.

4. BRAND AS A SOURCE OF COMPETITIVENESS OF POLISH JEWELRY BRANDS

4.1. OVERVIEW

The development of brand's competitive potential is given an extremely high priority when it comes to luxury brands. In this case, the value of a brand accounts for the overwhelming portion of shareholder value [Mazurkiewicz 2012a]. Brand strength is equally important here since its relative relevance in the luxury goods market reaches 100% [Urbanek 2008, p. 49]. Despite the broad acknowledgement of the increasing role of brand in gaining the edge over competitors, competitive potential of Polish luxury brands has not been explored so far. The current research aims to fill this gap.

Top 3 Polish jewelry brands have been chosen as a the object of the study since they are perceived by the majority of Poles as a manifestation of luxury (Table 5).

Table 5. The most valuable Polish jewelry brands – Top 3

Brand	2012		2011		Value change
	Brand value [million PLN]	Overall position	Brand value [million PLN]	Overall position	
Apart	246.5	56.	218.4	57.	13%
W. Kruk	73.5	142.	64.3	161.	14%
Yes	62.7	157.	60.1	170.	4%

Source: Mazurkiewicz 2012a.

Apart, W. Kruk and YES form a segment of the luxury market which is far more less vulnerable to changes occurring in the aesthetic paradigm than fashion or accessories. The research gives therefore a better idea of brand's ability to compete successfully in the long run.

4.2. METHODOLOGY

The study consisted of 3 phases. After the secondary data concerning the performance of Polish jewelry brands analyzing, customer survey was conducted. The questionnaire consisted of 16 questions. It was completed by 150 respondents (50 from each of the three brands) who were shopping in one of the jewelry shops located in the mall. The specification of study population has been shown in Table 6.

Table 6. Characteristics of study population

Brand	Gender (%)		Age (%)					
	female	male	< 25	25–29	30–34	35–39	40–44	> 44
Apart (nA = 50)	64	36	4	8	30	22	14	22
W. Kruk (nWK = 50)	66	34	4	4	2	10	32	48
YES (nY = 50)	76	24	8	28	30	20	12	2

N = 150

Source: own elaboration.

4.3. RESULTS

Consumer buying behaviors

The choice of one jewelry brand is determined mostly by the quality (61.33%) and the uniqueness of its products (41.33%). The presence of brand ambassadors (27.33%) may also affect purchase decision. The mission statement of a particular jewelry brand is the least likely to be taken into consideration (4.67%). The respondents are most frequently in possession of two (46.67%) or one (29.33%) jewelry brands. Only 5.33% of the study population declares to have more than three of these. It is worth mentioning that, if a customer is attached only to one jewelry brand, it is usually Apart.

Brand image associations

The study of brand personalities has indicated that Apart is generally associated with sophistication, excitement and competence. W. Kruk is, in turn, perceived to be competent, mature and totally unexciting, whereas YES tends to give an impression of excitement, sophistication and sentimentality.

Potential of popularity

Apart is seen to be the market leader in terms of brand popularity (93.70% of maximum score).

Table 7. Potential of popularity of Polish jewelry brands

Dimension of popularity	Evaluation criteria	Max	Apart	W.Kruk	YES
Brand market share	The share of brand in the total value of Polish jewelry market	8.00	8.00	4.00	4.53
	Number of retail stores	4.00	4.00	1.75	2.36
	Overall	12.00	12.00	5.75	6.89
Brand awareness	Top-of-mind brand awareness	5.00	3.80	1.95	1.75
	Spontaneous brand awareness	3.00	2.94	2.28	1.95
	Overall	8.00	6.74	4.23	3.70
Potential of popularity		20.00	18.74	9.98	10.59

Source: own elaboration.

Apart has gained the largest share in the Polish jewelry market (15%) and built the densest network of stores (183). It is top-of-mind brand for 76% customers of competitive brands who are mostly women (75%). Additionally, almost all respondents (98%) have mentioned Apart spontaneously when asked about Polish jewelry brand. There is a large gap between the leader and its follower which amounts to 47.05% of the maximum score. YES, with 8.5% share of the market, has developed its distribution network on the basis of franchising. 35% of non-YES customers perceives the brand as top-of-mind whereas 65% of them name it spontaneously. W. Kruk has achieved 7.5% market share and now its offer is available in 80 stores.

Potential of attractiveness

Apart is the leader of brand attractiveness classification. It has got the highest scores in both the distinction of brand identity and customer satisfaction.

Table 8. Potential of attractiveness of Polish jewelry brands

Dimension of attractiveness	Evaluation criteria	Max	Apart	W.Kruk	YES
Brand identity distinction	The existence of the substantial reason to purchase the brand	3.00	2.28	1.62	2.16
	Brand trust	3.00	2.51	2.24	2.32
	Quality-price relationship	3.00	2.38	2.00	2.35
	The presence of recognizable brand ambassador	2.00	2.00	0.00	2.00
	The duration of brand presence in the market	1.00	0.17	1.00	0.18
	The uniqueness of selected brand assets	8.00	6.43	4.40	6.24
	Overall	20.00	15.77	11.26	15.25
Customer satisfaction	Customer satisfaction with the use of the product	3.00	2.47	2.23	2.12
	Customer satisfaction with several features of brand proposition	12.00	9.22	6.74	9.00
	Overall	15.00	11.69	8.97	11.12
Potential of attractiveness		35.00	27.46	20.23	26.37

Source: own elaboration.

Apart's edge over the runner-up is very small (3.11% of the maximum score). YES poses a serious threat to Apart in the field of brand identity distinction and customer satisfaction. W. Kruk is perceived to be the least attractive jewelry brand. The lack of brand ambassadors together with typical product portfolio make W. Kruk customers ca. 25% less satisfied with its offer.

76% of Apart's customers point out specific reasons for the purchase. These are: wide range of products (23.68%), quality (23.68%), exclusiveness (21.05%), well-known brand ambassadors (18.42%) and brand availability (13.16%). Women mostly choose Apart because they find it exclusive whereas men purchase the brand due to the high quality of its jewelry. As many as 72% of YES customers recognize its unique brand identity. The main reasons behind the purchases of YES jewelry are: the mix of classic and modern designs (47.22%), brand communication in social media (25.00%), the quality of jewelry (13.89%). Only about a half of W. Kruk customers is able to indicate the specific reason of the choice. It usually comes down to the classic design (29.63%), traditions associated with brand (29.63%) and product quality (29.63%).

Both Apart and YES take advantage of celebrity endorsement. The exclusive character of Apart's jewelry is reinforced by the popularity of Polish supermodel – Anja Rubik – whereas YES's balance between classic and modernity is supported by the image of Magdalena Frąckowiak.

W. Kruk has been selling jewelry for 173 years. Although Apart and YES are perceived as relatively young (30 and 32 years of business activities), they react better to market changes. Since the quality of Apart's products meets the expectations of its customers to a great extent, it is considered to be the most trustworthy jewelry brand. It is also characterized by the highest level of uniqueness (Table 9). However, this superiority may be shortly lost to YES. Therefore, Apart aims to strengthen its competitive position by providing customers with the offer which is better tailored to their needs and expectations (Table 10). Apart's customers are characterized by the highest level of satisfaction in terms of product quality, product range, the frequency of new product releases and retail stores availability. YES is constantly trying to get the edge over the leader with the use of qualified customer service as well as sophisticated after-sale service. As for luxury brand, W. Kruk performs very poorly when it comes to the level of customer satisfaction with overall sale service, product range and the frequency of new products releases.

Table 9. The uniqueness of brand assets

1 – the lowest score, 10 – the highest score		Average	Standard deviation	Mode
Brand name	Apart	8.58	1.17	9
	W. Kruk	5.78	1.29	6
	YES	7.94	1.45	8
Brand logo	Apart	7.68	1.29	8
	W. Kruk	4.80	1.55	4
	YES	6.54	1.46	6
Product design	Apart	8.82	0.82	8
	W. Kruk	5.68	1.26	6
	YES	9.08	0.72	9
Raw materials	Apart	8.76	1.09	8
	W. Kruk	5.94	1.17	6
	YES	5.76	1.35	5
Packaging	Apart	7.88	1.58	8
	W. Kruk	6.34	1.67	6
	YES	8.46	1.47	9
Interior decor of retail stores	Apart	6.50	2.38	3
	W. Kruk	6.00	0.75	6
	YES	8.72	1.06	9

1 – the lowest score, 10 – the highest score		Average	Standard deviation	Mode
Marketing communication	Apart	8.44	1.13	7
	W. Kruk	4.68	1.26	6
	YES	7.86	1.25	8
Web site	Apart	7.60	1.67	9
	W. Kruk	4.80	1.44	6
	YES	8.04	1.23	9

Source: own elaboration.

Table 10. The level of customer satisfaction

1 – the lowest score, 10 – the highest score		Average	Standard deviation	Mode
The use of brand (product)	Apart	8.22	0.94	8
	W. Kruk	7.42	1.17	8
	YES	8.08	0.98	8
Product quality	Apart	8.16	1.05	8
	W. Kruk	7.88	0.79	8
	YES	7.52	0.98	8
Product range	Apart	8.88	0.84	9
	W. Kruk	4.84	1.43	5
	YES	7.72	1.10	8
Frequency of new product releases	Apart	8.40	1.37	10
	W. Kruk	4.48	1.19	4
	YES	7.64	0.91	7
Retail stores availability	Apart	8.36	1.21	8
	W. Kruk	4.38	1.68	3
	YES	6.22	0.94	6
Customer service	Apart	6.40	1.83	7
	W. Kruk	5.88	1.12	6
	YES	8.76	0.86	9
Extra services	Apart	5.90	1.47	7
	W. Kruk	6.26	1.48	6
	YES	7.14	1.27	7

Source: own elaboration.

Potential of preferences

With 74.36% of the maximum score, Apart is considered to be the market leader in terms of customers' preferences. It has built its competitive advantage on the basis of brand loyalty since there are no significant differences between the perceived level of quality of domestic jewelry brands. The majority of Apart's customers makes one purchase per year whereas W. Kruk is usually bought every 2–3 years. There are usually two different jewelry brands in a Polish household. However, Apart's customers are far less likely to purchase another piece of jewelry offered by a different Polish brand.

Table 11. Potential of preferences of Polish jewelry brands

Dimension of preferences	Evaluation criteria	Max	Apart	W.Kruk	YES
Value-price relationship	Perceived product quality	9.00	7.04	6.62	6.95
Brand loyalty	Number of jewelry brands in household	8.00	5.26	4.20	4.46
	Premium price level	8.00	8.00	6.34	6.86
	Propensity to recommend the brand	7.00	5.66	4.21	5.31
	The frequency of brand purchases	7.00	2.66	1.90	2.80
	Propensity to buy another product of the brand	6.00	4.85	3.50	4.48
	Overall	36.00	26.42	20.15	23.90
Potential of preferences		45.00	33.46	26.78	30.85

Source: own elaboration.

Apart's users are prepared to be charged with the highest price premium (ca. 30.30%). They are also more willing than others to recommend and repurchase the brand. However, YES is also given a high level of brand loyalty, which together with its increasing brand attractiveness pose a real threat to the leader.

Summary

Apart is seen as the most competitive brand in the Polish jewelry market. Its competitive edge has been built mainly due to the popularity of the brand. However, since the image of YES has started to be perceived as more and more attractive, Apart's superiority has been seriously threatened. Although first in the market, W. Kruk has not been able to develop an appealing brand identity and thus has not taken advantage of the power of brand loyalty. None of Polish jewelry brands has achieved a monopoly position in the market. In terms of correlations which occur between particular elements of the competitive potential of luxury brand, it has been indicated that the higher the perceived quality of the product, the higher premium price customers are willing to pay. Moreover, the level of buyer's willingness to recommend the particular brand is affected by three principal variables: the level of trust that customer has towards the brand, the diversity of product range offered by the brand, and the frequency of new product releases. Finally, the more often new products are introduced to the offer, the more willing customers are to choose the particular brand again.

Managerial implications

As the competition between businesses intensifies, intangible assets are becoming the only source of company's uniqueness [Skrzypek 2003, p. 64]. The organizational resource, which is believed to create the most effective synergies, is brand [Jog, Suszyński 2001, p. 4]. Its tasks have evolved significantly over the last 25 years. As a consequence, brand has started to be considered as a basis of permanent relationships between the company and its various shareholders [Urbanek 2008, pp. 45–46]. Theorists together with practitioners have agreed to see brand as an inimitable source of competitive advantage [Płociński 2012]. Moreover, they pointed out that the continuous creation of brand's competitive potential is the only way to achieve strong and more sustainable market position which poses a real threat for competitors. Hence, measurement of competitive potential of brand has started to act as an indicator of brand's ability to compete efficiently in the market. In addition to providing numbers of shareholders with functional and emotional benefits, brands equipped with high competitive potential are capable of creating significant barriers to entry into markets [De Chernatony 2003, p. 23]. For this reason, the relative importance of brand tends to be the highest in the case of luxury goods market [Urbanek 2008, p. 49].

The measurement of competitive potential of Polish jewelry brands based on consumer survey has demonstrated that there is no brand that may be regarded as entirely monopolistic. The brand which competes most successfully in the given area is Apart. The leader of the overall classification ranks also as a top in terms of the potential of popularity, attractiveness and preferences. Apart's competitive potential exceeds the runner-up – YES – by 12%. Taking into account the fact that Apart's supremacy is much lower in the field of brand attractiveness (1.09%), it is anticipated that both brands will use more and more innovative ways to increase the effectiveness of competitive rivalry. The result achieved by W. Kruk makes 56.99% of the maximum score and does not pose a threat to the other two brands. All in all, the direction of activities which affect brand equity should be based on the correlations that exist between several components of brand's competitive potential, as indicated in the research. The results of the study may serve as a basis for the development of Polish luxury brand which is fully efficient in terms of competitive rivalry. Furthermore, it would be reasonable to use the measurements in strategic decision making in Apart, YES, W. Kruk.

It is believed that the role of brand in creating and sustaining competitive advantage will increase substantially in the next few years. Given the fact that potential customers tend to use social media to obtain current information about brands, it is the quality of brand communication on the Web that will significantly affect future purchasing decisions [Walker, Naylor et al. 2012].

Limitations

It should be kept in mind while deducing managerial implications of the research that some products offered by Polish jewelry brands are not perceived to be luxurious. Minimum price, above which each type of jewelry is regarded as luxury, depends on respondents' characteristics such as gender, age, the level of income. Additionally, there is no evidence that each customer that has been surveyed has ever used the bought item. This might have affected the overall responds.

Further research

More work is needed to determine how the components of brand's competitive potential identified here interact with the value of both brand and a company. In particular, in further conceptual and empirical work the focus should be given to the ethical dimension of brand. Since CSR activities are increasingly affecting the way in which the value of an organization's is perceived, the activities which make brand socially responsible should be taken into account when estimating its competitive potential. Further research is also needed to broaden the generalizability of the findings to other types of consumers and categories, particularly fashion and FMCG.

REFERENCES

Aaker D. (1992). The value of brand equity. *Journal of Business Strategy*, Vol. 13, No. 4.
Aaker D. (1993). *Managing Brand Equity*. New York: The Free Press.
Aaker D. (1996a). *Building Strong Brands*. New York: The Free Press.
Aaker D. (1996b). Measuring brand equity across products and markets. *California Management Review*, Vol. 38, No. 3.
Aaker D. (2010). *Brand Relevance: Making Competitors Irrelevant*. Hoboken: Jossey-Bass.
Aaker J. (1997). Dimensions of brand personality. *Journal of Marketing Research*, Vol. 34.
Altkorn J. (1996). Wizerunek firmy jako marka. *Marketing w Praktyce*, No. 4.
Altkorn J. (1999a). *Strategia marki*. Warszawa: Polskie Wydawnictwo Ekonomiczne.

Altkorn J. (1999b). *Strategie marki w marketingu międzynarodowym: pomocnicze materiały dydaktyczne*. Kraków: Wydawnictwo Akademii Ekonomicznej.

Altkorn J. (2004). *Podstawy marketingu*. Kraków: Instytut Marketingu.

Batra R., Ahuvia A., Bagozzi R. (2012). Brand love. *Journal of Marketing*, Vol. 76, No. 2.

Clark K. (2004). *Brandscendence: Three Essential Elements of Enduring Brands*. Chicago: Dearborn Trade/A Kaplan Professional Company.

De Chernatony L. (2003). *Marka. Wizja i tworzenie marki*. Gdańsk: Gdańskie Wydawnictwo Psychologiczne.

De Chernatony L., Christodoulides G., Roper S., Abimbola T. (2008). Brand management. *European Journal of Marketing*m, Vol. 42, No. 5–6. Bradford: Emerald Group Publishing.

Domański T. (2005). Strategie rozwoju marki własnej na rynku polskim. *Handel Wewnętrzny*, No. 2.

Dzinkowski R. (2000). The measurement and management of intellectual capital: An introduction. International Federation of Accountants. *Management Accounting*, Vol. 78, No. 2

Edwards H. (2006). *Kreowanie marek z pasją*. Kraków: Oficyna Ekonomiczna.

Farhana M. (2012). Brand elements lead to brand equity: Differentiate or die. *Information Management & Business Review*, Vol. 4, No. 4.

Fehle F., Fournier S., Madden T. (2006). Brands matter: An empirical demonstration of the creation of shareholder value through branding. *Journal of the Academy of Marketing Science*, Vol. 34, No. 2.

Gambetti R., Graffigna G., Biraghi S. (2012). The Grounded Theory approach to consumer-brand engagement. *International Journal of Market Research*, Vol. 54, No. 5.

Gierszewska G., Romanowska M. (1994). *Analiza strategiczna przedsiębiorstwa*. Warszawa: Polskie Wydawnictwo Ekonomiczne.

Haig M. (2004). *Brand Roylaty: How the World's Top 100 Brands Thrive & Survive*. London: Kogan Page.

Interbrand (2012). Brand Valuation: The financial value of brands. *Brand Channel*. http://www.brandchannel.com/papers_review.asp?sp_id=357 [accessed: 2012].

Jog V., Suszyński C. (2001). *Zarządzanie finansami przedsiębiorstwa*. Warszawa: Centrum Informacji Menedżera.

Kall J. (2001). *Silna marka. Istota i kreowanie*. Warszawa: Polskie Wydawnictwo Ekonomiczne.

Kotler P. (1999). *Marketing. Analiza, planowanie, wdrażanie i kontrola*. Warszawa: Felberg.

Mallik S. (2009). *Brand Management*. Jaipur: Book Enclave.

Mazurkiewicz P. (2012a). Chińczycy walczą o znane marki. *Rzeczpospolita*. http://www.ekonomia24.pl/artykul/830129-Chinczycy-walcza--o-znane-marki.html [accessed: 2012]

Mazurkiewicz P. (2012b). Dobra inwestycja, która przy okazji cieszy oko. *Ekonomia24. pl*. http://www.ekonomia24.pl/artykul/942065.html?print=tak&p=0 [accessed: 2013].

Mazurkiewicz P. (2012c). Marki własne wciąż tanie, ale coraz lepszej jakości. http://www.ekonomia24.pl/artykul/795533-Marki-wlasne-wciaz-tanie--ale-coraz-lepszej-jakosci.html [accessed: 2012].

Mazurkiewicz P. (2012d). Światowe marki atakują Polskę. *Ekonomia24*. http://www.ekonomia24.pl/artykul/794122-Swiatowe-marki-atakuja-Polske.html [accessed: 2012]

Meyers H., Gerstman R. (2002). *Branding @ the Digital Age*. Gordonsville: Palgrave Macmillan

Patkowski P. (2010). *Potencjał konkurencyjny marki*. Warszawa: POLTEXT.

Płociński M. (2012). Globalne marki wypierają polskie. *Rzeczpospolita*. http://www.rp.pl/artykul/962820-Globalne-marki-wypieraja-polskie.html [accessed: 2013].

Porter M.E. (1999). *Strategia konkurencji. Metody analizy sektorów i konkurentów*. Warszawa: Polskie Wydawnictwo Ekonomiczne.

Porter M.E. (2008). *Competitive Advantage. Creating and Sustaining Superior Performance*. Nowy Jork: Simon and Schuster.

Skrzypek E. (2003). *Wpływ zasobów niematerialnych na wartość firmy*. Vol. 2. Lublin: Uniwersytet Marii Curie-Skłodowskiej.

Stahl F., Heitmann M., Lehmann D., Neslin S. (2012). The Impact of Brand Equity on Customer Acquisition, Retention, and Profit Margin. *Journal of Marketing*, Vol. 76, No. 4.

Suszyński C. (2007). *Przedsiębiorstwo. Wartość. Zarządzanie*. Warszawa: Polskie Wydawnictwo Ekonomiczne.

Taylor D., Nichols D. (2010). *The Brand Gym: A Practical Workout to Gain and Retain Brand Leadership*. Hoboken: Wiley.

Urbanek G. (2002). *Zarządzanie marką*. Warszawa: Polskie Wydawnictwo Ekonomiczne.

Urbanek G. (2004). Zwiększanie efektywności strategii budowy marki. *Marketing i Rynek*, No. 11.

Urbanek G. (2008). *Wycena aktywów niematerialnych przedsiębiorstwa*. Warszawa: Polskie Wydawnictwo Ekonomiczne.

Walker Naylor R., Cait Poynor, Lamberton; West P. (2012). Beyond the "Like" Button: The impact of mere virtual presence on brand evaluations and purchase intentions in social media settings. *Journal of Marketing*, Vol. 76, No. 6.

NATALIA LENIEC
Jagiellonian University
Institute of Economics and Management
Chair of Standardized Management Systems

PACKAGING AND ITS ROLE IN THE POLISH CONFECTIONERY MARKET

INTRODUCTION

The rapid evolution of both packaging materials and packaging methods in the late 50's has resulted in the emergence of a new branch of industrial design – packaging design. At the same time, Marketing has been widely recognized as a new field of business activities. Consequently, marketers have started to consider packaging as a driving force behind the sales productivity. In the present paper the question of packaging is discussed in terms of utilizing packaging design in driving sales of confectioneries. Among the fundamental goals of the research the following ones can be distinguished:

- identification of relations between packaging and the elements of marketing mix;
- review of functions performed by packaging;
- specification of psychological impact of packaging on purchasing decisions;
- review of legal regulations concerning packaging design of food and beverages;
- exemplification of packaging's role in the Polish confectionery market including identifying the most attractive elements of packaging design.

1. PACKAGING AND THE MARKETING MIX

According to traditional marketing approach, four basic elements of the marketing mix can be identified. These are: product, price, place and promotion [Kotler 2004, p. 97]. There are two radically different ways of expressing interrelations which occur between packaging and the components of the marketing mix formula.

Philip Kotler and Theodore Levitt consider packaging as an integral part of the product. In order to understand the suggested line of reasoning, the concept of the product is about to be shortly explained. In marketing, a product is anything that can be offered to a market that might satisfy a want or need [Kotler et al. 2006, p. 17]. Not only are physical products included here but also services, places, organizations and ideas. Hence the majority of products shall be considered as the combination of both tangible and intangible elements. It is worth noting that the performance of a product in particular market is primarily determined by the extent to which it meets customer needs and expectations [Altkorn 1996, p. 114]. For this reason, the moving forces behind customer buying decisions are reflected in Kotler's product framework [Hales 1999, p. 43]. The author uses five levels in order to explain the idea of an integrated value which is delivered to customers. These are: core product, generic product, expected product, augmented product, and potential product. According to this concept, packaging is seen as an integral part of the product. When combined with the core product, it contributes to customers' perception at the generic level [Mruk, Rutkowski 1999, p. 23]. In that sense, packaging acts as an attribute which is absolutely necessary for a product to function.

The other group of marketers considers packaging as the fifth component of the marketing mix [Cichoń 1996, p. 146]. In this case, packaging is seen as a separate object of market transactions. Since it is not believed to be a part of any product's level, packaging does not reflect core benefits that make up a product.

Regardless of the theoretical approach, packaging design is influenced by the interrelations occurring between the remaining components of the marketing mix. All activities related to the creation of packaging have to be integrated into the overall marketing strategy in order to ensure its consistency and induce synergies. Therefore, issues which should be given a particular attention will be shortly discussed here.

1.1. PRODUCT

Packaging undoubtedly coexists with a product. Hence there are three fundamental reasons behind the changes in packaging design [Hales 1999, p. 43]. Firstly, packaging improvements may be associated with the product quality improvements. Secondly, they may give an impression of product's novelty. Finally, they might serve as the source of competitive advantage. In terms of strategic implications, packaging modifications may result in the emergence of a new product (e.g. liquid soap) or a new market (e.g. pre-packaged motor oil). In each case, the modification of packaging must be preceded by the analysis of product's characteristics, form, shape and size. These features may stimulate or restrict the use of packaging materials.

1.2. PRICE

Packaging is believed to have an indirect effect on price. In most cases, the cost of packaging contributes to the overall cost of manufacturing a particular product [Mruk, Rutkowski 1999, p. 94]. However, since the competition has intensified, the pricing formula has become more complex. Firstly, it is no longer rare that the cost of one packaging exceeds the value of its content. Secondly, companies have started to downsize packaging in order to leave prices at the same level [Hales 1999, p. 48]. As a result, the importance of packaging has been recognized at the strategic level (especially in pricing strategies).

1.3. PLACE

Packaging plays an important role in both distribution channels and points of sale. First of all, pre-packaged goods can be stored safely. The extended period of storage enables wholesalers as well as retailers to take an advantage of inventory management and respond flexibly to changes in demand. Moreover, packaging protects the content and reduces the losses during transportation. It is also useful when grouping standardized products into batches. Finally, packaging makes it easy to identify different products in various distribution channels. Consequently warehouses are managed effectively and customer service is improved. In order benefit from the use of packaging, the characteristics of various distribution channels and points of sales must be reflected in packaging design. It is worth mentioning that if one product is distributed through competitive distribution channels, it is reasonable to differentiate its packaging [Mruk, Rutkowski 1999, p. 93].

1.4. PROMOTION

Packaging is simply the best tool to engage customer attention and drive purchase intent. It is capable of appreciably affecting customer's behaviors before, during and after a purchase. First, packaging enables a buyer to identify and recognize the product which has drawn his attention earlier, e.g. in

TV commercial. Then, graphics, shapes and colours are used to persuade a customer to make a purchase. Packaging acts here as the basis for individual perceptions of product's functional features. It arouses interest in the product, provides relevant information and realizes unconscious needs of the target group. Hence it is called *'silent salesman'* [Szlak 2004]. It should be noted here that the persuasive role of packaging is of greater importance to fast-moving consumer goods (FMCG) than capital goods. Finally, after a purchase is made, packaging aims to maximize buyer's satisfaction with product use. It therefore affects the level of customer loyalty. The use of packaging along with other promotional tools enables a company to take an advantage of synergies (Table 1).

Table 1. Packaging and promotional tools

Advertising	• the same message is delivered to customers by both packaging and advertising • the same graphics is used in advertising and packaging design • synergies are achieved if packaging is placed in advertising • packaging is the cheapest advertising carrier
Sales promotion	• *cents-off deal*: a product is offered at a lower price; price reduction is marked on packaging • *price-pack deal*: more of a product is offered for the same price; a certain percentage of premium content is be marked on packaging • *contests, sweepstakes, games*: a product is offered with a ticket which entitles its user to participate in several competitions ; coupons are placed inside or outside packaging • *samplings*: a product is offered with a free sample; samples are usually attached to the surface of packaging • *designed to re-use*: a product is offered with a packaging that may be re-used; this type of packaging encourages customers to make regular purchases
Public Relations	• packaging gives the first impression of the image of a company • information relevant to various shareholders (i.e. logotype, quality symbols, environmental icons) is placed on packaging

Source: Hales 1999, pp. 64–72; Szymczak, Ankiel-Homa 2006, pp. 12–13.

Since there are significant interactions between packaging and other elements of the marketing mix, packaging is believed to add substantial value to the market offer. Indeed, it enables customers to easily dose the content, re-use the product and storage it safely. Strategically, packaging innovations increase the level of perceived product quality which, in turn, provides manufacturers with a temporary edge over competitors [Fishel, King Gordon 2007, pp. 32–36]. Packaging may also serve as a basis for market creation and acquisition. For example, the introduction of both aerosol containers and vacuum packages resulted in irreversible changes in consumption patterns.

2. THE FUNCTIONS OF PACKAGING

The role of packaging in the business area has significantly evolved over the last few decades. Packaging's function was initially limited to the protection of the content [Cichoń 1996, p. 17]. However, as the global market saturated, customers have started to use emotional rather than rational evaluation criteria when purchasing [Hales 1999, p. 9]. Therefore, it has been necessary to diversify primary functions of packaging in order to compete successfully. As a result, tasks performed by packaging are currently of interest to three fields of science: Commodity Science, Ecology and Marketing [Cichoń 1996, p. 18].

Primary functions of packaging concern mainly its technical nature [Hales 1999, p. 12]. Protective function essentially involves protecting contents from the external environment and vice versa. Storage function is fulfilled every time each product is stored in different locations. It applies to both before and after the package contents have been used. Packaging has also a crucial impact on the efficiency of transport. It facilitates the formation of cargo units so that it is always easy to pick up and load batches.

Secondary functions of packaging relate to communications [Mruk, Rutkowski 1999, s. 88]. The sales function involves enabling or promoting the sales process and making it more efficient. Promotional function aims at attracting buyer's attention. Packaging design is believed here to have an positive impact on the purchasing decision. The main objective of service function is to provide customers with details about the content and use of a particular good. Moreover, once the content has been used, packaging may also fulfill further tasks. Finally, packaging acts as the basis for ensuring quality and product liability. This guarantee function is heavily related to legislative requirements.

In order to address environmental problems, packaging performs ecological functions [Cichoń 1996, p. 28]. They essentially relate to the extent to which packaging containers or packaging materials may be re-used once the content has been utilized.

This study aims to investigate secondary functions of packaging performed in the Polish confectionery market.

3. THE IMPACT OF PACKAGING DESIGN ON PRODUCT PERCEPTION

The primary function of FMCG packaging is to attract customers [Calver 2007, p. 8]. The package is considered here to act as a brand ambassador. In that sense, it should sell itself. This means every company needs to have a strong brand identity so that each packaging is capable of communicating clear, concise and relevant information to the target audience [Stewart 2009, p. 38]. Packaging design requires also a creative idea and an accurate assessment of long-term financial consequences with respect to both micro and macro environment. A comprehensive look at the packaging life cycle – from design and manufacturing until its disposal – ensures its consistency with company's goals.

Most successful packages are those which reflect attitudes and behaviors of the target group [Calver 2007, p. 28]. For this reason, designers use highly sophisticated segmentation techniques. The profile of a customer is largely based on demographics and psychographics [Fishel 2003, p. 12]. It aims to explain why customers buy the particular product. By doing so, it is possible to understand and anticipate the actions of the target audience [Fishel 2003, p. 19]. All these information is then presented in the mood board. It primarily consists of pictures and symbols which best represent customers' aspirations [Stewart 2009, p. 41]. It is the way buyers perceive these icons that is next translated into packaging design.

During the process of perception customers absorb stimuli and then use them to interpret the world [Solomon 2006, p. 67]. In terms of packaging design, three stages of the perception process may be distinguished: stimulus exposure, attention, and interpretation.

Whenever a stimulus reaches buyer's sensory receptors, the exposure phase is induced. Both characteristics of stimuli and customers' attitudes are of great importance here. They simply determine whether the signals transmitted by the packaging are likely to be noticed or ignored. The power of each stimulus depends primarily on its [Solomon 2006, p. 85]:
- *size*, e.g. large inscriptions placed on the packaging attract customer attention faster than those written with the use of relatively small font;
- *colour*, e.g. white packaging of chocolate bar stands out from the brownish ones;
- *location*, e.g. the information about the contest is noticed faster when placed on the front of the packaging than at the back of it;
- *novelty*, e.g. liquid and spray candies are far more likely to draw customer's attention than ordinary goodies.

Once the stimulus has been exposed, buyer's attention is likely to be drawn to the packaging. Since the target audience interprets stimuli selectively, signals transmitted through the packaging should be perceived as extraordinary. After buyer's interest in the product has been raised, customers concentrate on the packaging while ignoring other things [Solomon 2006, p. 82]. The duration of the attention phase depends heavily on buyer's:

- *Experience*: perceptual filters, developed as a result of past experience, decide which of the signals emitted by the packaging are processed by the customer;
- *Vigilance*: the state of mind which makes it possible for the buyer to identify stimuli related to his/her current needs. For example: a person who rarely buys boxes of chocolates pays also no attention to their packaging as long as there is no need to give them as a gift. Similarly, a chocolate bar attracts the attention of a hungry customer who stands in line at the supermarket even if it is not on a shopping list.;
- *Adaptation*: the point at which people stop responding to the signals as they are already familiar with them. Whenever a signal is adopted, manufacturers should choose to introduce new stimulus so that the product attracts customers again.

In order to understand how quickly customers become insensitive to the particular elements of packaging design, it is reasonable to indicate factors which influence the process of stimulus adaptation [Solomon 2006, p. 83]:

- *stimulus intensity*: low-intense stimuli (e.g. blurred colours of packaging) tend to be less powerful and less durable than high-intense stimuli;
- *stimulus duration*: stimuli which require a significant period of exposure in order to be processed (e.g. on-package recycling information) get customer accustomed to the packaging as a whole;
- *stimulus distinction*: simple stimuli (e.g. monochromatic pack) tend to be ignored quickly since there are no details which may attract customer attention;
- *stimulus exposure*: frequent exposures of the stimuli (e.g. at each checkout) make buyers familiar with the product;
- *stimuli interrelations*: stimuli that are not relevant to the target audience (e.g. bar codes) tend to be overlooked.

After the sensory reception, each stimulus is subject to interpretation. This process draws on elements such as emotions, memory, motivation, personality and attitude. It comprises of two different subprocesses of information processing: 'bottom-up' and 'top-down'. The first one integrates simple elements of signals that come to a customer from the environment. The second one is related to the perceptual synthesis which is strongly affected by customer experience. Hence the choice of packaging depends on both sensory factors and buyer's long-term memory.

The perception process results in customer action. It is therefore of great importance to companies to understand the manner in which customers perceive the product and its packaging. Once it is done, packaging design is capable of driving and maximizing sales.

4. LEGAL REGULATIONS
ON CONFECTIONERY PACKAGING

There are several regulatory requirements for packaging design which have been introduced on behalf of the European Union. They apply to different stages of packaging life cycle:

- *packaging conception* – e.g. regulation No 1935/2004 on materials and articles intended to come into contact with food and repealing Directives 80/590/EEC and 89/109/EEC;
- *raw material transformation and packaging manufacturing* – e.g. Commission Directive 2003/94/EC laying down the principles and guidelines of good manufacturing practice in respect of medicinal products for human use and investigational medicinal products for human use;
- *packaging filling* – e.g. Directive 2000/13/EC relating to the labelling, presentation and advertising of foodstuffs. Regulation (EC) No. 1830/2003 concerning the traceability and labelling of food and feed products produced from genetically modified organisms and amending Directive 2001/18/EC;
- *valorisation and recycling packaging waste* – e.g. Directive 94/62/EC on Packaging and Packaging Waste, as amended by Directive 2004/12/EC.

Since focus has been given to the use of CSR policies, packaging has become a subject of public interest [Hales 1999, p. 131]. Companies are therefore encouraged to take up voluntary activities aiming at meeting customers' expectations and eliminating fraud procedures. In order to make customers fully aware of these CSR initiatives, businesses have started to display such information on labels which are usually printed directly on packaging. As a result, three fundamental types of labels have evolved: qualitative, descriptive and informative [Hales 1999, p. 133]. Qualitative labels include icons which reflect the level of product quality. These quality symbols are exclusively reserved for products that meet certain requirements. Descriptive labels, in turn, provide basic information about product characteristics such as brand name, net weight or methods of manufacturing. Finally, informative labels present the full range of information related to a particular product. They enable a customer to learn about serving suggestions, nutrition facts, the frequency of application etc. The choice of the most appropriate label depends heavily on the type of product and the channels through which it is sold. In order to support the image of a company, each label should be characterized by the optimal amount of information, impeccable printing, and the right balance between packaging's shape and its colors [Cichoń 1996, p. 126].

All food and beverages are subject to mandatory labeling. It is Directive 2000/13/EC which clarifies labeling, advertising and presentation requirements for these product categories. Most importantly, 'the labeling and methods used must not be such as could mislead the purchaser as to the characteristics of the foodstuff, its nature, identity, properties, composition, quantity, durability, origin or provenance, method of manufacture or production' (Directive 2000/13/EC). Moreover, it is not allowed to attribute to the foodstuff effects or properties which it does not possess. Finally, labels must not suggest that the foodstuff possesses special characteristics when in fact all similar foodstuffs possess such characteristics. Domestic regulations are in line with the European Commission requirements. According to them, food manufacturers are obliged to provide specific information on labels. These include: trade name, ingredients, allergy advice, net weight, expiry date, storage conditions, product origin, batch number, and manufacturer's address. Moreover, a universal barcode is placed on each packaging [Mruk, Rutkowski, p. 99]. The right to use the EAN code (European Article Numbering) is granted to countries that have joined the International Article Numbering Association (IANA). Poland has joined IANA in 1990 and uses prefix 590. Since then both manufacturers and retailers use bar code scanning in order to control inventories and sales.

5. PACKAGING AND ITS ROLE IN THE POLISH CONFECTIONERY MARKET

5.1. OVERVIEW

Since packaging is believed to serve as a powerful tool for communication and branding, it is considered to be vital to the FMCG market [Don 2013]. The development of packaging design is given an extremely high priority when it comes to confectioneries. The reason for this is that sweets remain at the top spot for impulse purchases [Glaberson 2011]. Indeed, functionality, convenience and sustainability are driving Polish packaging market for confectioneries. However, best practices regarding the use of packaging design to trigger the purchase of sweets remain undefined. This research aims to fill this gap.

The main objective of this paper is to present students' preferences for packaging design of a chocolate bar. According to the Polish Classification of Activities, the confectionery market consists of three fundamental segments: bakery, chocolate and candies. The total value of all three segments is estimated at 9.65 billion PLN. Bakery and chocolate make the largest contribution in the growth of the market (increase of 9.5% and 8.5% respectively). Hence manufacturers of both categories are seen to be the most powerful market players.

Table 2. Top manufacturers of bakery and chocolate in the Polish confectionery market

Chocolate manufacturers		
	Share in the overall sales value (1.3 bn PLN)	Share in the overall sales volume (49.1 m kg)
Kraft Foods Poland	36%	30%
LOTTE Wedel	24%	22%
Private labels	13%	22%
Others	27%	26%
Bakery manufacturers		
	Share in the overall sales value (1.1 bn PLN)	Share in the overall sales volume (65.2 m kg)
Kraft Foods Poland	34%	26%
Private labels	22%	32%
Bahlsen Group	15%	15%
Others	29%	27%

Source: own elaboration.

Sweets are most often purchased at supermarkets (21% of total market value, 24% of total sales volume), groceries (25% and 23% respectively), and hypermarkets (17% and 19% respectively). Since the value of pre-packaged chocolate bars represents the largest portion of total market value (18.1%), they have been chosen as the object of the study. This category of sweets accounts for 18.0% of the overall sales volume (estimated at 255.62 million kg).

According to AC Nielsen industry report, chocolate is usually bought at supermarkets (36% of total sales value) and medium-sized groceries (21.9%).

5.2. METHODOLOGY

After the secondary data concerning industry performance had been analyzed, the customer survey was conducted. The questionnaire consisted of 13 questions. It was completed by 100 respondents who were shopping at one of the supermarket chains. At every stage of the research the focus was given to a random selection of respondents. Hence high level of sample representativeness has been achieved. Characteristics of study population has been shown in Table 3. They stay in line with the structure of students' population and higher education in Cracow.

Table 3. Characteristics of study population

	Number (share) of respondents*	Gender		Modes of study	
		female	male	stationary	non-stationary
Jagiellonian University	46 (46%)	31 (68%)	15 (32%)	31 (67%)	15 (33%)
AGH University of Science and Technology	33 (33%)	10 (30%)	23 (70%)	24 (73%)	9 (27%)
Cracow University of Economics	21 (21%)	13 (64%)	8 (36%)	10 (49%)	11 (51%)

* Values in brackets refer to the size of the entire study sample (n = 100)

Source: own elaboration.

Packaging design of chocolate bars has been examined with the use of elements shown in Figure 1.

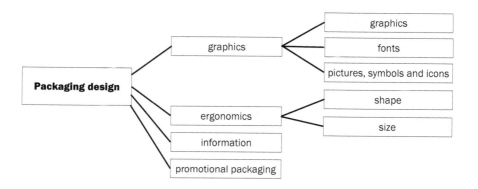

Figure 1. Elements of packaging design

5.3. STUDENTS' PREFERENCES TOWARDS CHOCOLATE PACKAGING

Students who buy chocolate account for 98% of the general population. The results presented in this paper do not apply to customers who have never bought any chocolate before.

Chocolate is believed to be purchased by the overwhelming portion of students (98%). These are both women (54%) and men (46%). Bars are bought by 60% of students whereas cookies – only by 14% of them. Other categories of sweets are not popular among students. Interestingly, the choice of confectionery goods is determined mostly by personal habits (46%), price (41%), advertising (28%) and product quality (24%). It should be emphasized that only 23% of students pay attention to packaging when selecting confectioneries. These are only women.

Graphics

For over half of the respondents (51%) pictures displayed on packaging are crucial when choosing a chocolate bar. In addition, almost every second student (47%) pays attention to the colour of packaging. These are mainly women (96%). What is more, the colour of pre-packaged chocolate bar serves as a primary selection criteria for the majority of women (81%). The possibility to open/re-close is, in turn, essential for 44% chocolate buyers. These are mostly men (67%). The shape of chocolate bar is far more likely to be taken into consideration by women whereas the visibility of brand logo – by men. The type of font is significant for every fourth student (mostly female) whereas packaging material is of high importance for every fifth chocolate buyer (mostly male). Only 14% of the respondents pay attention to the quality of information presented on a packaging. Most of these are women (71%).

Table 4. Factors determining the choice of packaging

Factor	The percentage of chocolate buyers (n = 98)	Of whom	
		women	men
Pictures	51%	48%	52%
Colour	47%	96%	4%
Possibility to open / re-close	44%	33%	67%
Shape	39%	76%	24%
Visibility of brand logotype	29%	18%	82%
Font	24%	63%	38%
Packaging material	19%	26%	74%
Quality of information	14%	71%	29%

The outcomes do not add up to 100% since the respondents were given the option of indicating their top-three alternatives.

Source: own elaboration.

The colour of packaging tends to inform customers about the flavour of chocolate. Colours, which are most frequently attributed to various chocolate flavours, have been presented below.

Table 5. Colours determining the flavour of chocolate

Colour	The most common flavour attribution
Brown	milk (70%)
Black	dark (86%)
Green	nuts (77%)
Silver	coconut (54%)
Red	strawberry (77%)
Purple	raisins&nuts (70%)
Gold	toffee (63%)
White	white (93%)

Source: own elaboration.

It is worth mentioning that in the opinion of the majority of students (77%) all these colour-flavour associations should be applied only to these graphic objects which distinguish one chocolate flavor from another. The minority (23%) of the respondents find it useful to cover the whole packaging with a particular colour.

Ergonomics and shape

There has been identified no form of a chocolate bar which would encourage over a half of the respondents to purchase a new brand of chocolate. However, triangle chocolate bar appears to be of the great interest. If introduced, women's purchases would be affected to a greater extent. Men would, in turn, be more encouraged to try new brand of chocolate if it's packed in a triangular prism. Other shapes of chocolate bar are not perceived as influential.

Table 6. Shapes of chocolate bars which would trigger the purchase of new brand

Shape	The percentage of chocolate buyers	Of whom	
		women	men
Triangle	46%	67%	33%
Triangular prism	23%	30%	70%
Circle	11%	82%	18%
Horizontal rectangle	10%	40%	60%
Square	6%	33%	67%
Vertical rectangle	2%	50%	50%

Source: own elaboration.

Size

Almost every student buys chocolate (98% of study population). In most cases (79%), the weight of chocolate bar is between 51–100 grams. Interestingly, none of the respondents chooses chocolate bars which weigh less than 50 grams or more than 200 grams. Chocolate bars weighing 51–100 grams or 101–150 grams are bought equally often by women and men. On the other hand, only women purchase chocolate bars weighing below 50 grams. Moreover, 82% of students who buy chocolate far more often than other sweets choose these of a weight from 51 to 100 grams.

Information

The majority of students consider quality symbols to be the most significant source of front-side information. These icons are of the highest importance for 77% of male chocolate buyers. In the opinion of over half of the respondents, expiry date should be positioned on the front of chocolate packaging. This type of information is almost equally important for both women and men. Almost every second student would like to see calories per serving icon on the front of pre-packaged chocolate bar. It is also the most desirable type of front-side information among female buyers (76%). Finally, presenting net weight on the front of pre-packaged chocolate meets the expectations of 37% students. There is no need to include other types of information on the front of chocolate packaging.

Table 7. Elements which should be displayed on the front of pre-packaged chocolate bar

Element	The percentage of chocolate buyers (n = 98)	Of whom	
		women	men
Quality symbols	64%	46%	54%
Expiry date	57%	46%	54%
Calories per serving	48%	87%	13%
Net weight	37%	53%	47%
Serving suggestion	11%	100%	0%
Nutrition facts	4%	25%	75%
Country of origin	3%	33%	67%
Storage conditions	2%	50%	50%
Allergy advice	2%	50%	50%

The outcomes do not add up to 100% since the respondents were given the option of indicating their top-three alternatives.

Source: own elaboration.

The average frequency of the use of information is about 2.7 which means that students sometimes take advantage of the information provided by one packaging in order to make a better purchase. Expiry date is most often paid attention to. Nutrition facts, net weight and quality symbols are also frequently used. The findings also show that, as might have been expected, women seek information about calories per serving far more often than men. Other information is used rarely in consumer decision making process.

Table 8. The average frequency of the use of information presented on packaging*

Type of information	Average (n = 98)	Among	
		women	men
Expiry date	4.46	4.59	4.30
Nutrition facts	3.57	3.91	3.16
Net weight	3.50	3.63	3.34
Quality symbols	3.21	3.44	2.93
Calories per serving	3.07	4.06	1.86
Country of origin	2.35	2.31	2.39
Storage conditions	1.99	2.20	1.73
Serving suggestion	1.78	2.00	1.50
Allergy advice	1.54	1.69	1.36

* 1 – never, 5 – always

Source: own elaboration.

For the majority of students (86%) icons, symbol and pictures serve as the main source of chocolate flavor. Written information (76%) and the colour of packaging (50%) are also considered to be important sources of chocolate flavor (50%). However, graphic objects tend to be noticed in the first place. Interestingly, in order to identify the flavor of chocolate, women take a look at graphic objects at first (71%) whereas men – at written information (50%). Moreover, female buyers (72%) use the colour of packaging as a source of chocolate flavor far more often than men (22%).

Table 9. The sources of information about the flavour of chocolate

Source	The percentage of chocolate buyers (n = 98)
Graphic objects	86%
Written information	76%
Colour	50%
Font	2%

The outcomes do not add up to 100% since the respondents were given the option of indicating their top-three alternatives.

Source: own elaboration.

Promotional packaging

The majority of students (71%) usually go for promotional packaging in order to take part in contests, sweepstakes or games. Lottery codes and coupons attract 80% of men and 65% of women, indeed. Cents-off deals are the most popular promotional packagings among female chocolate buyers (70%). Interestingly, men are more prone to choose a packaging which is designed to be re-used whereas women – the one that offers price-pack deal. Every third student pays attention to samplings, regardless of gender.

Table 10. The types of promotional chocolate bars

Type of promotional packaging	The percentage of chocolate buyers (n = 98)
Contests, sweepstakes, games	71%
Cents-off deal	60%
Designed to re-use	57%
Price-pack deal	37%
Samplings	32%

The outcomes do not add up to 100% since the respondents were given the option of indicating their top-three alternatives.

Source: own elaboration.

Since promotional packagings attract the vast majority of students, companies have started to use them as a basis of product differentiation in the Polish confectionery market [Table 11].

Table 11. Promotional packagings of the most popular chocolate bars

Type of promotional packaging	Leading brand
Contests, sweepstakes, games	Alpen Gold (70%)
Cents-off deal	Milka (59%)
Designed to re-use	Goplana (39%)
Price-pack deal	Wedel (81%)
Samplings	Lindt (71%)

Source: own elaboration.

The most successful packaging of chocolate bar in the Polish confectionery market

None of selected chocolate packagings is considered to be attractive to more than 36% of students. Lindt – the leader of general classification – has gained its market superiority mainly due to the use of unique graphic objects and sophisticated fonts. These two elements have significantly increased customer willingness to buy a bar of Lindt's chocolate. On the other hand, the runner-up of the ranking – Milka – has taken the advantage of both packaging's functionality and logotype visibility. Wedel aims to follow in leaders' footsteps and closes the Top 3 with the highest level of packaging's functionality. Other brands are not believed to compete successfully in the field of packaging design.

Table 12. The attractiveness of chocolate packaging across various brands

Brand Evaluation criteria	Lindt	Terravita	Wawel	Wedel	Goplana	Alpen Gold	Milka	Overall
Functionality	4%	1%	0%	43%	2%	8%	42%	100%
Visibility of brand logotype	6%	0%	4%	3%	0%	20%	66%	100%
Font	42%	0%	5%	32%	2%	0%	19%	100%
Graphic objects	69%	4%	3%	11%	0%	4%	8%	100%
Wilingness to buy	56%	0%	2%	21%	0%	2%	18%	100%
Share in overall classfification	36%	1%	3%	22%	1%	7%	31%	100%

Source: own elaboration.

Managerial implications

Since Polish confectionery market is growing rapidly, companies use more and more sophisticated tools to achieve market leadership. As 59% of students admit to buying sweets on impulse, packaging design is considered to be a primary source of competitive advantage for confectionery manufacturers [Glaberson 2011].

Compliance with the legal regulations concerning food and beverages labeling is the prerequisite for fair competition. The edge over competitors is achieved mainly by taking advantage of secondary functions of packaging which relate to the perceptual level of communication. Since packaging design attracts customer attention, creates a unique scenery at the point of sale, and drives purchase intent, it is believed to be an effective sales tool.

Although many researches consider promotional role of packaging as essential to FMCG manufacturers, recent studies suggest that only 23% of students pay attention to packaging when purchasing confectioneries. It should be emphasized that this group consists mostly of women. Buyers' habits (46%) and price (41%) are still the main criteria for the selection of sweets.

Interestingly, the more often students pay attention to packaging when selecting sweets, the more often they take into account the colour of pack-

aging when choosing chocolate bar (r = 0.507). Moreover, the more often attention is paid to packaging:
- the less often individual habits are taken into consideration when selecting confectioneries (r = −0.406);
- the less often price is taken into account when choosing sweets (r = −0.307);
- the less often brand is taken into consideration when selecting confectionery goods (r = −0.237).

Limitations

It should be emphasized that students' preferences for packaging design have been identified with the use of customer survey. In order to fill in the questionnaire respondents needed to consider each of the given answer options. This means that the majority of the results presented in this paper relate to the rational reasons for purchasing confectioneries. Since sweets are usually bought on impulse it is highly probable that the use of a different research method (e.g. experiment) would demonstrate the greater significance of packaging in the confectionery market.

Further research

The results of this study provide a useful insight for packaging designers. However, more work is needed to determine which elements of packaging design drive purchase intent. The impact of incremental changes in packaging design on sales volume should also be discussed. Finally, it is highly recommended to estimate the extent to which packaging affects the image of a company.

REFERENCES

Ahvenainen R. (2003). *Novel Food Packaging Techniques*. Cambridge: Woodhead Publishing Limited, pp. 5–22.
Altkorn J. (1996). *Podstawy marketingu*. Kraków: Instytut Marketingu, pp. 113–118, 157–161.
Calver G. (2007). What is Packaging Design? Mies: RotoVision SA, pp. 4–40, 68–150.
Cichoń M. (1996). *Opakowanie w towaroznawstwie, marketingu i ekologii*. Wrocław: ZNiO.
Don A. (2013). *Packaging vital to the FMCG market*. Packaging Hub, http://www.packaginghub.org/feature/packaging-vital-fmcg-market [accessed: 17th July 2013].
Fishel C. (2003). *Design Secrets: Packaging*. Massachusetts: Rockport Publishers Inc., pp. 1–30.
Fishel C., King Gordon S. (2007). *The Little Book of Big Packaging Ideas*. Massachusetts: Rockport Publishers Inc., pp. 1–41.

Glaberson H. (2011). Confectionery Still Top for Impulse Buys, Survey. *Confectionery News*, http://www.confectionerynews.com/Markets/Confectionery-still-top-for-impulse-buys-survey [accessed: 13th July 2013].

Hales C.F. (1999). *Opakowanie jako instrument marketingu*. Warszawa: PWE.

Jedlicka W. (2009). *Packaging Sustainability: Tools, Systems, and Strategies for Innovative Package Design*. New Jersey: John Willey & Sons Inc.

Jerzyk E. (2006). Nowoczesne opakowanie – design, funkcjonalność i informacje. *Opakowanie*, No. 2, p. 24–26.

Jerzyk E. (2007). Wykorzystanie opakowania jako kreatora wizerunku produktu i przedsiębiorstwa. *Zeszyty naukowe Gnieźnieńskiej Wyższej Szkoły Humanistyczno-Menedżerskiej Millenium*, No. 1, pp. 75–83.

Kotler P. (1994). Opakowanie. In: M. Belka (ed.). *Marketing. Analiza, planowanie, wdrażanie i kontrola*. 6th ed. Warszawa: Gebethner & Ska, pp. 420–422.

Kotler P. (2004). *Marketing od A do Z*. Warszawa: Polskie Wydawnictwo Ekonomiczne S.A.

Kotler P. (2005). *Marketing*. Dom Wydawniczy REBIS Sp. z o.o., pp. 438–441.

Kotler P., Armstrong G., Brown L., Adam S. (2006) *Marketing*. 7th ed. Prentice Hall: Pearson Education Australia.

Kozak A. (2007). Produkt dobrze pakowany. *Fresh & Cool Market*, No. 6, p. 28.

Mruk H., Rutkowski I.P. (1999). Marka i opakowanie. In: *Strategia produktu*. Warszawa: PWE, pp. 84–111.

Solomon M.R. (2006). *Zachowania i zwyczaje konsumentów*. 6th ed. Gliwice: HELION, chapters 1–4, 9.

Stewart B. (2009). *Projektowanie opakowań*. Warszawa: Polskie Wydawnictwo Naukowe.

Szlak J. (2004). Niemy sprzedawca. *Marketing przy kawie*, www.marketing-news.pl/theme. php?art=153 [accessed: 17th October 2010].

Szydzińska K. (2006). Opakowanie – niemy sprzedawca. *Marketing w Praktyce*, www. egospodarka.pl/12963,Opakowanie-niemy-sprzedawca,1,20,2,o.html [accessed: 17th October 2010].

Szymczak J., Ankiel-Homa M. (2006). Możliwość wykorzystania opakowań w strategii rozwoju produktu. *Opakowanie*, No. 2, pp. 12–13.

Szymczak J., Ankiel-Homa M. (2004). Warstwa wizualna opakowań jednostkowych – kreatorem wizerunku produktów kosmetycznych. *Opakowanie*, No. 8, part. I, pp. 28–30.

Zientek-Varga J. (2008). Kupowanie klienta znakami. *Fresh & Cool Market*, No. 11, pp. 26–28.

KINGA BAUER
Jagiellonian University
Institute of Economics and Management
Chair of International Accounting

RESTRUCTURING VENTURES IN COMPANIES AT RISK OF BANKRUPTCY

INTRODUCTION

Achieving and maintaining competitive advantage forces companies to be flexible and creative which allows them to implement efficient transformations in terms of production, operating principles and organizational structure. Nevertheless it is not only development of a company that is related to its continuous adjustment to changes occurring in the company environment.

Fundamental objective of a company is to survive. However, it does not imply that it is sufficient for an organization to maintain its production on the same quantitative and technological levels of the same products for the same clients. If a company does not develop it is bound to fall consequently as it is unable to adapt to market changes. In a long term perspective it needs to strive toward growth through investments, modernization of technologies, manufacturing new products [Wędzki 2003, p. 17].

Inability to solve problems quickly and efficiently, imperception of the need to constantly introduce changes adapting the organization and company operations to new market conditions may cause serious crisis posing threat not only to development but also to survival of the company [Nalepka 1999, p. 7, Borowiecki 1998, p. 22; Mączyńska 2009, p. 23].

Threat to continue operations may be noticed by the managers only at the time when crisis forces to file a bankruptcy petition. Should a company – debtor stand a chance to satisfy claims of creditors to a greater extent than in case of bankruptcy leading to liquidation of the bankrupt's assets, the court shall declare bankruptcy leading to conclusion of agreement. In order to deem likely before the court that the entrepreneur – debtor is in a condition to continue business activity it is required to carefully plan restructuring ventures and to develop agreement proposals along with justification.

Discussion included in the hereby study is based on the conviction that debtor who files a bankruptcy petition leading to conclusion of agreement does not only see legal and economical reasons for implementing it but also is determined to undertake actions in order to maintain the possibility to continue operations. On account of it, the debtor will undertake all (legitimate) actions to prove that they are able to satisfy the claims of creditors and to further conduct business activity. The efforts as part of co-operation with court mean that the debtor will signify that the debtor will strive to provide the best possible information which will increase data transparency of the bankruptcy procedure. In particular it will be reflected in defining directions and means to implement restructuring undertakings as well as in co-operation with court supervisor.

The main objective of the present study is to analyze restructuring ventures of companies at risk of bankruptcy. Attaining this aim may serve to assess the risk of crisis re-occurring as:
- analysis of company's areas of operation which require remedy is prerequisite to conducting effective restructuring,
- restricting a company exclusively to restructuring through insolvency plans may be threatening for its existence in long term.

As part of achieving the main objective attempts were made in order to answer the following questions:
- did the co-operation according to the court supervisor proceed smoothly?
- did the debtor attempt to identify the reasons for the ensuing crisis?
- does the justification of agreement proposal include all subsections stated in article 280 of the Bankruptcy and Reorganization Law (BRL), if not which ones do the simplifications apply to?
- do the changes concern financial or operational restructuring?
- do the managers of the company at risk of bankruptcy declare implementing changes of developmental nature or only remedial ones?

In order to answer the above questions research has been conducted in district courts, in departments conducting insolvency proceedings. The research is a pilot study and comprise part of own research of the author connected with managerial aspects of bankruptcy proceedings. For the purpose of the hereby study the research included documentation of initial, and in case of proceedings leading toward agreement also proper insolvency proceedings collected by the courts conducting them. In these trials restructuring undertakings were indentified. Analysis included 24 cases which is 3.3% of all bankruptcies announced in 2011, in case of 18 of them court announced bankruptcy leading toward agreement which constitutes 17.5% of all bankruptcies leading toward agreement announced in the year of research. Absolute small size of the sample does not allow to statistically generalize conclusions for the entire population of companies at risk of bankruptcy.

1. RESTRUCTURING IN ECONOMIC AND MANAGEMENT SCIENCES

1.1. THE ESSENCE OF COMPANY RESTRUCTURING

Restructuring is the body of changes within a company in reaction to the changing environment of the organization. The purpose of these alterations is to streamline operations of the company.

Restructuring is a multi-dimensional process. It may take place simultaneously in several areas of company operations such as [Brandenburg 2010, p. 97]:

- technical – technological,
- organizational,
- economic,
- legal.

Restructuring can be undertaken in every stage of business life cycle as property, organization and economic changes should take place always when it is necessary.

Restructuring includes activities which aim at survival of the company in short term and its development in longer perspective. Literature of the subject distinguishes the following types of restructuring [Nalepka 1999, p. 23]:

- creative; preceding changes in the business environment and aiming at creating changes,
- anticipating; which results from the company management expecting certain changes to occur and which allows to implement them in advance,
- adaptive; being a speedy reaction to changes which have already taken place in business environment,
- remedial; which is a type of adaptive restructuring. It is however introduced later as an activity to restore the company operation effectiveness.

Remedial restructuring is conducted in companies of poor economic condition, while the remaining types, creative, anticipating and adaptive, in efficient organizations willing to increase their competitiveness. Hence these three types are usually considered jointly as development restructuring (offensive).[1]

Consequently, as far as the manner of restructuring is concerned, two types of this process can be distinguished – remedial and development

---

[1] Some sources treat adaptive restructuring as a separate type being less radical than remedial at the same time being less creative than development one.

[Nowak 2009]. Nevertheless it needs to be highlighted that for companies in crisis remedial restructuring is the starting point.

Remedial restructuring may take place [Nalepka 1999, p. 27]:
1) as part of the current company potential by:
   - streamlining management process,
   - improving work organization,
   - increasing product quality,
   - raising employees competencies,
   - developing motivation system;
2) as part of reduced ("lean") company potential by:
   - elimination of inefficient parts of operations,
   - sale of unused assets,
   - utilize assets with participation of other individuals or entities,
   - limiting production range,
   - employment reduction.

Activities as part of development restructuring concern in particular [Nalepka 1999, p. 27]:
   - starting new spheres of action,
   - change of production range,
   - change o markets,
   - exchange of suppliers,
   - exchange of manufacturing technique and technology,
   - perfecting organization structure and management process.

Restructuring can also be divided into financial and operational. Operational includes changes in terms of its implementation and methodology as well as change of organization and management of physical and human resources of the company. Financial restructuring involves also capital and cost structure along with sources of financing business activity. In real life operational and financial restructuring are closely related. Changes in operational activity affect financial sphere. On the other hand, change of managing financial means affects resources and the way a company operates [Garstka 2006, pp. 27–28].

In bankruptcy proceedings restructuring may be restricted to discharging liabilities guarantee. However if the company is expected to survive after agreement execution, deep changes of operational nature should also be implemented.

1.2. COURSE OF RESTRUCTURING PROCESS

In market economy companies are diversified on the grounds of their legal form, nature, size, trade, etc. Diversity of companies, their needs and positions influence the course of restructuring processes they undertake.

Effectiveness of restructuring process requires customization of introduced changes. Its course is also influenced by the type and area of restructuring activities [Brandenburg 2010, p. 97].

In the restructuring process three main stages can be singled out such as [Pacholski, Cempel, Pawlewski 2009, p. 6]:

1) identification of the company condition,
2) restoration of capability to generate profits allowing the company to survive,
3) implementing mechanisms protecting against loosing the ability to generate profits.

Identification of the current state of a company is of fundamental importance for the restructuring process. It provides information about the nature and scale of company problems what at the same time is the basis for further stages of the process. This stage makes use of financial and strategic analysis methods and if they are not sufficient detailed techniques of individual functions of an organization are used. For companies experiencing serious crisis appropriate diagnosis of current situation is linked with verifying if there are grounds for filing a bankruptcy petition. Hence, it is simultaneously a stage preceding filing a bankruptcy petition.

After identification of the restructuring need, assessment of the present situation and market position of a company and after strategic analysis it is required to develop restructuring programme which should cover [Brandenburg 2010, p. 98]:

- action plans specifying scope of scheduled changes and individuals responsible for executing them,
- financial plans that is results of restructuring expressed in units of account expected,
- risk analysis,
- schedule of implementing the plan.

In case when it is the debtor to file a bankruptcy petition the planned restructuring ventures should be a part of agreement proposals. Agreement proposals must concern liabilities related issues, yet their justification should include restructuring programme for all sub-systems of company which might cause problems in executing agreement and in surviving of the company after finalized bankruptcy proceedings.

In the next stage the company executes restructuring activities. This stage in bankruptcy proceedings may start already at the initial bankruptcy proceedings, however its major part falls for the proper bankruptcy proceedings. Implementing restructuring activities can and should take place after finalized bankruptcy proceedings especially in case of development activities.

Furthermore, it is also necessary to introduce mechanisms protecting against loosing capability to generate expected profits and in case of continuing operations after finalized bankruptcy proceeding – to prevent crisis situations.

1.3. VENTURES OF REMEDIAL AND DEVELOPMENT RESTRUCTURING[2]

Restructuring ventures should apply to such company sub-systems as:
1) company mission and objectives,
2) people,
3) structure,
4) resources and technology,
5) other activities.

Restructuring ventures concerning individual sub-systems of an organization depend from the type of restructuring – if it is of remedial or development nature.

Ventures as part of remedial restructuring concerning company **mission and objectives** are usually developed by company management and their character is mostly adaptive. They should lead to warding off the vision of bankruptcy by improving current financial situation. It needs to be emphasized here that for debtors filing bankruptcy petition it will mean efforts avoiding bankruptcy leading to liquidation of assets thanks to restructuring conducted as part of proceeding leading to conclusion of agreement.

The newly created mission and objectives of the company undergoing development restructuring usually take shape of formalized programmes prepared together with consulting companies and approved by management. It embraces aspects connected to company development, increasing profits, raising competitiveness or change of operations scope.

Various approach in case of both types of restructuring concerns the issue of **human resources**. Remedy of a company usually forces substantial reduction of employment, starting from non-production staff and often, due to restricting scope of operations, also production workers directly. Crisis forces employers not only to discontinue salary increases but mostly to lower the remunerations.

Companies in development stage approach the employees-related issue in a different manner. Not only do they focus on utilizing present potential of employed staff but also on investments and raising their professional qualifications and strengthening motivation system. Furthermore, offensive strategy may be connected also with hiring additional employees, finance, marketing or new technologies specialists.

---

[2] Division in terms of company sub-system and detailed discussion of restructuring ventures has been dealt with by J. Pasieczny [1997, pp. 33] and later quoted, completed and modified in numerous other papers [among others Nalepka 1998, pp. 28–28, Nalepka 1999, pp. 29–30; Garstka 2006, pp. 25–26; Dźwigoł 2007, pp. 21–22]. Discussion of this subsection has also been broadened by own conclusions of the Author of the present paper (in particular those relating to restructuring in bankruptcy proceeding).

Structure remedial may require among others:
- closedown or joining some organizational units,
- assignment of organized parts together with their economic and legal independence,
- creating responsibility centres, changing operating principles and those concerning holding individuals accountable, development of controlling.

Restructuring of development nature shall determine structure of a company mostly by simplifying it, making it more flexible, by increasing independence of some individuals or by rationalization of IT system.

Remedial restructuring influences ventures in terms of **resources and technology** by:
- restricting or suspending investments,
- sale of redundant assets and more efficient use of those left in the company,
- activities as part of improving quality of produced goods, tightening requirements applicable to suppliers,
- utilizing owned property in undertaking new, risky ventures.

Development restructuring will shape resources and technology by:
- striving after quality improvement,
- investments in new technologies,
- undertaking both viable and company-specific ventures (in crisis situation in order to survive a company may be active in areas not corresponding to its profile only to make profit),
- activities of the organization and management area – streamlining logistic processes, applying management accounting and controlling,
- environment protection activities (which may also improve financial condition).

Other activities as part of restructuring ventures in case of company remedy concern mostly financial issues such as reduction of obligations, attempts to obtain additional means, or negotiations regarding entered agreements which allow to shorten the receivables turnover ratio and extend deadline for meeting payment obligations. In a situation when bankruptcy proceeding is in progress in court the greatest emphasis is placed on activities related to change in obligations payment conditions.

Restructuring ventures – development may concern activities such as financial restructuring, ownership changes and creating new business entities.

To sum up restructuring ventures of a company in its remedial stage are related to reduction of employment, property and obligations as well as activities aiming at greater efficiency with the use of owned resources. Development stage of a company results in new investments in tangible and intangible assets along with processes improving quality, organization and management.

Companies experiencing serious crisis filing a bankruptcy petition in order to survive need to introduce restructuring ventures of remedial nature. Nevertheless, organizations at this stage of company lifecycle should develop strategy of further development. Planning exclusively remedial activities carries a risk that after executing agreement company might not be able to survive in the market conditions. Efficient performance of bankruptcy proceeding not infrequently results from debt reduction. What is more, the process may substantially reduce resources of bankrupt company. Hence, without developing strategy of operations the risk of failure reoccurring still exists.

2. RESTRUCTURING LEGAL BASIS IN BANKRUPTCY PROCEEDING LEADING TO CONCLUSION OF AGREEMENT

Changes in the Bankruptcy and Reorganization Law (BRL) which came into force as of 2 May 2009 are intended to help saving the companies experiencing only temporary financial difficulties. If companies are in a position to satisfy claims of creditors to a greater extent thanks to rehabilitation proceeding or one leading to agreement with creditors, the court will not deprive the organization of the possibility to continue their business activity [Kański 2009].

Bankruptcy proceeding leading to conclusion of agreement is conducted with the aim to satisfy claims of creditors and to restore the company ability to compete on the market. In order to do that company restructuring is necessary. Agreement proposals, which are required to include debtor's liabilities restructuring plan, are submitted to court. Agreement proposals (both before and after the court announcement of bankruptcy) may be filed by the bankrupt, court supervisor, administrator or creditor (BRL, Art. 267–269).

Agreement proposal should specify one or several manners of restructuring obligations along with justification. They may include postponing repayment of obligations, splitting them into instalments, reducing total amount of obligations, debt for equity swap – be it shares or interests depending on the legal form of the debtor, exchange or change or waiving provision securing the specified debt [Działocha-Świetlikowska et al. 2003]. Agreement may also concern satisfying claims of creditors by liquidation of the bankrupt's assets and may stand for take-over of the assets by creditors or other method of liquidation (BRL, Art. 271).

Pursuant to Art. 280 of BRL

reasoning of agreement proposals should:
1) describe the company conditions with particular specification of its economic and financial, legal and organizational situations;
2) analysis of the market sector where the bankrupt's company operates including market position of competition;
3) methods and sources of funding for executing agreement taking into account expected incomes and expenses in the time of executing the agreement;
4) level and risk structure analysis;
5) persons responsible for executing agreement (names and surnames);
6) evaluation of alternative manner of restructuring obligations;
7) system of securing rights and interests of creditors for the time of executing agreement.

With the consent of supervising judge it is possible to restrict agreement proposal justification (provided the company specific allows it and it does not affect proper execution of agreement).

The scope of reasoning of the agreement proposals included in Art. 280 of BRL applies mostly to restructuring of obligations (in particular items 3, 5, 6 and 7). It is due to the fact that the reasoning is required to be one of the grounds for the decision if the company is able to execute the agreement and satisfy claims of creditors to an extent greater than in case of proceeding leading to liquidation of assets of insolvent debtor.

Nevertheless, the article refers also to such aspects of restructuring as identification of current state of the company and of its situation not as an entity operating separately from other market players but also in relation to its external environment (items 1, 2 and 4).

To sum up, although the BRL regulations greatly stress restructuring of insolvent debtor's obligations, they do not however restrict the possibilities to attempt restructuring from a far broader and strategic perspective.

3. IDENTIFICATION OF RESTRUCTURING UNDERTAKEN BY COMPANIES AT RISK OF BANKRUPTCY

3.1. SAMPLING PLAN

Research of company restructuring ventures was conducted in 3 courts:
- District Court for Kraków-Śródmieście in Kraków, VIII Commercial Department for Bankruptcy and Reorganization (17 cases),

- District Court for Katowice-Wschód in Katowice, in X Commercial Department (6 cases),
- District Court in Tarnów, in V Commercial Department (1 case).

Research on identification of companies restructuring ventures are part of the Author's own studies on economic aspects of bankruptcy proceedings of organizations.

As part of attaining the aim of the present paper, detailed analysis included bankruptcy proceeding records of cases in which the court announced bankruptcy in 2011 (as in these cases the risk of bankruptcy was later confirmed with the court decision). Records of cases in which companies undertook restructuring ventures and filed bankruptcy petitions leading to conclusion of argument regardless if the court, having examined the case in preliminary bankruptcy proceeding, decided to announce bankruptcy leading to conclusion of agreement or leading to liquidation of insolvent debtor's assets.

The research results are of pilot character. Analysis included 24 cases which is 3.3% of all bankruptcies (723) announced in 2011. The study included cases in which ventures should be undertaken due to the efforts of the debtor to announce bankruptcy leading to conclusion of agreement. The sampling plan embraces:

- 18 cases in which the court announced bankruptcy leading toward agreement which constitutes 17.5% of all (103) cases dated in 2011 for which this type of bankruptcy was announced.[3] The group contains 15 cases in which petition for announcing bankruptcy leading toward agreement was filed and the court acceded to the petition and 3 cases in which the debtor files petition for proceeding leading toward liquidation of insolvent debtor's assets however the court announced agreement proceeding.
- 5 cases in which the debtor filed petition for announcing bankruptcy leading toward agreement, yet the court decided to announce bankruptcy leading toward liquidation of insolvent debtor's assets.
- 1 case in which the debtor filed petition for announcing bankruptcy leading toward liquidation of insolvent debtor's assets and the court considered the petition favourably. This particular case however is adequate for analyzing restructuring as the debtor attempted to prove their ability to continue activities and to satisfy creditors' claims to an extent greater than in case of liquidation bankruptcy.

As far as the 18 companies in case of which the court announced bankruptcy leading toward agreement are concerned, analysis covered not only the restructuring ventures undertaken in the initial but also in the proper bankruptcy proceeding.

---

[3] The sample is numerous percentage-wise however due to its small absolute number it does not allow for fully justified generalization of conclusions embracing entire population.

In the studied sample bankruptcies according to legal forms were as follows:
- 17 limited liability companies (70.8%),
- 3 entrepreneurs (12.5%),
- 2 general partnerships (8.3%),
- 1 joint-stock company (4.2%),
- 1 other form of business activity (limited partnership) (4.2%).

The above share of organizations according to the legal forms is similar to the entire population of bankruptcies announced in 2011.

3.2. CO-OPERATION BANKRUPTCY PROCEEDING

As part of the research analysis covered co-operation between the temporary administrator/administrator and debtor/bankrupt as one of the factors potentially influencing successful bankruptcy proceeding. The grounds for determining if the co-operation was satisfactory are reports of the temporary administrator/administrator in the part evaluating the attitude of debtor/bankrupt.

In the analyzed records of bankruptcy proceedings:
- In 6 cases it is clearly stated by the administrator that entrepreneur undertook full co-operation.
- In 15 cases explicit statement is missing, however records analysis indicates that the co-operation of temporary administrator/administrator with debtor/bankrupt proceeded without any mishaps.
- In 1 case following the request of the administrator management by the bankrupt entity was withdrawn as their activities did not guarantee proper execution of agreement.
- In 2 cases temporary administrator was not appointed and in the proper proceeding it was not specified.

When it comes to the co-operation between temporary administrator/administrator and debtor/bankrupt in vast majority of cases it proceeded unhindered what deserves a positive evaluation.

3.3. IDENTIFICATION OF REASONS FOR THE ENSUING COMPANY CRISIS

In 22 cases debtor made an attempt to identify the reasons for the company crisis. In 2 cases it was restricted to statement that the entity was insolvent as it was unable to settle its obligations promptly.

Among the most frequent reasons given by debtors for the ensuing crisis was the fact that their problems result from the global economic crisis (14

cases). In all analyzed cases for their failure debtors blame external conditions beyond their control, such as:
- drop of demand caused by the global economic crisis,
- conventional penalties for not meeting agreement deadlines (e.g. deadlines missed due to unfavourable weather conditions or unjustly calculated by contractors),
- change of credit policy of banks (e.g. restriction of new loans),
- dishonest contractors and partners,
- illness and death in family and costs related with them,
- change of consumer behaviour (e.g. decline of reading level),
- drop of debtor's product prices resulting from competition growth, crisis or fashion change,
- increase of the resources prices,
- rise of costs of business activity (e.g. fuel prices),
- unfavourable currency exchange rate or fluctuation of currency rate,
- insolvency of contractors,
- inefficient and incompetent staff (e.g. lack of initiative on the part of the employees in their approach towards client, mistakes in accounting),
- decisions of officials (e.g. tax inspections which used different interpretation of the law or disclosed accounting mistakes, sentences for contractors for untimely execution of work, delayed administrative decision regarding construction permit),
- exceptional occurrences (e.g. acts of nature or waterworks failure which damaged equipment).

Opinions of administrators and expert witnesses attract attention to reasons like:
- missing pricing calculations, missing any cost < benefit analysis when making decision,
- flawed business decisions,
- "domino effect" or "credit spiral" effect,
- lack of financial basis.

According to the Author's evaluation, company crisis may be caused by company management errors. Analyzed records may prove other economists' research results regarding low management competencies. The studied sample includes only SME[4] companies. Despite attempts to improve competencies of this sector[5] entrepreneurs, the problem of inadequate education, of both those managing small companies and their employees has been proven

---

[4] For the micro, small, medium and large enterprise groups, classification criterion pursuant to the *Act on Freedom of Business Activity.*

[5] Attempts to improve the knowledge of SME entrepreneurs were taken e.g. as part of Sectoral Operational Plan "Human Resources Development" for the years 2004–2006. In the period 20% of all trainings concerned issues related to company management [Szałaj 2010, pp. 197–200].

with numerous scientific researches [Woźniak 2006; Gierusz, Martyniuk p. 93; Polaczek 2010, p. 390].

To summarize, entrepreneurs make the attempt to identify reasons of insolvency, however most commonly they search them in the company environment without acknowledging, or trying to hide, own responsibility for the given situation.

3.4. ELEMENTS OF JUSTIFICATION OF AGREEMENT PROPOSALS

The agreement justification proposals only in 13 cases included all subsections stated in Art. 280 BRL. The element which is most often missing in the justification of agreement proposals is the one concerning analysis of risk level and structure – it was entirely missed in 7 cases. While in 10 out of 13 cases which discussed all subsections risk analysis was limited to:
- statement that risk is low or virtually non-existent,
- short listing of risks connected to further business activity of debtor/ bankrupt (e.g. inflation risk, lack of payments from contractors, prolonging contracts execution time, risk of loosing employees, or of hiring staff with low qualifications).

Next in order missing element of justification of the agreement proposals is evaluation of alternative method of obligations restructuring. In 6 cases it was entirely omitted and in further 6 debtor/bankrupt stated only that "the proposed restructuring method is the best which is why they do not give any alternative one."

Moreover, the issue of a system protecting creditors' rights and interests for the time of executing agreement was skipped four times, while three times the economic and financial as well as organizational situations were vaguely analyzed and market sector analysis was missing twice.

In the studied sample only one case of preparing reasoning for agreement proposals used management sciences achievements creating a full analysis of economic – financial – organizational situation, detailed analysis of the market sector and risk analysis implementing SWOT method.

It should be stressed that from the legal regulations perspective the current state of justifying agreement proposals needs to be regarded as correct because with the official receiver's consent it is possible to limit the reasoning of the agreement proposals as long as in the official receiver's opinion it will not affect proper execution of the agreement. However, analyzing company's chances to survive after finalized bankruptcy proceeding, situation when debtor/bankrupt is unable to positively evaluate their economic and financial situation, strengths and weaknesses, opportunities and threats carries a risk of failure after executed agreement.

3.5. AREAS AND CHARACTER OF PLANNED RESTRUCTURING VENTURES

Among the organizations of which the bankruptcy proceeding records were analyzed, there were restructuring ventures concerning all areas resulting from the management sciences. In some instances the ventures included merely ventures of remedial nature; however cases with planned development changes were noted too.

Restructuring venture concerned both the financial and operational restructuring.

Financial restructuring concerned among others:
- reduction, postponing payment or splitting obligations into instalments,
- recovering amounts due,
- improving current liquidity by winning external sources of financing – loans, entering agreements for factoring services,
- increasing share capital,
- reduction of fixed and variable costs of business activity,
- increasing income.

Operational restructuring concerned among others:
- changes of employment – reduction or more rational use of the employed staff potential in terms of quality and efficiency, strengthening of both financial and non-financial motivation systems,
- scope of activities – change in the operation profile, liquidation of centres generating loss, change of distribution channels,
- company material resources – sale of redundant assets and more efficient use of those left in the company,
- marketing – especially changes of marketing strategy by using Internet marketing tools and potential of employed staff.

Statement of restructuring ventures divided by company sub-systems they concerned and their nature – remedial or development can be found below.

Mission and objectives

a) ventures of remedial nature:
- improvement of the current financial situation and warding off the vision of bankruptcy,
- change proposals were developed by the management of the debtor/ bankrupt company;

b) ventures of development nature:
- expanding scope of operation and increasing income,
- developing formalized restructuring programmes approved by the management of the bankrupt entity,
- commissioning audits and preparation of action plans to an external company.

People
a) ventures of remedial nature:
- employment reduction,
- lowering remunerations level,
- retraining employees,
- expanding scope of duties and responsibilities;

b) ventures of development nature:
- change of human resources management strategy,
- hiring new employees.

Structure
a) ventures of remedial nature:
- liquidation of centres generating loss,
- expansion and strengthening of marketing services;

b) ventures of development nature:
- change of distribution channels,
- simplification and rationalization of organization structures (e.g. restructuring of accounting department, outsourcing of accounting services).

Resources and technology
a) ventures of remedial nature:
- sale of redundant property,
- rational management through reduction of operational costs (e.g. introducing saving programmes related to the use of utilities, purchase of products and services, renting production and office space, withdrawal from services of external companies – law office, collection agencies),
- starting activities different from the to-date company profile due to inability to keep the previous one or due to greater profitability of these activities (e.g. selling new products, utilizing new forms of sale – commission, on-line, subcontracting services from customer-provided materials, capitalizing on renting fixed assets),
- tightening requirements applicable to suppliers;

b) ventures of development nature:
- change of suppliers (e.g. diversification of sources, direct import from manufacturers),
- introducing procedures concerning management and accounting and implementing management accounting (e.g. outsourcing of accounting services, estimating costs of business activity, cost < benefit analysis, applying prices calculations, economy forecast, budget planning),
- investments in fixed assets,
- installation of environment-friendly appliances (to reduce costs of business activity with positive influence on the environment at the same time).

Other activities
a) ventures of remedial nature:
- splitting them into instalments, postponing payment term and reduction of obligations,
- activities aimed at improving liquidity, concluding a factoring agreement, additional bank loans and negotiations to extend the term of trade credit,
- ownership changes (e.g. conversion of debt to shares, establishing a partnership which will be winning orders when the indebted company no longer can take part in tenders),
- reduction of other in-kind costs and representation and advertising expenses,
- attempts to recover amounts due from contracting parties,
- pressurizing the founding body to obtain financial support by increasing share capital;

b) ventures of development nature:
- change of marketing strategy (e.g. addressing client with promotional actions, participation in trade fairs, active pricing management, current market monitoring , analysis of customer and competitors' behaviour introducing marketing action with the use of the Internet on EU markets),
- active searching new markets,
- improving organizational structure by simplifying it,
- ownership changes (e.g. reducing the number of shareholders),
- attempts to win external investor.

4. SYNTHETIC CONCLUSIONS FROM THE STUDIES

In all analyzed cases planned restructuring ventures concerned financial area. It results from the concept of bankruptcy proceedings the aim of which is to satisfy claims of creditors. Hence, all of the proceedings included agreement in which debtor/bankrupt proposed postponing payment, splitting into instalments and reduction of obligations.

Financial restructuring without thorough changes in terms of operations carries a risk of repeated crisis. In three analyzed cases debtor/bankrupt limited their proposal to payment of obligations and recovery of amounts due. In the remaining cases the changes also refer to the operations, however:

- in four cases they are related exclusively to sale or transfer of assets ownership rights to the creditor,
- in seven cases they concern greater changes but only of economical character,
- in ten cases they refer to broader changes exceeding economical character.

The nature of the study does not allow for justified generalization of conclusions to the entire populations, however the fact that only 42% of entities declared operational changes of scope exceeding economical character is a foundation to conduct further research in this field as it signals potential risk of re-occurring crisis in the company.

In all of the analyzed cases the planned restructuring, in line with the bankruptcy proceeding concept, related to the area "mission and objectives" (improvement of the current financial situation and warding off the vision of bankruptcy) and to the "other activities" area (by proposals to delay payment, split into instalments and reduce obligations). Nevertheless, only 3 companies undertook ventures of development character in the "mission and objectives" area and 6 organizations in the "other activities" area.

In 23 cases the agreement proposals were developed by the entity management. In one case an external company was hired to audit the company and prepare restructuring plan.

In the area "People" 13 companies planned changes including two ones planning both remedial and development changes. The major alterations in this area concerned employment reduction – planned in 10 cases which amounts to 42% of studied cases.

In the area "Structure" only 3 companies undertook restructuring ventures, including 2 of remedial and development nature, while only 1 of solely developmental character.

Changes in terms of "Resources and technology" were planned by 21 companies including 13 which planned only remedial ones, 7 organizations both remedial and development and 1 only development. The greatest number of companies planned:
- operational costs reduction (10 cases, being 42%),
- reducing resources (7 cases that is 29%),
- undertaking activities different from the to-date profile (6 cases that is 25%).

Furthermore, in 5 cases (i.e. 21%) the plans included changes in this area of development nature concerning the management and accounting methods. In 4 cases tools of management accounting were implemented. According to the author of the study implementing management accounting should be a common practice in companies. However the study results indicate that the practice of implementing tools of management accounting in Poland is still unsatisfactory. In the analyzed bankruptcy proceedings simplified tools of management accounting were used (budget planning, cost calculation, pricing calculation, costs < benefits analysis). However due to the company size (micro and small) application of these tools can be regarded as changes of development nature.

There is a prospect that a company after finalizing stage of remedial restructuring undertakes also development activities. Nevertheless, results of conducted research indicate that at the initial stage of bankruptcy proceeding (in cases where records of proper bankruptcy proceeding were studied also in later stages of proceeding) only a part of managers of companies at risk of bankruptcy is aware of and demonstrates the need of development changes. Furthermore, the scope of proposed (and/or implemented) restructuring activities may indicate that evaluation of the current condition and of the necessity to introduce changes is insufficient.

Meeting legal requirements without implementing ventures resulting from theory and practice of company's functioning is at risk of another crisis re-occurring which this time the company might not survive.

SUMMARY

Currently, the aspect changing the most is the mere pace of change. Business environment is undergoing constant, intensive changes which influence the conditions companies operate in. These changes carry the changes for development, opportunities for range-related, technological and organizational changes, opening to new markets, etc. If a company wants to survive it needs to submit to changes, monitor environment and introduce new solutions. If it does not grow in the long term it may face serious crisis or even bankruptcy and total liquidation.

In conclusion, changeability of the environment in which companies operate causes that permanent introduction of changes is a prerequisite not only for their development but also for their survival. Restructuring is even more required when crisis has already arisen in company and has lead to court's announcement of bankruptcy.

It should be emphasized that Bankruptcy and Reorganization Law imposes on companies in bankruptcy proceeding certain minimum requirements in terms of restructuring namely, presenting agreement proposals which satisfy creditors' claims to the greatest, ideally 100% extent.

Still, proceeding toward conclusion of agreement means that a company does not cease to exist. If it is to survive after the bankruptcy proceeding it is prerequisite to introduce thorough changes in the company to prevent the crisis situation from re-occurring. If organizations wish to operate in long term they have to develop remedial restructuring plan of the company, both the one required by the regulations restructuring of obligations, and restructuring of operating strategy dictated by rational management. These are stabilizing activities the purpose of which is restoring the company's lost efficiency. It is also necessary to continuously adjust to changes taking place in the economic environment of the company.

Company crisis may lead to file petition for bankruptcy. Simultaneously, it may be a valued stimulus for introducing changes and further development of the company.

The research results indicate that the present state is satisfactory from the point of view of implementing legal regulations. There were, however, problems with identifying the causes of the crisis and conducting comprehensive analysis of strengths and weaknesses of companies as well as opportunities and threats for their operation.

The research sample, due to its size, does not allow for statistical generalisation of conclusions in order to cover the whole population of companies at risk of bankruptcy. Nonetheless, the research results give a clear signal that there is a need for further research in this area.

REFERENCES

Act on Freedom of Business Activity of 2nd July 2004. Journal of Laws from 2004, No. 173, item 1807.

Bauer K. (2010). Kryzys finansowy a restrukturyzacja przedsiębiorstw w stanie upadłości, *Procesy transformacji przemysłu i usług w regionalnych i krajowych układach przestrzennych*, Prace Komisji Geografii Przemysłu Polskiego Towarzystwa Geograficznego, Warszawa–Kraków.

Borowiecki R. (1998). Restrukturyzacja przedsiębiorstwa jako proces zwiększania efektywności jego działania. In: R. Borowiecki (ed.). *Restrukturyzacja a poprawa efektywności gospodarowania w przedsiębiorstwie*, Kraków.

Brandenburg H. (2010). *Projekty restrukturyzacyjne. Planowanie i realizacja*. Katowice: Wydawnictwo Akademii Ekonomicznej w Katowicach.

BRL, Act of 28th February 2003, Bankruptcy and Restructuring Law. Journal of Laws from 2003, No. 60, item 535.

Cabała P., Bartusik K. (2006). *Restrukturyzacja w jednostkach gospodarczych*. Kraków: Wydawnictwo Akademii Ekonomicznej w Krakowie.

Durlik I. (1998). *Restrukturyzacja procesów gospodarczych. Reengineering. Teoria i praktyka*. Warszawa: Agencja Wydawnicza „Placet".

Działocha-Świetlikowska A., Kowalski A., Kućmin B., Talarek U. (2003). *Upadłość i likwidacja przedsiębiorstw osób fizycznych i spółek osobowych w aspekcie prawnym i praktyce podatkowej oraz księgowej*. Warszawa: Difin.

Dźwigoł H. (2007). *Model restrukturyzacji organizacyjnej przedsiębiorstwa górnictwa węgla kamiennego*. Warszawa: Difin.

Garstka M. (2006). *Restrukturyzacja przedsiębiorstwa. Podział przez wydzielenie*. Warszawa: CeDeWu.pl Wydawnictwa Fachowe.

Gierusz B., Martyniuk T. (2008). Czynniki determinujące zdolność finansową małych przedsiębiorstw. In: T. Wiśniewski (ed.). *Czas na pieniądz. Zarządzanie finansami. Inwestycje i wycena przedsiębiorstw. Finance, rynki finansowe, ubezpieczenia, No. 13.* Szczecin: Wydawnictwo Nauk Ekonomicznych i Zarządzania Uniwersytetu Szczecińskiego.

Grzybowska K. (2010). *Reorganizacja przedsiębiorstw. Zarządzanie zmianą organizacyjną*. Poznań: Wydawnictwo Politechniki Poznańskiej.

Kański T. (2009). Czy znowelizowane przepisy o upadłości usprawnią postępowanie naprawcze. *Gazeta Prawna*, No. 95.

Krawiec F. (2007). *Zasadnicza zmiana drogą do sukcesu przedsiębiorstwa XXI wieku*. Warszawa: Difin.

Krzos G. (2006). *Business Processs Reengineering a pozycja konkurencyjna przedsiębiorstwa*. Wrocław: Wydawnictwo Akademii Ekonomicznej im. Oskara Langego we Wrocławiu.

Mączyńska E. (2009). Wstęp. In: E. Mączyńska (ed.). *Meandry upadłości przedsiębiorstw. Klęska czy druga szansa?* Warszawa: Szkoła Główna Handlowa w Warszawie.

Nalepka A. (1998). *Zarys problematyki restrukturyzacji przedsiębiorstw*. Kraków–Kluczbork: Oficyna Wydawnicza: Drukarnia ANTYKWA s.c.

Nalepka A. (1999). *Restrukturyzacja przedsiębiorstwa. Zarys problematyki*. Warszawa–Kraków: Wydawnictwo Naukowe PWN.

Nowak E. (2009). *Zaawansowana rachunkowość zarządcza*. Warszawa: Polskie Wydawnictwo Ekonomiczne.

Pacholski L., Cempel W., Pawlewski P. (2009). Reengineering. *Reformowanie procesów biznesowych I produkcyjnych*. Poznań: Wydawnictwo Politechniki Poznańskiej.

Pasieczny J. (1997). Restrukturyzacja – wczoraj, dziś, jutro. *Przegląd Organizacji*, No. 9.

Polaczek R. (2010). O potrzebie wyceny małego przedsiębiorstwa. In: D. Zarzecki (ed.). *Czas na pieniądz. Zarządzanie finansami. Inwestycje i wycena przedsiębiorstw. Finance, rynki finansowe, ubezpieczenia, No. 25.* Szczecin: Wydawnictwo Nauk Ekonomicznych i Zarządzania Uniwersytetu Szczecińskiego.

Raport Coface nt. upadłości firm w Polsce w 2011 roku http://www.coface.pl/CofacePortal/ShowBinary/BEA%20Repository/PL/pl_PL/documents/Raport_upadlosci_caly_2011_COFACE [accessed: 2013].

Suszyński C. (1999). *Restrukturyzacja przedsiębiorstw*. Warszawa: Polskie Wydawnictwo Ekonomiczne.

Szałaj M. (2010). Doskonalenie kadry przedsiębiorstw jako kierunek działań finansowanych ze środków Europejskiego Funduszu Społecznego. In: *Raport o stanie małych i średnich przedsiębiorstw w Polsce w latach 2008–2009*. Warszawa: Polska Agencja Rozwoju Przedsiębiorczości.

Waściński T. (2010). *Finansowa diagnoza procesów restrukturyzacji przedsiębiorstwa w aspektach ekonomicznej wartości wiedzy*. Warszawa: Dom Wydawniczy ELIPSA.

Wędzki D. (2003). *Strategie płynności finansowej przedsiębiorstwa. Przepływy pieniężne a wartość dla właścicieli*. Kraków: Oficyna Ekonomiczna,.

Woźniak M.G. (2006). *Rozwój sektora małych i średnich przedsiębiorstw w Polsce a wzrost gospodarczy*. Kraków: Wydawnictwo Akademii Ekonomicznej w Krakowie.

ANNA DYLĄG

Jagiellonian University
Institute of Economics and Management
Chair of Standardized Management Systems

COOPERATION – COMPETITION. PSYCHOLOGICAL PERSPECTIVE

INTRODUCTION

For the needs of this chapter, cooperation and competition are viewed from psychological perspective. Cooperation is seen as a kind of relation which yields more positive outcomes, and which requires more complex social, cognitive, motivational and moral skills. Also competition which is "a part of everyday life" [Deutsch 2000, p. 28], as long as it is fair and "healthy," remains a promoted social behavior. Effective, constructive competition in cooperative context also requires development of complex skills (both at the individual and group levels), and it can be a positive experience for involved parties. Only destructive form of competition seems to bring more costs than advantages resulting in most negative effects.

Literature and research on human competitive – cooperative behavior bring many interesting issues that can be formulated as several questions. For instance:

- What effects (social and work related, at the individual and organizational level) are produced by competition and cooperation?
- How competition and cooperation are related – should cooperation be viewed as the superior or "more ethical" to competition?
- What are psychological determinants of an effective cooperation?

In the first section of this chapter, psychological definition of competition and cooperation will be presented as proposed by Deutsch [2000]. Then, comparison of the main characteristics of these behaviors will be presented. Next, competition – cooperation continuum will be discussed from a perspective of Kohlberg's concept of human moral development [1984]. In further sections, cooperation and competition will be viewed as evolutionary based mechanisms, conflict resolution styles, and stress coping strategies.

Finally, the mentioned above mechanisms will be discussed at the team and individual levels looking for psycholgical determinants and useful concepts explaining their nature.

1. MECHANISMS OF COMPETITION AND COOPERATION – "SINK OR SWIM TOGETHER"[1]

While the one working on a computer clicks Thesaurus typing the word "cooperation," the program will automatically list several synonyms to the term, such as: collaboration, assistance, help, support, teamwork, mutual aid, etc. As an antonym of the "cooperation" Thesaurus will show "antagonism" with such synonyms as: competition, rivalry, opposition, aggression, war, struggle, fight. From this quick overview of a popular Windows lexicon it could be concluded that "cooperation" is phrased positively and remains associated with "good," desired or ethical behavior while "competition" is associated with negative phrases and "bad" or unethical behavior.

What is meant by cooperation and what is meant by competition in psychological sense? How are they related and induced? What effects do they bring? How do these orientations develop during the course of life? Psychological analysis of cooperation and competition in several aspects, give some answers to these questions.

1.1. DEFINITION

Cooperation and competition may be viewed at as two distinct orientations which are usually mixed in a number of everyday life situations [Deutsch 2000]. Deutsch's theory is based on two fundamental issues: (i) goal interdependence and (ii) the type of action taken. Both can be positive or negative and both are seen by the author as "polar ends of continua" [Deutsch 2000, p. 22]. Additionally they affect three basic social psychological processes: substitutability, attitudes and inducibility, which are jointly responsible for major reactions taking forms of competition or cooperation. Deutsch explains that people can be linked either way – liking or disliking, being bound together or

---

[1] Morton Deutsch uses this saying in illustrating his theory of cooperation and competition (2000, p. 22)

fighting against each other, sharing and dividing work or disorganizing and discouraging one another, etc. The course of action they take is determined by an inborn tendency to respond positively toward beneficial stimuli and negatively toward harmful environment. As Deutsch puts it (p. 24), cooperation implies the positive attitude that "we are for each other" while competition is activated by the negative attitude that "we are against one another".

1.2. COMPARISON

In order to better illustrate differences between cooperation and competition several characteristics were selected and described below (see Table 1).

Table 1. Cooperation and competition – selected differences

Characteristic	Cooperative orientation	Competitive orientation
Group identity	"Us" (unity)	"We – They" (antagonism)
Goals	Mutual goals	Individual goals
Orientation	"win – win" (I swim – you swim)	"win – lose" (I swim – you sink)
Attitudes towards problems	"Problems are ours," problem as a challenge, the whole group makes an effort to solve it, most effective solution is being sought	"It's your / somebody's else business," problems are left at the individual level, group members keep away from problems of others'
Power and knowledge	Mutual development, "you know more – I know more," sharing of ideas, power and solutions, everybody learns	Individual advantage, hidden knowledge, the conflicting parties seek to enhance their own power and to reduce the power of others
Communication	Effective: exchange of ideas, mutual understanding, open discussion, acceptance of opposite point of views, constructive feedback	Impaired: conflicting parties seek to gain advantage by misleading, false promises, disinformation, destructive critique
Level of trust	High	Low
Productivity and performance	Coordination of effort, complementary roles, work and effort divided, specialization	Poor coordination, duplicating one another's effort, increased workload and high costs of control
Work climate	Friendly, helpful climate, social support, work engagement, mutual inspiration	Coercion, threat, deception, lack of help and lack of social support, risk of stress and burnout, destructive conflicts
Time perspective	Long-term	Short-term
Conflict resolution	Effective conflict resolution with the use of flexible styles[2], constructive discussions	Inflexible styles, often external authority required in order to resolve conflicts

Source: adopted from Deutsch 2000, pp. 25–26.

---

[2] See further in this chapter – Kilman's typology of conflict resolution strategies.

The differences described above can be observed at both individual, group (team) and organizational level. Harmful behaviors and practices can affect both, people working in small teams as well as within / between larger groups. According to the "Crude Law of Social Relations" [Deutsch 2000, p. 29] positive relation (cooperation) arises from similarities in beliefs, values and attitudes inducing positive emotions and effects[3] (as trust, friendliness, common interests and alike). On the other hand negative relation (competition) induces the opposite: distrust, unfriendliness, coercion, etc. It has been evidenced elsewhere that people at work share and transmit both positive and negative emotions – on the basis of mechanism called "emotional contagion" [i.e. Barsade 2002]. Thus it can be expected that working in cooperative environment increases individual positive exchange and collaborative effort, while experience of unhealthy competition may lead to self-defence, withrdawal or open conflicts.

1.3. DEVELOPMENT

There are theoretical concepts explaining relations between those two psychological orientations also from a perspective of continuum in human (moral) development. One of the main questions to be raised here is: how do cooperative / competitive norms and behaviors develop and relate? Is each individual "capable" of showing both orientations, with a special respect to cooperation? Are people focused upon one orientation or do they develop to the stage of a more complex and "better" behavior (cooperation) throughout their life?

Such thinking leads to the life-span theories, like somewhat controversial Kohlberg's theory of human moral development. According to the concept, competition – cooperation orientation may be determined by a particular stage of the moral reasoning a person operates at. The figure below (Figure 1) presents stages and levels of human moral develoment with reference to competition – cooperation framework.

Kohlberg [1984] believed that individuals progress in their moral reasoning development moving from one stage to another. The process is generally the same across different cultures, and people differ in respect of the highest stage obtained. He identified six particular stages classified into three more general levels, with the process starting in early childhood and continuing through adolescence till adulthood. In this sense Kohlberg's theory belongs

---

[3] Negative linkage can occur however even in the context of value similarities. This may happen in the value conflict situation, for instance when the supply of valued resources are scarce (see Dyląg et al. 2013).

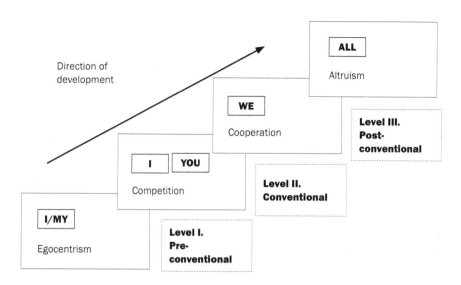

Figure 1. L. Kohlberg's concept of moral reasoning
Source: own elaboration.

to a larger group of stage theories where human development is perceived as a movement from lower to higher phases or from simple forms to more complex behaviors; additionally the initial periods are seen as fundamental for the entire process of successful development [i.e. Freud, Piaget, Erikson; also see Sandy and Cochran 2000, p. 320, for detailed comparison of social cognitive approaches to development].

In Kohlberg's concept the first level is called "pre-conventional." It encompasses two stages that can be characterized respectively by rules of: (1.1) obedience and punishment and (1.2) individualism, instrumentalism and exchange. At this phase of development (generally in elementary school age) individuals comply with social norms mainly because some authority (like a parent or a teacher), who is a source of threat to them – expects so. In the second stage of the Level 1, individuals start to develop thinking in terms of their own best interests ("my business first" which is viewed as behavior morally reasonable).

At the second, "conventional" level of moral reasoning, the rules of (2.1) approval of others (being a "good" girl / a "good" boy) and (2.2) law and order become most important. Kohlberg believed that most people in society operate at this level.

The third, "post-conventional" level of moral development is – according to Kohlberg – generally not available for majority of people. This is probably one of the most controversial points in his theory, along with believe in universality of moral stages and the specific course of the human moral development (as a systematic move from one stage to another up the hierarchy shown above, see: Czyżowska 2008). At this level of moral development Kohlberg placed two such stages as (3.1) understanding of social mutuality and a genuine interest in the welfare of others, and (3.2) respect for universal principle and the demands of individual conscience.

Following Kohlberg's way of thinking it could be concluded that both competition and cooperation may form a continuum starting from individualistic or even egocentric forms of behavior, which is by Deutsch believed to yield rather a destructive form of competition. Then, through individualistic behaviors (not necessarily destructive) a person would be able to show a constructive competition, also guarded by rules of law and order (still "my business first" as the most important rule). Finally, the cooperation could start beginning with "healthy exchange" of interests up to a deep, mutual exchange of social support, knowledge sharing, and creative problem solving via discussion and taking into account the best interests of both sides as well as acceptance of varied values systems. Altruistic forms of behavior based on the motives of selfless "giving" rather than selfish "taking" or even a balanced "give and take" exchange – seem rare in business area and could be even perceived naïve, unless they take a form of an organized philanthropy or charity. On the other hand – as it will be shown below – emotional costs and expanses of cooperation may be higher than costs of individualistic competition, especially in the situation where stress is involved and there is a risk of loosing own resources while helping the team at the same time.

2. DETERMINANTS OF COOPERATION AND COMPETITION

2.1. EVOLUTIONARY POINT OF VIEW – GENDER DIFFERENCES

From evolutionary point of view gender plays an important role in such behaviors as competition and cooperation. Physical, psychological and social conditions of men and women resulted in division of tasks: traditionally females took care of children and house keeping, while males protected families and society from external threats, as well as supplied food. Women were expected to show mildness, patience and support to each other in a group, while men were expected to be strong and brave individuals. Thus, one could hypothesise that women are better prepared to cooperate and men are better prepared to compete. In an experiment study conducted by Van Vugt, De Cremer and Janssen [2007], the competitive and cooperative behaviors related to gender were tested ("male-warrior hypothesis"). Outcomes of the research supported the hypothesis that men's social behavior is more strongly intergroup driven than women's. Men showed they were more likely to "cooperate in order to compete and win," especially under conditions of perceived external danger. It meant that men contributed more to their group when their group was competing with other groups, if there was no intergroup competition. The situation of an intergroup threat did not seem to affect women social behaviors. Cooperation of women may be less intergroup driven, however their group identity as well as collaboration within the group seems generally stronger then males. Such gender differences are probably well rooted in evolutionary origins – evolutionary psychologists argue that human cooperation is the product of a long history of competition and colaboration between rival groups [Van Vugt, De Cremer, Janssen 2007].

2.2. CULTURAL CONTEXT – INDIVIDUALISTS VS COLLECTIVISTS

Individualism is often referred to as one of the main dimensions explaining cultural differences [see Wagner 1995, Triandis 1995, Hofstede and Hofstede 2007]. Individualism – collectivism continuum has formed a theoretical framework for a large number of cross-cultural studies. It may be also useful for explaining cooperation – competition dynamics with special attention to multicultural work environment [Boros et al. 2010]. Research show that collectivists conform more to group norms than individualists, and form more cooperative groups. On the other hand, individualists seem more interested in their individual goals and their cooperation is instrumental. They do not however significantly differ from collectivists in their levels of cooperative behavior. When they can only achieve their individual goals in groups, they tend to do so [Wagner 1995]. Triandis et al. [1988] stated that collectivists were more willing to cooperate, especially with ingrups, where they would rather avoid an open conflict and competition. Individualists could easily initiate an open conflict or disagreement, either with internal or external group members.

The results of mentioned above studies conducted by Boros and colleagues [2010] show that group dynamics are different depending upon vertical or horizontal forms of individualism and collectivism. Vertical individualism (VI) is observed when people view themselves as unequal and independent, while horizontal individualism (HI) when they feel equal but independent. In vertical collectivism (VC) members perceive groups as unequal, but interconnected, while in horizontal collectivism (HC) people view themselves as equal and connected (see Table 2).

Table 2. Individualism and collectivism – vertical and horizontal

High on feeling independent	VI VERTICAL INDIVIDUALISM (unequal and independent) – avoiding style of conflict management is more frequently used – weaken cooperation	HI HORIZONTAL INDIVIDUALISM (equal and independent) – more cooperative conflict resolution strategy is used – better cooperation
Low on feeling independent (connected)	VC VERTICAL COLLECTIVISM (unequal but connected) – more cooperative conflict resolution strategy – better cooperation	HC HORIZONTAL COLLECTIVISM (equal and connected) – cooperation is better – avoiding a contending conflict management and coping styles are used less
	Low on feeling equal (unequal)	High on feeling equal

Source: own elaboration based on Boros et al. 2010.

In her studies Boros found that in situation of HC (members feel equal and connected), cooperation is better, as well as the avoiding and contending (dominating) conflict management and coping styles are used less. When people view themselves as unequal and independent (VI) there may arise more chance for hidden or open competition while cooperation may weaken. Also in such cicumstances the avoiding style of conflict management is more frequently used. High group variety in views of being unequal, but intercon-nected (VC) also leads to more cooperative conflict resolution strategy, and probably better teamwork in general.

2.3. CONFLICT RESOLUTION STYLES

A substantial number of literature focuses upon conflicts and the way they are resolved [for instance Deutsch and Coleman 2000; Liberman 2004; Bala-wajder 1992, 1994; Chełpa, Witkowski 2004]. In his earlier works Deutsch distinguished three forms of relationship individuals can develop towards groups. Cooperative relationship appears when individual goals are positively correlated with the group goals, negatively correlated links result in competi-tion, and individual goals can be separated from the group goals – which he referred to as individualism [Triandis et al. 1988]. Low concern for ingroup needs, goals and relationship Trandis and coauthors highlight as one of the key aspect of individualism (at least in American culture), although the social skills of making new friends easily, can be also high [Triandis et al. 1988, p. 325].

Concern for people within a group versus concern for tasks to be performed is a basic framework for other models, including conflict resolution styles. For instance the Thomas-Kilmann Conflict Mode instrument (TKI) is based on the Blake and Mouton managerial grid concept [Stoner, Freeman, Gilbert 2001]. Both dimensions were adopted, forming axes of assertiveness and cooperativeness (see: http://www.kilmanndiagnostics.com). The TKI identifies five different styles of managing conflict situations [Balawajder 1998]: (1) competing (highly assertive, non cooperative), (2) collaborating (highly assertive, highly cooperative), (3) compromising (intermediate assertiveness and cooperativeness), (4) avoiding (unassertive, uncooperative), and (5) accommodating (unassertive, cooperative) – see Table 3.

Table 3. Kilman's styles of conflict management

HIGH ASSERTIVENESS	(1) competing		(2) collaborating
		(3) compromising	
	(4) avoiding		(5) accommodating
LOW	COOPERATIVENESS		HIGH

Source: Chełpa, Witkowski 2004, p. 163.

According to the model shown above, an individual has got a choice of five different modes of behavior that can be used during the conflict situation. When neccesary it is sometimes most recommneded for the one to compete, and sometimes the best strategy is to accommodate or avoid. Although cooperation seems the best option of all (it is usually correlated with high performance and high team satisfaction), it may not always be possible to obtain. It depends on the maturity of organization, team and the person. Choosing the most adequate strategy usually depends on power, resources, skills, stress coping strategy and goals to be obtained. Also, behavior of the other parties involved, and costs to be paid, as well as other obstacles should be taken under consideration. At individual level, sometimes a person does not show respective skills or the conflict is too difficult to resolve (like a value conflicts type, for instance). Some cultures or leaders may not let people have a choice in conflict resolution strategy, or sometimes the price of a certain alternative would be too high. One of the goals of the TKI is a diagnosis of preferred conflict style at the individual or group level, as well as individual and organizational development through adequate incorporating of a wide range of strategies.

2.4. STRESS AND TIME MANAGEMENT

Under conditions of increased time pressure and perceived stress in contemporary organizations, the quality of social relations is likely to suffer
most. Despite the fact that mutual understanding, respect, care and social support are of the highest needs in periods of increased workload, at
the same time, these aspects are most likely to be ignored or postponed. As
it is almost impossible to demonstrate an equal, parallel interest in task and
relations at the same moment, thus a time and stress management should be
aimed at both: task effectiveness as well as towards a compensation of socio-
emotional deficits. Effective co-operation should thus allow periods of lower
productivity giving space and priority to socio-emotional recovery, which
in fact is a good investment in long-term effectiveness within organization.
Also from time tactics advisors, it can be concluded that different tasks in
relation to time resources should be managed according to rational rules.
Instead of running from one activity to another, speeding up in time and
fighting with increasing stress, an individual is advised to plan, act, delegate
or to postpone and even resign of a task if possible [Covey 2007].

As Maslach and Leiter notice, one of the main causes of burnout, decrease
in work engagement and stress in contemporary organizations remain increased workload and raised quality standards, in the absence of supportive
community and decreasing autonomy over ones work [Maslach and Leiter
2010, 2011]. In order to improve employees' well-being and work engagement as well as to reduce the risk of stress and burnout, the authors suggest
undertaking several steps aimed at better job-person fit in six key areas.
These areas include: workload, control over one's work (autonomy), rewards,
community, fairness and values. Development of trust and supportive community within organization takes time and effort. Maslach and Leiter [2010]
propose several steps in this process which include:
- analysis of the climate and social relations at work,
- definition of a problem if there is a perceived misfit in the area (i.e.
  alienation, poor communication, ineffective conflict management, etc.),
- goal setting, prioritizing (i.e. education, integration),
- action taking,
- monitoring and control.

*Coping with stress and burnout – cultural determinants of individual
strategies*
Steven Hobfoll's way of thinking of stress and coping [2006] may give a new
perspective in reflection on competition – cooperation continuum. Hobfoll
views stress as culture related phenomena, where structures, roles and processes determine its perception and preferred coping style. Culture rooted

factors (like individualism) are among possible mechanisms explaining differences in burnout levels between several western European countries, Poland and the US [Maslach, Schaufeli, Leiter 2001]. Data collected at the level of national samples consistently show that the latter ones (Poland and the US) are somewhat similar in respect of the burnout level examined, and significantly different (higher) compared to the studied European countries. A possible explanation focuses upon higher levels of individualism believed to characterize Polish and American populations compared to more collectivistic European respondents with better social environment within organizations. Naturally, work related factors, as work organization, workload, work climate, health and safety issues, and alike are also under consideration. In addition, Maslach and Leiter [2010, 2011] also described a hard reality of contemporary workplaces (mainly American and global corporations), where employees are too frequently exposed to increasing workload and poor autonomy, lack of teamwork and social support.

Although the mentioned above authors claim that unfriendly work environment will raise the risk of burnout, there are some arguments that involving too much into supportive, cooperative, team-oriented stress coping strategies may increase the risk of burnout itself [Hobfoll 2006]. Hobfoll's model of conservation of resources (COR) gives some hints to understand this paradox. Author discussed costs and benefits of several coping strategies claming that involving into cooperative behaviors may be more stressful and less effective than indiviualistic styles.

Multidimensional model is a theoretical framework for Hobfoll's consideration (see Figure 2).

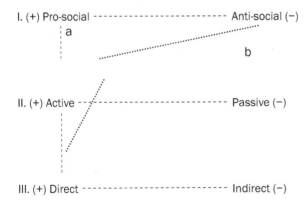

Figure 2. S. Hobfoll's strategic approach to stress coping
Source: based on Hobfoll 2006, p. 172.

The figure above shows three independent dimensions forming a theoretical framework for Hobfoll's conceptualization. Author identified 9 strategies yielded out of combinations among those dimensions (assertiveness, cooperation, seeking social support, avoidance, instinct, indirect/manipulative behaviors (behind somebody's back), cautious behaviors, anti-social behaviors, aggressiveness). For instance, a combination of all three dimensions at their positive ends (I + II + III +), which is pro-social, active and direct coping (profile "a"), describes such strategies as assertiveness and cooperation. While for instance a combination reflected in profile "b" (I – II + III +) shows aggressive coping strategies.

It is generally agreed that pro-social, active, assertive – supportive behaviors help to reduce stress, enhance cooperation and innovativeness at individual, team, organization and even regional levels (i.e. creating social capital, see Laursen, Masciarelli, Prencipe 2012). Nevertheless – as it was mentioned above – investing in teamwork, especially when individual resources are scarce – may lead to negative results like increase in stress and burnout. The study described below illustrates this relation.

In one study[4] a research on highschool teachers' stress coping strategies was conducted. All respondents (54 teachers) were employed in the same organization – a high school in Central Poland (Stalowa Wola). With the use of SACS questionnaire developed by Hobfall [2006] it was shown that among nine stress coping strategies described above, only cooperation and avoidance were significantly related to one or two burnout scales [as defined by Maslach 1998]. Cooperation was positively related to emotional exhaustion while avoidance to both: emotional exhaustion and cynicism. In the case of cooperative coping style, it was low but significant correlation of .285. Compared to the positive correlations of avoidance coping strategy and burnout dimensions (avoiding positively correlated to emotional exhaustion [.323] and to cynicism [.297]) – it did not seem a logical pattern, unless the wording of coping scales was considered. It appeared that cooperation subscale involed many items related to self-sacrifice and giving more to others then to the self (instead of more assertive or self-oriented behavior). This kind of imbalance between satisfying the needs of individual and the needs of others as a priority, may explain the effect of linking cooperation positively with emotional exhaustion.

Team level characteristics

Effectively collaborating teams seem to poses certain characteristics and/or to obtain a certain level of maturity. Cooperation develops in time and re-

---

[4] Unpublished Master thesis, Joanna Pyrkosz "Wypalenie zawodowe i style radzenia sobie ze stresem u nauczycieli liceum ogólnokształcącego w Stalowej Woli", Jagiellonian University 2009.

quires many internal resources. Teams and organizations operate in a wider context like others groups, specific culture, law restrictions, etc.; the environment nowadays is complex, demanding and unpredictable [Katzenbach and Smith 2001].

- Belbin model

Several concepts highlight different aspects of team functioning. For instance Belbin [2003] concentrated on team roles performed individually. The central issue in his model of team effectiveness is complementary role handling, meaning that successful group of people avoid duplicating each others work and effort. Instead, different team members perform according to their natural best potential, and if not possible, they perform according to the second best potential. As Belbin puts it: "...a team is not a bunch of people with job titles, but a congregation of individuals, each of whom has a role which is understood by other members. Members of a team seek out certain roles and they perform most effectively in the ones that are most natural to them..." (see http://www.belbin.com).

Belbin identified 9 such roles, as well as he described the strenghts and weaknesses of each. The roles relate to idea creation, team climate, realization of tasks, control over it, and criticism about group actions. In Table 4 (below) there are described roles and their main characteristics showing potential limitations of each.

Table 4. Belbin team roles

Role	Main characteristic (weaknesses)
1) Plants	– could be unorthodox or forgetful
2) Resource investigators	– might forget to follow up on a lead
3) Monitor evaluators	– could be overly critical and slow moving
4) Co-ordinators	– might over delegate leaving themselves little work to do
5) Implementers	– might be slow to relinquish their plans in favour of positive changes
6) Completer finishers	– could be accused of taking their perfectionism to the extremes
7) Teamworkers	– might become indecisive when unpopular decisions need to be made
8) Shapers	– could risk becoming aggressive and bad-humoured in their attempts to get things done
9) Specialist	– may have a tendency to focus narrowly on their own subject of choice

Source: http://www.belbin.com.

In effective cooperation at a team level, Belbin's model highlights an individual potential, as well as the structure or configuartion of the entire group. If the team is designed well, it may be expected to work efficiently with a healthy balance on both, the needs of task and the needs of people [Bales 1965]. An analysis of a group effectiveness also requires combining situational internal and external context.

--------------------------------- work context ---------------------------------

- group structure   ------>
- team built on individual, natural potential   ------> EFFECTIVE COOPERATION
- skilled leadership   ------>

------------------------------ external environment ------------------------------

Figure 3. Effective cooperation in Belbin's model
Source: own elaboration.

- Tuckman model

In Tuckman's model [1965] it is assumed that groups go through a number of phases or stages. It means that each group, in order to become an effective team, requires a certain amount of time and experience, in order to develop. First, the group members want to know each other better, then the most dominating personalities crash and some conflicts arise. Next, the group needs to develop a degree of interdependence in order that it may achieve its tasks and be satisfying to its members; also it has to learn to deal with conflicts if it is to survive. While there are various differences concerning the number of stages and their names – most often the four or five stage model is presented (see Figure 4).

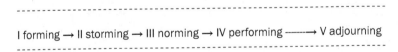

I forming → II storming → III norming → IV performing ------→ V adjourning

Figure 4. Tuckman team development model
Source: Tuckman and Jensen 1977.

First, there were four stages in Tuckman's model – forming, storming, norming and performing. He was later to add the fifth stage – adjourning [Tuckman and Jensen 1977]. The last stage is often described as 'mourning' given the loss that is sometimes felt by former participants. The process can be stressful, and the symptoms of depression may show (particularly where the dissolution is sudden and unplanned) [Stoner, Freeman, Gilbert 2001]. The model itself suggests that effective cooperation and teamwork develops in time, with some difficult experience or moments, like stage II – storming. Nevertheless, the negative phase seems to strenghen the group and its memebers, if only they are able to go through the crisis.

• Blanchard PERFORM model
In Blanchard model of best performing team, seven key characteristics are mentioned [Carew, Parisi-Carew, Blanchard 2007]. They may be described as follows (see Table 5):

Table 5. Blanchard PERFORM model

Characteristic	Description
P – purpose and values	Values and norms are combined and harmonized at each level, organization and individuals have got a clear vision, mission, and precise instructions.
E – empowerment	Creativity, engagement, risk taking and participation are the key elements; employee engage in realization of organizational goals using effective procedures based on continuous development.
R – relationships and communication	Open communication, constructive critique, feedback and support are visible; people openly share ideas and brainstorm; actively discuss the best possible solutions.
F – flexibility	Leadership may be shared if needed, organization highlights the need for creativity, thinking different and drawing conclusions from failures.
O – optimal productivity	High standards and reasonably effort, optimal use of resources, monitoring of processes, focus upon goals and verification with organizational mission, vision and values.
R – recognition and appreciation	Reward, recognition and appreciation form a sound basis for an effective motivation. Employees feel motivated, satisfied and engage in the future goals.
M – morale	High morale, trust and enthusiasm make work easier, better and nicer. Stress and risk of burnout is reduced, employees believe in organizational values and mission; they feel a part of the organization.

Source: Carew, Parisi-Carew, Blanchard 2007.

The model itself describes both, the determinants and consequences that characterize the most effective organizations. This usually happens on many levels: each employee, a leader, team and organization as a whole. For instance "purpose and values" characteristic, at the organizational level is verbalized as its mission, and on the team level it takes a form of clear goals to be obtained. Leader formulates precise instructions and directs team toward common purpose, while each individual engages in team and organizational mission – harmonizing individual values with organizational ones. It was shown in the research on value fit/misfit that congruence of individual and organizational values is related to employees' work engagement, while conflict between a person and organizations in terms of values was correlated with negative consequences, as burnout [Dyląg et al. 2013]. Also, one can see that both aspect of effective teams are present in the model: concern for tasks and productivity (i.e. O) and concern for people (i.e. R), [Robbins 2004].

2.7. SELECTED INDIVIDUAL CHARACTERISTICS

In order to effectively cooperate with others, especially under conditions of increased work pace and standards, the one needs to be well prepared in terms of developed skills or competencies. Also to be able to keep so called "work-life" balance, as well as to experience high (subjective) quality of life, it is important to find a healthy way to live a "wise life."

Czapiński defines wisdom as an ability to comfort and equalize both, individual needs with the needs of the others (2004). It is also close to the concept of assertiveness which can be nicely quoted as "I'm OK – You're OK," meaning ability to build equal, partner relations with people [Alberti and Emmons 2007]. As shown above, team or organizational effectiveness require a number of individual assets at the level of leaders and group members. Collaboration is often linked to a wide range of specific characteristics or competencies. They also are referred as "individual effectiveness skills" or "socio-emotional competencies." They form a long list of concepts, qualities, features and behaviours as: emotional intelligence [Mayer and Salovey 1993; Cooper and Sawaf 2000], self-management and time management (for instance Covey 2007), change management [Clarke 2009], effective stress coping, coherence [Hobfoll 2006; Antonovsky 2005], conflict management [Deutsch and Coleman 2000; Haman and Gut 2008], communication and negotiation skills [Nęcki 2000], etc. The detailed description of the mentioned above topics is far beyond the scope of this chapter.

CONCLUSION

Cooperation and competition are related psychological processes or orientations, which develop in different directions and time periods. Cooperation seem to require longer time to grow, as well as more skills, both at the individual, team or organizational level. Competition may also require the highest standards, unique skills and much effort, although it seems more one-sided: the goal and effect is the main – and often the only – focus. Less concern is placed upon people, with the main concern placed upon results and performance. It is always recommended to think of these mechanisms as possible alternatives – either as the stages of individual/group development (cooperation following competition), or as two distinct forms of many possible behaviors (meaning variety of parallel coping styles). The choice of a certain strategy should depend on the context, skills and goals to be obtained, as contemporary times require outstanding flexibility and creativeness. Nevertheless it is always worth to consider the "win-win" or assertive – collaborative (active, pro-social) approach, which appears the most recommended option from the literature review.

REFERENCES

Alberti R., Emmons M. (2007). *Asertywność.* Gdańsk: Gdańskie Wydawnictwo Psychologiczne.

Antonovsky A. (2005). *Rozwikłanie tajemnicy zdrowia – jak radzić sobie ze stresem i nie zachorować.* Warszawa.

Balawajder K. (1998). *Komunikacja, konflikty, negocjacje w organizacji.* Katowice: Wydawnictwo Uniwersytetu Śląskiego.

Balawajder K. (1992). *Konflikty interpersonalne: analizy psychologiczne.* Katowice: Wydawnictwo Uniwersytetu Śląskiego.

Balawajder K. (1994). *Rozwiązywanie konfliktów międzyludzkich.* Katowice: Wydawnictwo Uniwersytetu Śląskiego.

Bales R.F. (1965). The equilibrium problem in small groups. In: A.P. Hare, E.F. Borgatta, R.F. Bales (eds.). *Small Groups: Studies in social interaction.* New York.

Barsade S.G. (2002). The ripple effect: Emotional contagion and its influence on group behavior. *Administrative Science Quarterly,* No. 47, pp. 644–675.

Belbin R.M. (2003). *Twoja rola w zespole.* Gdańsk: Gdańskie Wydawnictwo Psychologiczne.

Boros S., Meslec N., Curseu P.L., Emons W. (2010). Struggles for cooperation: conflict resolution strategies in multicultural groups. *Journal of Managerial Psychology,* Vol. 25, No. 5.

Carew D., Parisi-Carew E., Blanchard K. (2007). *Przywództwo wyższego stopnia.* Warszawa: Wydawnictwo Naukowe PWN.

Chełpa S., Witkowski T. (2004). *Psychologia konfliktów. Praktyka radzenia sobie ze sporami.* Biblioteka Moderatora.

Clarke L. (2009). *Zarządzanie zmianą.* Wydawnictwo Emka.

Cooper R., Sawaf A. (2000). *EQ – Inteligencja emocjonalna w organizacji i zarządzaniu.* Wydawnictwo Emka.

Covey S.R. (2007). *The 7 Habits of Highly Effective People.* Rebis.

Czapiński J. (2004). *Psychologia pozytywna. Nauka o szczęściu, zdrowiu, sile i cnotach człowieka.* Warszawa: Wydawnictwo Naukowe PWN.

Czyżowska D. (2008). O celu i granicach rozwoju moralnego. *Analiza i egzystencja,* Vol. 8.

Deutsch M. (2000). Cooperation and Competition. In: M. Deutsch, P.T. Coleman (eds.). *The Handbook of Conflict Resolution. Theory and Practice.* San Francisco, 21–40 (Polish edition by Kraków: Jagiellonian University Press, 2005).

Dyląg A., Jaworek M., Karwowski W., Kożusznik M., Marek T. (2013). Discrepancy between individual and organizational values: Occupational burnout and work engagement among white-collar workers. *International Journal of Industrial Ergonomics*, January.

Haman W., Gut J. (2008). *Docenić konflikt. Od walki i manipulacji do współpracy*. Helion.

Hobfoll S.E. (2006). *Stres, kultura i społeczność. Psychologia i filozofia stresu*. Gdańsk: Gdańskie Wydawnictwo Psychologiczne.

Hofstede G., Hofstede G.J. (2007). *Kultury i organizacje*. Warszawa.

Katzenbach J.R., Smith D.K. (2001). *Siła zespołów, wpływ pracy zespołowej na efektywność organizacji*. Kraków: Oficyna Ekonomiczna.

Kohlberg L. (1984). Essays in Moral Development. In: *The Psychology of Moral, Development*. New York: Harper and Row.

Laursen K., Masciarelli F., Prencipe A. (2012). Regions matter: How localized social capital affects external knowledge acquisition and innovation. *Organizational Science*, Vol. 23, No. 1, pp. 177–193.

Liberman D.J. (2004). *Sztuka rozwiązywania konfliktów*. Gdańsk: Gdańskie Wydawnictwo Psychologiczne.

Maslach C., Schaufeli W.B., Leiter M.P. (2001). Job burnout. *Annual Review of Psychology*, No. 52, pp. 397–422.

Maslach C. (1998). A Multidimensional Theory of Burnout. In: C.L. Cooper (ed.). *Theories of organizational stress*. New York: Oxford University Press, pp. 68–85.

Maslach C., Leiter M.P. (2010). *Pokonać wypalenie zawodowe. Sześć strategii poprawienia relacji z pracą*. Warszawa: Wolters Kluwer Polska.

Maslach C., Leiter M.P. (2011). *Prawda o wypaleniu zawodowym. Co robić ze stresem w organizacji*. Warszawa: Wydawnictwo Naukowe PWN.

Mayer J.D., Salovey P. (1993). The Intelligence of Emotional Intelligence. *Intelligence*, Vol. 17, pp. 433–442.

Nęcki Z. (2000). *Negocjacje w biznesie*. Wyd. Antykwa.

Robbins S.P. (2004). *Zachowania w organizacji*. Warszawa: Polskie Wydawnictwo Ekonomiczne.

Sandy S.V., Cochran K.M. (2000). The Development of Conflict Resolution Skills in Children: Preschool to Adolescence. In: M. Deutsch, P.T. Coleman (eds.). *The Handbook of Conflict Resolution. Theory and Practice*. San Francisco, pp. 316–341.

Stoner J.F., Freeman R.E., Gilbert D.R.J.R. (2001). *Kierowanie*. Warszawa: Polskie Wydawnictwo Ekonomiczne.

Triandis H.C. (1995). *Individualism and Collectivism*. Boulder, CO: Westview Press.

Triandis H.C., Bontempo R., Villareal M., Masaaki A., Lucca N. (1988). Individualism and collectivism: cross-cultural perspectives on self-ingroup relationships. *Journal of Personality and Social Psychology*, Vol. 54, No. 2, pp. 323–338.

Tuckman B.W. (1965). Developmental sequence in small groups. *Psychological Bulletin*, No. 63, pp. 384–399, http://dennislearningcenter.osu.edu/references/GROUP%20 DEV%20ARTICLE.doc. [accessed: May 2013].

Tuckman B.W., Jensen M.C. (1977). Stages of small group development revisited. *Group and Organizational Studies*, No. 2, pp. 419–427.

Van Vugt M., De Cremer D., Janssen D.P. (2007). Gender Differences in Cooperation. *Psychological Science*, Vol. 18, No. 1.

Wagner J.A. (1995). Studies of individualism-collectivism: effects on cooperation in groups. *Academy of Management Journal*, No. 38, pp. 152–172.

IRENA ŚWIĄTEK
Jagiellonian University
Institute of Economics and Management
Chair of Standardized Management Systems

COMPETITION-ORIENTED ORGANIZATIONAL CULTURE AS A FACTOR FOSTERING THE DEVELOPMENT OF WORKAHOLISM

INTRODUCTION

One of the most current problems of the business administration is effective management of human resources. Since in the 21st century the access to material, financial and informational resources is no longer limited, people who can manage these resources in a more or less effective way have become the factor responsible for the attainment of a competitive advantage. Their knowledge, skills, personality traits and functional fit to their work positions determine the effectiveness of organizational goals fulfilment. The problem of functional fit is not a novelty for HR management specialists. Over two decades ago, Pettigrew and Whipp emphasized that it is very important for the management team to care about their employees and that it is necessary to take some strong measures in the area of matching employees to their positions according to their suitability as well as in the area of verifying their competence, creating training and development opportunities, motivating and creating rewarding systems. In their opinion, formulating a shared paradigm of human resources management would allow these actions to become closely related to each other [Armstrong 1996, p. 44].

What is interesting, despite the extreme focus on effective human resources management, many HR specialists and managers repeatedly fail to notice a very serious threat of workaholism. The reason of such a state of affairs could be sought in the lack of fundamental knowledge of the fact that work can become a source of problems. After all, this activity is regarded as socially beneficial, while diligence is a much desired personal trait which enables to satisfy one's economical needs, helps in developing certain structures and contributes to increasing the capital of a company as well as of a country.

Social and economic changes rendered work not only as a tool for gaining goods, but also a goal in itself – it became the means of self-fulfilment and a source of self-esteem, strengthened by own development and by building the sense of own competence. With such a common approval to professional activity, additionally supported by corporate standards, an intensive work is rarely perceived as a threat. It is commonly held that a workaholic is a perfect find for a company. Organizational culture, which is more and more frequently considered as the most modern tool for HR management [Ostrowska 2006, p. 79], is openly used by many companies in order to actively shape attitudes of their subordinates, inducing them to excessively burden themselves with work. Such norms and patterns are promoted especially in the companies the culture of which favours individualism and encourages competition between employees.

The aim of this article is to explore the phenomenon of workaholism, to point out some organizational mechanisms which boost maladaptive work-related behaviour and also to present negative consequences brought by workaholism to an individual and an organization.

1. WORKAHOLISM – A WORK PATHOLOGY OR A HEALTHY STYLE OF PROFESSIONAL FUNCTIONING?

The spread of the view that workaholism can be considered as a healthy style of professional functioning was most probably prompted by the results of research conducted by Marilyn Machlowitz and published at the beginning of the 1980's. Basing on these results, a conclusion was drawn that workaholics are very productive and satisfied with their work. Before the subsequent critical analysis of that research proved it to be inadequate and lacking in reliability, workaholism started to be identified with a phenomenon beneficial to a company and socially desirable [Wojdyło 2003, pp. 39–40]. These beliefs were supported by various classifications present in the literature of the subject which introduced "healthy" kinds of workaholism; such classifications were created, inter alia, by Tomas Naughton and Kimberly Scott, Keirsten Moore and Marcia Micelli [Malinowska 2008, p. 94].

In order to answer the question whether some forms of workaholism may be indeed beneficial to a company, it is crucial to verify two key issues – the definition of workaholism and the fact that not every hard working person should be considered as a workaholic. The original criterion for the diagnosis of workaholism, presented by Mosier, was merely the quantitative one, namely the amount of working hours had to exceed 50 hours per week [Wojdyło 2010, p. 12]. Despite the subsequent discoveries concerning this addiction which allowed to verify and reject that criterion, it is commonly believed that in order to describe someone as a workaholic it is necessary and at the same time completely sufficient to observe that they spend a lot of time at work. Therefore it is necessary to define the true nature of workaholism. The concept itself has been functioning in the literature for only just over forty years. It was introduced by Vicar Wayne Oates, a man who struggled with the problem of being addicted to work himself. The term itself originates from two words: "work" and "holism," which literally mean "[being] entirely the work" [Golińska 2008, p. 11]. The etymology itself brings to attention the extreme concentration of individual's activity on their work, suggests the sense of pressure and lack of control over their behaviour. Oates clearly emphasized these two elements in his definition of a workaholic: "[...] a workaholic is a person whose need for constant work becomes so excessive that it causes visible disorders and violation to their physical condition, personal happiness, interpersonal relationships and social functioning" [Chodkiewicz 2011, p. 297]. Similar aspects of the definition of work addiction were indicated by Robinson: "workaholism is a compulsive need to work, occurring despite of lack of external pressure, manifesting itself in setting requirements to oneself, being unable to regulate own work-related habits and by excessive commitment to work resulting in other forms of life activities being neglected" [Golińska 2008, p. 23]. The relatively recent history of research conducted on workaholism places this field on its discovery stage. Therefore it is not surprising that so many different theoretical ways of approaching this topic can be found. Nevertheless, the scholars reach agreement as far as fundamental issues and the mechanisms of that syndrome are concerned, and although workaholism has not been yet formally included in the psychopathological classifications such as ICD–10 and DSM–IV, it is treated as an addiction to an activity [Wojdyło 2010, pp. 20–24].

In order to develop addiction to work, an individual must have certain personality predispositions. People who lack these predispositions do not demonstrate a tendency to excessively burden themselves with work. When external conditions force them to overwork themselves, they may react with developing situational workaholism, and even though they would work long hours in an intensive way and impairing their own welfare, that behaviour would be contradictory to their inner standards. As soon as the situation or the circumstances change, such people would be relieved to return to their normal style of functioning in which work is balanced with other aspects of life. However, if a person has certain personality predispositions to become addicted, the situation will look completely different. The external conditions may activate their cognitive processes and emotions, resulting in the development of maladaptive behaviour associated with work [Lubrańska 2008, p. 29; Wojdyło 2010, p. 25–31]. Since that behaviour would be triggered by internal, and not external compulsion, it would not disappear when the circumstances change, just the opposite – this person will get engaged in even more intensive work and over time will become a prisoner of own compulsive behaviour.

The factors predisposing to the development of workaholism can be classified into two groups; these are temperamental factors and experiences from the period of early childhood. The research conducted by Hornowska and Paluchowski [2007] proved the existence of a vital link between workaholism and the following three temperamental features: high level of arousability (resulting from a low activation threshold and high emotionality) [Hornowska, Paluchowski 2007, pp. 91–93], avoidance of negative reinforcements and high persistence of activity [Wojdyło 2010, p. 78]. As a result, an individual needs to be provided with only a low level of stimulation in order to function in an optimal way, is more prone to restlessness and anxiety and more endurable in completion of undertaken actions. A person of such predispositions may manifest an inclination to escape into work as into their safe and well-known field of activity and to minimize their anxiety of failure by compulsive commitment to professional activities. The experiences from the period of early childhood can also contribute to the development of workaholism. According to Killinger, workaholics tend to have the background of being brought up in dysfunctional families where relations between their members were regulated by maladaptive mechanisms [Killinger 2007, p. 23]. The key issue which becomes the basis for the development of negative behaviour patterns is addiction or obsession with something, manifested by at least one of the parents [Killinger 2007, p. 35]. Parenting style is also an important factor, namely the highly demanding or the highly neglecting one, whereas the first one appears as more dangerous. The families in which that style is implemented are characterized by focusing on responsibilities and by rejecting play as an unproductive waste of time [Hornowska, Paluchowski 2007, p. 32; Killinger 2007, p. 26]. Children are expected to meet very high requirements [Hornowska, Paluchowski 2007, p. 24; Killinger 2007, p. 26; Wojdyło 2003, p. 47]. There is no genuine care or support while love and acceptance are demonstrated conditionally, only when the children meet their parents' expectations [Guerreschi 2010, p. 132; Hornowska, Paluchowski 2007, p. 33]. The parents demand perfectionism from their children and demonstrate no acceptance to their mistakes or failures; expressing emotions in an open way and direct communication, especially as far as discussing problems is concerned, are non-existent [Killinger 2007, pp. 24–25]. It is quite common in such families that at least one of the parents is addicted to work; in such cases, the child's predispositions to workaholism result from identification and modelling of their behaviour, and are directly connected with the process of building their own self-esteem [Guerreschi 2010, p. 133; Hornowska, Paluchowski 2007, p. 36; Killinger 2007, p. 28].

What underlies the development of workaholism is a psychological mechanism, formed on the basis of the factors described above. It is founded on unconscious, deeply rooted beliefs constructed as a result of the accumulation of certain experiences allowing to arrange the knowledge about oneself and about the surrounding world. Growing up in a dysfunctional family may lead to the development of maladaptive key beliefs, predisposing to falling into an addiction. In case of workaholics, these beliefs will refer to their own helplessness, lack of competence and inadequacy, and will also result in low self-confidence. In an attempt to save their threatened self-esteem, an adult workaholic will continually repeat the deeply-rooted scheme they acquired during their childhood in which working hard and meeting excessive expectations made them feel worthy of love and attention.

Numerous research confirm the connection between workaholism and anankastic personality [Golińska 2008, pp. 73–80; Kalinowski et al. 2005, p. 94; Wojdyło 2010, pp. 81–82]. People with this kind of personality demonstrate such personality traits as excessive ambition, diligence, perfectionism, stubbornness, high level of self-control, rigidity of behaviour, scrupulousness and preoccupation with details [Wojdyło 2010, p. 81]. According to the research conducted by Golińska [2008], those workaholics who can be classified with the obsessive-compulsive personality type are inclined to devotion to work by the means of two main mechanisms: the fear of being defeated which is focused on interpersonal consequences of experiencing such a failure and the sense of compulsion associated with work [Golińska 2007, p. 79; Kalinowski et al. 2005, p. 94]. Overworking oneself functions as a restlessness and anxiety reducing mechanism which allows to compensate own low self-esteem by confirming own self-worth [Wojdyło 2003, p. 47]. There is also a vital difference between workaholics and non-workaholics as far as narcissistic tendencies are concerned. The results of Golińska's research proved that these tendencies contribute to the development of workaholism. In her opinion, narcissistic workaholics make use of their work to confirm their own belief concerning their extraordinary abilities as well as to satisfy their need to be admired by others. These traits influence their professional functioning style which is characterized by competitiveness and ruthlessness towards co-workers [Golińska 2008, pp. 79–80]. The research conducted by Poppelreuter [1996] as well as by Hornowska and Paluchowski [2007] pointed out the existence of the link between workaholism and Type A personality. Poppelreuter indicated the Type A personality with a high need for stimulation whereas Polish scholars opted for the connection between workaholism and a highly reactive Type A personality. The low reactive workaholics were characterized by Poppelreuter as ambitious, action-oriented and greedy for appraisal. They demonstrate competitive attitude and a tendency to impose excessive standards on themselves as well as to create the pressure of time and effectiveness. They are impatient, display a great need for dominance and desire to control their environment. These features make them subject to high stress levels [Wojdyło 2010, p. 82; Kalinowski et al. 2005, pp. 94–95]. On the other hand, Hornowska and Paluchowski tried to prove that workaholics with a low need for stimulation use their work for controlling the inflow of stimuli from the environment. Since they identify work with a safe and controllable area which provides them with an optimal activation level, they consciously decide to concentrate on it and, furthermore, they limit their participation in other fields of activity [Hornowska, Paluchowski 2007, pp. 90–94].

Although many scholars are trying to provide a full description of the workaholic's profile, such a unified and clear typology does not exist. Each attempt of creating such a definition contributes to the general knowledge of this syndrome, yet it describes it only partially. Irrespectively of the chosen classification, it needs to be remembered that development of the addiction to work is a gradual process during which an individual is moving step by step on the health – illness continuum, systematically walking away from their welfare and falling into a trap of more and more serious disorders. This is the reason why the symptoms, manifesting themselves at the beginning only in a very slight way, become more obvious and visible with time. Fassel described the three successive phases of developing an addiction to work. The initial one is characterized by the need for permanent commitment to professional activities. Since work is a source of positive reinforcement, an individual is trying to stay occupied at all times; as their reservoirs of energy seem endless during this phase, the time for rest becomes more and more limited. Interpersonal relations start to deteriorate while non-professional responsibilities are neglected. The second phase, called the critical one, begins as soon as the individual loses their control over their behaviour. Their work becomes a compulsion, yet it is still a great source of gratification, such as well-being and high self-esteem; it is not merely the main activity anymore as it becomes the "state of mind" of a workaholic who cannot stop concentrating their thoughts on it. At the same time they are trying to conceal their compulsion by inventing some reasons for their excessive professional activity. Unfortunately, in the long time perspective overloading oneself with prolonged hard work connected with lack of regeneration leads to exhaustion and various psychosomatic disorders. When a strained workaholic becomes less and less efficient and is unable to deal either with the load of responsibilities or with grudges from their neglected relatives, the crisis is inevitable. A work addict becomes impatient and aggressive, falls into depressive mood, withdraws from relations with others and blocks their own emotions. Despite being overloaded with work, it is impossible for them to resign from it as such attempts trigger withdrawal symptoms in the form of mental and physical complaints. The last phase implies entering the vicious circle scheme as the addiction becomes the way of dealing with all the problems, including those caused by the addiction itself. A workaholic becomes emotionally numb and withdrawn while any attempts to re-direct their attention from professional activity result in the outbursts of aggression. Although all their vitality is concentrated on their work, their extremely exhausted organism is unable to function in an efficient way which causes frustration and despair. Therefore a workaholic turns to substances which are supposed to help them to control the body and increase their efficiency or to abate their constant stimulation. This phase is often characterized by development of cross-addictions to alcohol, medications, drugs, nicotine or some other compulsive forms of activity. The vicious circle scheme repeated over and over again leads to a complete personal and physical disintegration of an addict who is now vulnerable to burnout, serious mental disorders and somatic illnesses, in extreme cases leading to psychoses or death caused by exhaustion, called by the Japanese "karoshi" [Golińska 2008, p. 21; Guerreschi 2010, pp. 136–139; Hornowska, Paluchowski 2007, pp. 22–23].

Taking into consideration the development phases of this addiction and its consequences, it is hard to agree with the statement that workaholism can be considered as a healthy and efficient style of professional functioning. Hence the question, why so many typologies describe a workaholic as a healthy and productive person? The reason for such a discrepancy may lie in the accuracy of the criteria chosen to select groups of people for the research since not every hard working person is addicted to work [Hornowska, Paluchowski 2007, pp. 18–23; Jachnis 2008, p. 202]. There are people who spend a lot of time working in an intensive way but at the same time they function in an optimal way, stay healthy and are satisfied with their lifestyle; such people are called enthusiasts of work [Wojdyło 2010, p. 25]. Although their work constitutes their key life activity, just like it is observed in case of workaholics, the enthusiasts are driven by a completely different motivation. Janet Spence and Ann Robbins distinguished workaholics from work enthusiasts when working on the first method of examining workaholism, the Work – BAT scale. Their distinction was based on three measurements: commitment to work, compulsion to work and satisfaction from work. High commitment and high satisfaction levels together with low compulsion level were characteristic of work enthusiasts, while in the case of workaholics high levels of commitment and compulsion to work were crucial. The difference in levels of satisfaction from work was a distinguishing feature for two types of workaholics: high satisfaction level was characteristic of enthusiastic worka-holics while the low one represented addicted workaholics. Nevertheless, the subsequent research conducted with the use of the Work – BAT scale in Japan proved that only the measurement of compulsion and satisfaction from work are necessary for the diagnosis of workaholism. Compulsion to work turned out to be the key factor as it is present in all the types or work addic-tion. Workaholics spend so much time working because they cannot stop it, while for the work enthusiasts it is a source of satisfaction; it pleases them and makes them feel personally fulfiled. They can become involved, both mentally and physically, in other forms of activity and derive pleasure from them, whereas workaholics, even when they do not work, they constantly think about it. It is like a drug for them and separation from the ability to fulfil their professional goals is a severe, unpleasant experience which causes withdrawal symptoms, just as in case of alcoholism [Golińska 2008, p. 55, Wojdyło 2010, p. 43].

2. COMPETITION-ORIENTED ORGANIZATIONAL CULTURE AS A FOSTERING FACTOR IN THE ESCALATION OF MALADAPTIVE BEHAVIOUR ASSOCIATED WITH WORK

Workaholism can be a subject to reinforcement by the means of different subjective and environmental factors. The latter ones include among others the work environment. In many organizations it can be observed that orga-nizational culture and the management team working for these organizations are used for promoting the model of behaviour in which the employees are expected to overwork themselves. Organizational culture understood as "a set of values held by a company, creating certain, often unwritten norms of behaviour which are expected from this company's employees" [Arm-strong 2000, p. 149] is defining ways of behaviour and methods of task fulfilment.

General analysis of cultural organizational models allows to distinguish two basic models: the western one which originated from the United States, and the eastern one which comes from Japan [Ostrowska 2006, p. 71]. The basis underlying each of these cultures comprises certain unconscious assumptions which constitute organizational axioms – incontestable beliefs which shape attitudes towards different areas of functioning within an or-ganization, such as the manner of working, quality of the services provided, customers, contractors, partners, superiors, authority, status, prestige, loyalty and other important elements [Armstrong 2000, p. 152].

In the American model, gaining profit plays the superior role while realization of new undertakings is perceived in the category of "the art of making money." Companies representing this model are open to innovations while their employees are expected to constantly prove themselves to be competent and enthusiastic, to demonstrate individualism and determination. Human resources management is conducted in an autocratic way, the power is centralized and decisions of the executives are not a subject to discussion. The relations between workers are ruled by clearly defined principles and it is common to continually increase the expectations towards employees and to encourage competition between them. Hence keeping own position in such a company is similar to fighting an endless battle for financial and professional success because only the best ones deserve appraisal. The kind of behaviour represented by workers of organizations characterized by this type of culture is colloquially described as a "rat race." This pejorative term referring to pointless efforts of laboratory rodents hustling down labyrinth paths is used as a metaphor of the atmosphere of stress and an authoritatively imposed compulsion which leaves an individual with no choice of alternative action. The eastern management model stands as an opposition to the organizational culture described above. Although profitability is still very important, in this model the core values are excellence of the work process, quality management and individual as well as social relations. Such an organizational culture is paternalistic and strongly collective – subordinates are not encouraged to demonstrate individual behaviour or competitiveness. It is common to set new goals and make decisions collectively. The tools for managers' work are emotional involvement and attention to the issues important to the employees. A great significance is ascribed to the actual shaping of the values and norms. The subordinates are guaranteed a lifelong employment and each of them may become a potential candidate to a managerial position as long as they succeed in reaching yet another step on the career ladder by demonstrating diligence, loyalty and attention to relationships with others [Harasim 2006, pp. 11–12; Ostrowska 2006, p. 71; Wasilewski 1994, p. 52].

The management style "imported" from the United States which promotes competition between workers is the one most frequently employed in European businesses, including Polish ones. In such companies it is more and more common to express approval to excessive professional activity in a direct way and to promote the values prompting competition and work ethics [Moczydłowska 2004, p. 111; Szaban 2003, p. 39]. Many organizations reinforce these values by the means of suitable motivation systems [Guerreschi 2010, pp. 133–134].This situation is intensified by high competition on the labour market and the increase of unemployment level which renders work positions as goods in still shorter and shorter supply.

Fassel and Schaef indicated six organizational features which foster development of workaholism. They are as follows: concentrating on productivity, focusing on achieving set short-term financial goals, treating employees like objects and managing them by the means of negative reinforcements, demonstrating no respect to private lives of employees, unfriendly and dehumanized work atmosphere as well as treating critical situations as a norm [Hornowska, Paluchowski 2007, pp. 39–40]. Most of these features are directly or indirectly present in the western culture of management, especially in these companies which promote competition between their workers.

The global trend of focusing on company's productivity and fast short-term profits seems to be the most important aspect from the list given above. Gaining profit is obviously the key objective for each business, but still, when all the management processes concentrate exclusively on accumulating capital, the human factor tends to sink into oblivion. In such conditions employees with predispositions to excessive burdening themselves with work may develop addiction to work. They demonstrate a great need to confirm their own self-worth which they achieve by the means of hard and persistent work, even more so because they want to meet other people's expectations. Therefore the values and norms determining the way of behaving accepted in the company have a key importance here. Szaban points out that these values can be defined as of double nature: on the one hand, they are officially written down, taking form of a mission, a vision or a list of regulations and procedures; on the other hand, they function in an informal way, inside common consciousness of the employees. Relevance of one of these forms depends not on the written records but on the organizational culture of a company and on the values with which employees can identify themselves [Szaban 2003, p. 13]. If these are the values fostering competition and work ethos, they may become a factor triggering development of workaholism [Hornowska, Paluchowski 2007, p. 38].

Organizations, in which the culture of reinforcing individualism and competition is present, tend to propagate the myth of a "work leader." That pattern corresponds to the beliefs and behaviour of a workaholic, fixed during their early childhood. If they are encouraged to burden themselves with work in an excessive way, the well-known scheme will be activated instantly. The maladaptive behaviour related to work may be additionally reinforced by various awarding and punishing practices employed by the management. Since workaholics are characterized by temperamental features and a need for acceptance from the environment, they are susceptible to various motivation techniques. Being officially rewarded for some forms of behaviour, such as competitiveness, distancing oneself from co-workers, overtime work and constant eagerness to undertake professional actions, will incline them to repeat that behaviour as often as it is possible [Hornowska, Paluchowski 2007, pp. 40–41]. Correspondingly, non-formal sanctions, such as being denied promotion or bonuses, employed by the management team as a punishment for behaving against their expectations, will induce workaholics to resign from functioning in a given way, especially in a case when that reprehensible behaviour concerned the use of time intended for rest and relaxation.

The patterns of behaviour involving excessive burdening oneself with work are very often promoted by managers because they hold responsibility for shaping their subordinates behaviour according to the values held by a company. It is possible for them to do that by the means of their entitlements following the position they hold or by the means of own authority, the influence of which is incomparably stronger than the code of conduct stemming from the formal power they were given [Ostrowska 2006, p. 76]. The danger of modelling is even greater if a charismatic and authoritarian superior suffers from workaholism themselves, which is a frequent disorder among people from the managerial rank. Another factor which increases the risk of developing an addiction is working on positions on which exceeding time limits of work is not a subject to control and at the same time the scope of responsibilities is considerable [Guerreschi 2010, p. 133; Kalinowski et al. 2005, pp. 87–88]. Those individuals who are characterized by a specific, low reactive temperament and therefore are able to function in an optimal way in highly stressful situations, are particularly prone to undertaking the work rhythm called by S.A. Hewlett and C.B. Luce the *extreme one*. They also demonstrate a tendency to perform duties burdened with high responsibility level, therefore they usually hold managerial posts. The basic criteria for distinguishing the extreme work rhythm are high incomes, prestigious professional position and working hours exceeding 60 hours per week. Moreover, the work manner of an individual needs to be characterized by at least five from ten following principles: physical presence at work for at least 10 hours per day, unpredictable rhythm and fast pace of work, the scope of responsibilities greater than the average one (resulting from performing a few functions at the same time), performing professional duties outside normal working hours, the unlimited accessibility to the clients, responsibility for losses and profits, responsibility for employees recruitment and mentoring, numerous business trips and handing over the reports to their direct superiors [Kuc, Żemigała 2009, pp. 27–28]. People who work according to the extreme work rhythm seek self-fulfilment, most frequently understood by them as holding a prestigious position as well as achieving professional and financial success. They like taking risk and feel a need for high stimulation which makes them seek competition and function under constant pressure created by themselves. According to Golińska, those workaholics who work in highly stressful environment contrast those with obsessive-compulsive tendencies; yet both of these personality types are based on a shared mechanism – a compulsion to function in a certain manner [Golińska 2008, p. 88].

In organizations characterized by focusing on productivity and competition, exploitation of the employees is a commonly accepted practice. Subordinates are considered as tools used to achieve certain goals, treated like objects. An employee is expected to demonstrate constant readiness to undertake professional tasks, even at the time designated for activities other than work [Kaczyńska-Maciejowska 2002, p. 49]. It is also common that the pressure is exerted on the subordinates to make them spend their free time with their colleagues (e.g. at parties and bonding events) which in turn reduces the possibility to spend time with their relatives [Kalinowski et al. 2005, pp. 92–93]. Taking into consideration the fact that workaholics frequently suffer from an intense conflict between work and other spheres of life, and that their perceived sense of life and satisfaction from it is quite low, it is noticeable that such pressure will result in lower commitment to family life and relationships [Wojdyło 2010, pp. 62–63]. This in turn entails far-reaching consequences. Killinger emphasized the power of negative impact of workaholism on the addict's family. Their co-addicted spouses feel used, lonely and neglected which often leads them to the brink of depression and mental breakdown. The children develop and reinforce dysfunctional patterns and unsuitable schemes concerning the way of family functioning, priorities, communication, control and power. The process of identification can also be disturbed because of the lack of an appropriate model. This brings an imminent danger of development of maladaptive work-related habits at the children and as a result they may acquire predispositions to become addicted to work [Killinger 2007, pp. 157–165].

Inequality in treatment of the workers of different sex can become a key issue when it comes to development of dysfunctional work-related patterns by women. Those women who aim at making a career are more likely to develop addiction to work as they have to not only struggle with the stereotype of the female role present in our culture, but also to overcome the dissonance resulting from the fact that they begin their professional careers from a lower position than men. Especially in organizations which promote competition achieving a certain position and professional status requires more effort and work from women than from men [Hornowska, Paluchowski 2007, pp. 36–38].

Competition is a factor which increases stress, intensifies the sense of compulsion and influences the increase of work persistence. The negative tension may trigger a number of various factors, such as setting the employees high requirements to meet, fast pace of work, pressure of time and results, the risk of unemployment as well as lack of the feeling of safety and financial stability with the incomes level and keeping the work position depending on the achieved work outcomes. A similar level of stress is experienced by a workaholic when their self-esteem level is decreased because they fail to meet the imposed expectations, lose respect, prestige or professional status. For those workaholics whose addiction to work is based on the personality background resulting from obsessive-compulsive features, stress and competition at work may constitute factors reinforcing the tendencies of compulsive behaviour. Nevertheless, even those people who do not demonstrate inclination for excessive burdening themselves with work, when forced to do so may develop situational workaholism [Hornowska, Paluchowski 2007, p. 38; Wojdyło 2003, p. 46].

The work atmosphere which promotes competition can also foster marginalization of the meaning of interpersonal relations as well as formalization of contacts between co-workers. The research conducted by Wojdyło [2010] showed that those addicted to work are characterized by low emotional competence, a tendency to control their emotions in an excessive way, rigidity of behaviour and inclination to avoid commitment and intimacy [Wojdyło 2010, p. 83]. The influence of such a deficiency in the area of emotional efficiency on the sustainment of the scheme of workaholism can be reinforced by the "over-competence" of the addicted, demonstrated by a very high work-related sense of self-effectiveness. The company's open consent to competitiveness allows them to limit their participation in interpersonal relations (which they cannot handle well) to minimum and at the same time it sanctions indifferent or even hostile behaviour exhibited towards co-workers [Wojdyło 2010, p. 83].

Another factor prompting the development of workaholism can be the company's policy concentrated on so called "fire fighting." If critical events constitute a part of the every-day routine, the employees will be forced to function in an environment of continuous stress and will have to demonstrate constant readiness to undertaking actions at the cost of neglecting their own needs and pushing other kinds of activities into the background [Hornowska, Paluchowski 2007, pp. 39–40].

3. ORGANIZATIONAL AND INDIVIDUAL CONSEQUENCES OF WORKAHOLISM

It is estimated that workaholics constitute about 5% of the population [Schultz, Schultz 2002, p. 449]; from the point of view of statistics, every twentieth person is addicted to work. Therefore, the probability of finding at least one workaholic in a medium-sized company is close to one hundred per cent. Many organizations show willingness to recruit employees who display a tendency to commit themselves to work as it seems to be the best solution to employ a person constantly concentrated on the company's businesses and eager to abandon all the other life activities for the sake of the professional ones. It is commonly believed by the managers that this is the way how a perfect employee should behave, although such beliefs are not confronted with facts. In the short-term perspective, workaholic behaviour may be beneficial for a company, but still, the negative consequences connected with employing a person addicted to work will affect that company sooner or later.

The way in which a person addicted to work behaves may be a source of many problems. It has to be remembered that a workaholic demonstrates a specific temperament and personality traits. Their key concern is to protect their sense of self-worth by the means of cognitive distortion which may in turn disturb the way they perceive their professional reality. Such features as excessive ambition, vaulting expectations, competitiveness, compulsive need for domination and control as well as utmost concentration on tasks combined with overlooking the human factor will eventually hinder co-operation and generate conflicts within a work team [Wojdyło 2010, pp. 62–63]. Extreme perfectionism and inability to share responsibilities with other employees may bring a workaholic to delay or even to sabotage professional activities because it would be very difficult for them to agree on lowering their performance standards or dispersing the control. Low emotional competence would incline them to keep distance while competitiveness and a need for recognition may render them rather ruthless and insensitive to emotions and problems of other people.

To protect themselves from suffering from stress caused by interpersonal relations or at least to lower the level of that stress, a workaholic applies various maladaptive manners of behaviour, such as avoiding confrontation, escaping into work, blocking the experienced and expressed emotions, expressing aggression in a passive way and such ways of behaviour which would trigger interpersonal conflicts [Wojdyło 2010, p. 70]. All the above manners of behaviour make it very difficult to maintain clear and direct relations with a workaholic or to effectively function with them within a work team.

Extreme concentration on being occupied leads to deficiency of control when workaholics find themselves in decisive situations. The research conducted by Natalia Mielczarek (2007) proved that they demonstrate a tendency to make rapid decisions allowing them to take immediate action. When a workaholic is left idle, they experience tension, and so the need to reduce it inclines them to make decision which would let them start working again as soon as it is possible; therefore they are likely to make ill-considered choices [Golińska 2008, pp. 85–86]. High level of self-control together with rigidity of behaviour, both features very characteristic of workaholics, make them encounter difficulties when creative actions are needed. They also lack flexibility and adaptability to changeable work conditions while fear of failure only increases compulsiveness of work and rigidity of behaviour.

In the perspective of a few years, being overworked and having no rest lead a workaholic to a complete physical and mental breakdown. The consequences for an individual may include experiencing professional burnout, nervous breakdown, depression, psychoses, serious somatic illnesses, development of new addictions and even death caused by exhaustion. The addiction affects also the organization which employed a workaholic. When effectiveness of a work addict drastically decreases, they start to make mistakes and fail to fulfil their duties on time. The costs of these mistakes is additionally increased by the cost of absences. In cases where a quick profit gain is a superior principle, it is usually necessary to replace that team member who fails to work efficiently. It is not a rare situation when the company has to pay the compensation and also cover the costs of a job vacancy, the recruitment process and introducing a new employee into the company. To add up to that, non-financial losses, such as lowered team morale, decreased efficiency and deterioration of organizational atmosphere have to be taken into consideration. If this kind of scenario occurs repeatedly, it may influence the general opinion about that company and may discourage the best candidates from applying to it.

SUMMARY

When analysing the phenomenon of workaholism and its consequences, it has to be remembered that one case can be viewed from a few various perspectives. Apart from the point of view of an individual, there is the point of view of an organization and also different time perspectives: a short-term and a long-term one. What is more, all the addictions are developed by the means of gratification which is present during the initial stage. Similarly, during its first stages workaholism can be a source of positive reinforcements and therefore a work addict may seem very pleased with their intensive work before they start making mistakes and before the exhaustion and psychophysical problems occur. Workaholic behaviour can also be quite beneficial for the organization for a certain period of time and it seems to be the right decision to employ a person for whom work constitutes their life priority. Nevertheless, with time it becomes clear that the way of functioning of a person addicted to work is starting to exert a negative influence not only on themselves and on their own work results, but also on professional relations and efficiency of their co-workers.

In the companies where the basic and superior principle is gaining profit, all the management-related processes aim at contributing to the accumulation of capital in a more or less direct way. The organizational culture of such companies demonstrates a number of characteristics which fosters development of workaholism; competitiveness is generally accepted and excessive burdening oneself with work is common, whereas the analysis of behaviour of an individual usually falls outside the field of interest. As long as the employee does not encounter a crisis which would be caused by the state of being overworked and which would imply financial loss to the company, it is doubtful that the behaviour of a work addict would become a subject to evaluation for their superiors. Finally, when the inevitable crisis arises, it will be more practical to replace that ineffective employee rather than to investigate the reason for their breakdown or to offer them support.

What is interesting, encouraging the kinds of behaviour which are associated with excessive work does not transfer itself into achieving above-average results in a long term perspective. The analyses of various organizations from the economic point of view showed that companies characterized by the eastern culture of management achieve better financial results and tend to be more successful in different areas of activity [Ostrowska 2006, p. 71]. Obviously there may be a number of different factors influencing such a state of affairs, but still, more and more management theoreticians and practitioners come to an agreement that the work environment in which co-operation, maintaining harmonious relationships and keeping balance between work and other areas of life are emphasized, contributes to both physical well-being and effectiveness of the employees.

BIBLIOGRAPHY

Armstrong M. (1996). *Zarządzanie zasobami ludzkimi. Strategia i działanie.* Kraków: Wydawnictwo Profesjonalnej Szkoły Biznesu.

Armstrong M. (2000). *Zarządzanie zasobami ludzkimi.* Kraków: Dom Wydawniczy ABC.

Chodkiewicz J. (2011). Pracoholizm a przeżywane konflikty, emocje oraz stres w pracy. In: L. Golińska, E. Bielawska-Batorowicz (eds.). *Rodzina i praca w warunkach kryzysu.* Łódź: Wydawnictwo Uniwersytetu Łódzkiego.

Golińska L. (2008). *Pracoholizm – uzależnienie czy pasja?* Warszawa: Difin.

Guerreschi C. (2010). *Nowe uzależnienia.* Kraków: Wydawnictwo Salwator.

Harasim W. (2006). Generacyjne aspekty zarządzania potencjałem pracy. In: W. Harasim (ed.). *Tendencje rozwojowe zarządzania zasobami ludzkimi.* Warszawa: Wyższa Szkoła Promocji w Warszawie.

Hornowska E., Paluchowski W. (2007). *Praca – skrywana obsesja. Wyniki badań nad zjawiskiem pracoholizmu.* Poznań: Bogucki Wydawnictwo Naukowe.

Jachnis A. (2008). *Psychologia organizacji. Kluczowe zagadnienia,* Warszawa: Difin.

Kaczyńska-Maciejowska R. (2002). Komu grozi pracoholizm? *Personel i Zarządzanie,* No. 15–16.

Kalinowski M., Czuma I., Kuć M., Kulik A. (2005). Praca, Wydawnictwo KUL, Lublin.

Killinger B. (2007). Pracoholicy – szkoła przetrwania, Dom Wydawniczy REBIS, Poznań.

Kuc B.R., Żemigała M. (2009). Ekstremalny rytm pracy menedżerskiej. *Przegląd Organizacji,* No. 2.

Lubrańska A. (2008). *Psychologia pracy. Podstawowe pojęcia i zagadnienia.* Warszawa: Difin.

Malinowska D. (2008). Pracoholizm wśród menedżerów – wada czy zaleta? In: Z. Uchnast (ed.). *Psychologia kierowania: rywalizacja – współdziałanie.* Lublin: Towarzystwo Naukowe KUL.

Moczydłowska J. (2004). Szaleństwo pracy. *Personel i Zarządzanie,* No. 9.

Ostrowska J. (2006). Kształtowanie kultury organizacyjnej a efektywność zarządzania zasobami ludzkimi. In: W. Harasim (ed.). *Tendencje rozwojowe zarządzania zasobami ludzkimi.* Warszawa: Wyższa Szkoła Promocji w Warszawie.

Schultz D.P., Schultz S.E. (2002). *Psychologia a wyzwania dzisiejszej pracy.* Warszawa: Wydawnictwo Naukowe PWN.

Szaban J. (2003). *Miękkie zarządzanie. Ze współczesnych problemów zarządzania ludźmi.* Warszawa: Wydawnictwo Wyższej Szkoły Przedsiębiorczości i Zarządzania im. Leona Koźmińskiego.

Wasilewski L. (1994). *Modele strategii jakości firm przemysłowych.* Warszawa: Instytut Organizacji i Zarządzania w Przemyśle.

Wojdyło K. (2003). Charakterystyka problemu uzależnienia od pracy w świetle dotychczasowych badań. *Nowiny Psychologiczne,* No. 3.

Wojdyło K. (2010). *Pracoholizm – perspektywa poznawcza.* Warszawa: Difin.

MAGDALENA JAWOREK
Jagiellonian University
Institute of Economics and Management
Chair of Standardized Management Systems

COOPERATION AND COMPETITION AS ELEMENTS OF INDIVIDUAL AND ORGANIZATIONAL VALUE SYSTEM AMONG MIDDLE TOP MANAGERS – PILOT STUDY

INTRODUCTION

Ever more researchers are interested in issues of values in work and organization context [e.g. Schwartz 1999; Ros et al. 1999]. Nowadays, one of the most acknowledged one is Shalom H. Schwartz who conducts research into values in cultural context. He defines values as "conceptions of the desirable that influence the way people select action and evaluate events." In other words, value system is a collection of norms, which constitute a moral code – indicator of what is good and desired, and what is bad, not acceptable, or even condemned. Values may be discussed with reference to individual (individual value system), and to smaller or bigger and more complicated group like company.

And just at organizational level values are an intrinsic element or basis of organizational culture [Chatman and Jehn 1994; O'Reilly, Chatman and Caldwell 1991; Sheridan 1992; Cameron and Quinn 2003], that serves realization of company mission, goals achievement, and development of ways of coping with problems in hard or even crisis times. In order to fulfill its function values should be shared by the greatest number of participants possible, even though managers have the most influence on its shape [Giberson et al. 2009]. Organizational values are employees' lodestar, especially new ones, and are an indicator of acceptable behaviors and attitudes.

Cooperation and competition are definitely significant values from the point of view of organization. Due to the skills of cooperation and interaction between members of organization or team within a company it is possible to realize many tasks or projects, which individuals would not be able to do on their own. In turn, competition serves motivating employees and arousing energy, what is rather difficult to achieve in a group,[1] and what allows to gain extraordinary results by individuals.

Yet, is it possible to combine cooperation, which should be based on mutual trust and loyalty to coworkers, with competition between each other, that results in dishonesty and insincerity and insincerity to others? How do employees place just cooperation and competition in their values system? What positions in hierarchy do both values take in organizational system? What other values are connected with cooperation and competition at individual and organizational level? And finally, is there discrepancy between these values at organizational and individual level? The present work serves answering these questions, but because of small size of the sample it is only a pilot study.

1. AIMS OF STUDY

First aim of the current study was identification of individual value system of specific professional group – middle top managers who work for one of the biggest bank in Poland. Next goal was to determine value system in organization, what subjects work for, and finally comparing these two systems – individual and organizational, with emphasis on discrepancy in values, especially: cooperation and competition. Moreover, relationships of cooperation and competition with other values both at individual and organizational level were tested.

2. METHODS

PARTICIPANTS

The study was conducted among managers purposely. They were selected to the work in that organization as well as on managerial positions very carefully, and their work experience was sufficiently long. So, they make an

---

[1] See: social loafing effect – *"the tendency to exert less effort when working on a group task in which individual contributions cannot be measured"* (Gilovich et al. 2006, p. 60).

example for new employees by virtue of organizational value system, being a means of conveying this value system, and having definitely better knowledge and awareness what is valued in organization.

Sample consisted of 54 participants – 27 women (52%) and 25 men (48%); two of them did not specify their gender. Average age of participants was 30 (SD = 4.19). The youngest person was 22, the oldest – 43. Respondents have worked in their present organization on average for about 4.67 years (SD = 3.17), the longest – 17 years; and in the current position – 2.4 years (SD = 2.32), the longest – 13 years.

MEASURES

The study was conducted with the use of a questionnaire, which was constructed basing on Schwartz Value Survey. The questionnaire consisted of 25 values relating to individual (part A – "important to me"), and organizational level (part B – "important to the organization I work for"). Answers were rated on a 6-point scale ranging from [–1] "opposed" to 4 "of supreme importance." Data collection was carried out on the training, which was part of a development program directed to managers with sufficient work experience in the organization and human resource management.

3. RESULTS

Data was analyzed with SPSS to compute correlations and descriptive statistics. Figure 1 displays detailed results concerning means in comparison of individual and organizational level.

ORGANIZATIONAL AND INDIVIDUAL VALUES

Values recognized by the studied managers as the most valued in their organization are:
- effectiveness (3.52),
- success (3.44),
- responsibility (3.41),
- self-discipline (3.35),

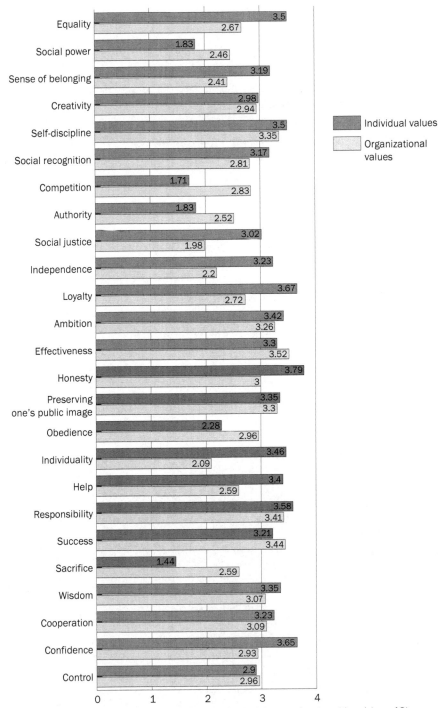

Figure 1. Means of values compared individual with organizational level (n = 48)
Source: own elaboration.

- preserving one's public image (3.3),
- ambition (3.26),
- **cooperation (3.09),**
- wisdom (3.07).

In turn, values recognized as the least significant in the studied managers' place work are: social justice (1.98). Competition also gained high mean of 2.83.

In regard to individual values, according to respondents, the most important are:

- honesty (3.79),
- loyalty (3.67),
- confidence (3.65),
- responsibility (3.58),
- self-discipline (3.5),
- equality (3.5).

The least important values for managers at individual level are: sacrifice (1.44), **competition (1.71)** and authority (1.83). Cooperation was recognized between "very important" and "of supreme importance." There are more values from individual level above "very important" than in case organizational ones – 18 values in 25 gained an average equal or above 3.0 (on organizational level – only 9).

DISCREPANCY IN INDIVIDUAL AND ORGANIZATIONAL VALUE SYSTEM

The widest gap between values at individual and organizational level concern: **competition**, social justice, independence, individuality and sacrifice (Figure 2). In turn, the arrowest discrepancy in these two value systems was gained in case of: creativity, preserving one's public image, control, **cooperation**, ambition and self-discipline.

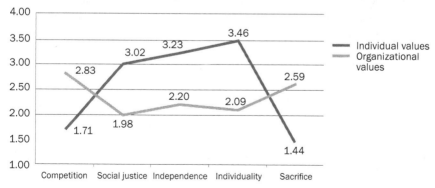

Figure 2. The widest gaps between organizational and individual values
Source: own elaboration.

RELATIONSHIPS OF COMPETITION AND COOPERATION WITH OTHER VALUES – INDIVIDUAL AND ORGANIZATIONAL LEVEL

When investigating relationships of competition and cooperation with other values, both at individual and organizational level some interesting relations may be observed (see: Table 1). Two values, i.e. effectiveness and success correlate positively with competition (respectively: r = .32 and .36) and cooperation at both levels (r = .36 and .35). Values related to only competition (but not to cooperation) in individual and organizational value system are: Authority (r = .67 and .65) and social power (r = .35 and .44). Whereas values which occured to be associated only with cooperation (but not with competition) at both levels are: preserving one's public image (r = .30 and .39), help (r = .30 and .43), and confidence (r = .50 and .46).

Some differences between organizational and individual value system were observed with regard to cooperation and competition. Competition, only at individual level (not at organizational) relates to creativity (r = .31), ambition (r = .35), and wisdom (r = .41). In organizational system values (but not in individual) self-discipline (r = .30), responsibility (r = .28), honesty (r = −.33), and individuality (r = −.30) are associated with competition. It is worth to note the negative relations in case of two last values and competition.

In turn, cooperation correlates with creativity (r = .41), self-discipline (r = .37), social recognition (r = .41) and obedience (r = .49) at individual level only, whereas at the organizational one with: equality (r = .33), ambition (r = .31), honesty (r = .34), responsibility (r = .40), sacrifice (r = .34) and control (r = .36).

Values, such as: sense of belonging, loyalty, social justice, and independence do not relate to any competition and cooperation at any level. It is surprising in case of lack of relationships between two first values and cooperation. It must be noticed that both values: cooperation and competition are not related to each other. Studied relationships fluctuate from weak (.28) to significant (.68).

Table 1. Correlations of Competition and Cooperation with other values, separately at individual (n = 48) and organizational (n = 54) levels

	Individual level		Organizational level	
	Competition	Cooperation	Competition	Cooperation
Equality	−.197	−.062	−.135	.326(*)
Social power	.354(*)	.147	.442(**)	−.153
Sense of belonging	.071	.199	−.047	.218
Creativity	.309(*)	.411(**)	.009	.232
Self-discipline	.12	.373(**)	.298(*)	.095
Social recognition	.246	.407(**)	.107	.219
Competition	1	.256	1	−.003
Authority	.675(**)	.284	.654(**)	−.119
Social justice	−.115	−.096	−.022	.170
Independence	.025	−.139	−.055	.170
Loyalty	−.096	.257	−.232	.200
Ambition	.355(*)	.204	.081	.310(*)
Effectiveness	.322(*)	.332(*)	.356(**)	.412(**)
Honesty	.046	−.044	−.332(*)	.345(*)
Preserving one's public image	.284	.297(*)	.038	.392(**)
Obedience	.395(**)	.488(**)	.500(**)	.058
Individuality	−.185	.25	−.303(*)	.223
Help	−.175	.304(*)	−.065	.430(**)
Responsibility	.005	.191	.280(*)	.402(**)
Success	.451(**)	.356(*)	.353(**)	.351(**)
Sacrifice	.439(**)	.233	.524(**)	.342(*)
Wisdom	.407(**)	.508(**)	.117	.430(**)
Cooperation	.256	1	−.003	1
Confidence	−.024	.509(**)	−.174	.461(**)
Control	.367(*)	−.112	.447(**)	.360(**)

*p < 0.01, **p < 0.001

Source: own elaboration.

4. DISCUSSION

The first aim of the present study was to identify the position of two values: cooperation and competition in individual and organizational value systems of managers. The second aim was to verify relationships these two values with others, and compare these relations at individual and organizational levels.

The studied individuals, personally value the most: honesty, loyalty, confidence, responsibility, self-discipline, and equality. Two of them, i.e. responsibility and self-discipline occurred in the group of organizational values. Apart from them, effectiveness, success, preserving one's public image, ambition, cooperation, and wisdom appeared as well. First group of values seems to be more universal, and to a greater extent is associated with characteristics which we expect from our close relatives, friends, and co-workers. The second group consists of values which are profitable for organization in the form of intensive work of employees.

Translating results into practice, organizational culture of company where studied managers work, is characterized by the expectation of success and goals achievement. Employees who are ambitious, very responsible, conscientious, self-disciplined, with strong need for development and achievement are highly valued in the organization. What is interesting, more important is skill of cooperation than need for competition, although the last one ranked very high also. Two organizational values found out in the group of the highest ranked individual values, i.e. responsibility and self-discipline, and next three were very close to the organizational ones: Preserving one's public image, cooperation, and ambition. It means, that studied managers seem to be fitted for their work place. They differ from organization to the highest degree in case of feeling of independence, individuality, and social justice.

Hence, the organization may become close to their employees by emphasis on these values, which are important for them and to a lesser extent for the organization, i.e. social justice, individuality, and independence. First of them means safety and a concern for others, two last ones – need for autonomy and having control over situation in the organization. Some studies confirmed that the level of congruence between organizational and individual values may be predictor of turnover [Vandenberghe 1999; O'Reilly et al. 1991]. So, it is worth to work on reducing gaps between organizational and individual system value and just selecting future employees in respect of person-culture fit.

Out of two key values from the point of view of the current work, i.e. cooperation and competition, only the last one ranked differently in organizational and individual value system. Skill of teamwork, coordination of efforts joined is a value almost to the same degree personal as organizational.

In turn, competition is perceived as a value needed in the organization, but in the individual value system it scores very low (lower is only sacrifice). Two issues are emerging. First, there is a gap between organizational and individual level in regard to competition. Some studies observed that values congruence may be related to job satisfaction, organizational commitment, and employees' intent to remain with employer [Westerman and Cyr 2004; Amos and Weathington 2008; Vandenberghe 1999; O'Reilly et al. 1991], whereas value mismatch leads to occupational burnout, and as further consequence to resignation from a job [Leiter, Jackson, Shaughnessy 2009].

Simultaneously, cooperation and competition are perceived as very important in the organizational value system. Both values give some profits for organization. Some tasks exceed abilities even of the best individual and in order to be accomplished they require coordination of efforts of the entire team. In turn, competition generates energy, what may lead to extraordinary results gained by individuals. Obtained correlations in current work show that both cooperation and competition are good for organization – both are associated with such values as success and effectiveness. Yet, is it possible to reconcile cooperation which should be based on mutual loyalty and confidence in co-workers, with competition associated with among others 'suspicious and hostile attitudes' or 'poor communication' [Deutsch 2006, p. 30]? Results of that study partly does not deny such combination – there is no negative correlation between these two values at both levels, as it would be expected (as well as positive relation). On the other hand, competition at both levels is associated, among others, with authority, social power, and above all – at organizational level negatively with honesty (!), what may exclude competitive and cooperative behaviors at the same time.

Deutsch distinguishes "destructive" and "constructive" competition, when in case of the last one – "the losers as well as the winners gain" and "winners see (...) that losers are better off, or at least not worse off than they were before the competition" [Deutsch 2006, p. 29]. In turn, Sagiv, Sverdlik and Schwartz [2011] suggest to assign individuals to character of tasks. Employees who emphasize power values should work in a competitive atmosphere, whereas individuals emphasize values associated with concern and care of others to tasks that require teamwork and cooperation.

To sum up, competition in the managers' individual value system is very low, otherwise at organization level where is valued as almost "very important." In turn, cooperation is significant both at individual and organizational level. In organizational value system competition is associated with authority, sacrifice, and obedience, whereas cooperation with: confidence, wisdom, and help. At individual level, the strongest relations competition were observed with authority, success, and sacrifice, and in case cooperation – confidence, wisdom, and obedience.

It must be emphasized, that it is pilot study, and results because of small sample should be treated with caution. However, it would be interesting to continue similar research but in larger sample, and in comparison with other occupational groups.

REFERENCES

Amos E.A., Weathington B.L. (2008). An analysis of the relation between employee-organization value congruence and employee attitudes. *The Journal of Psychology*, Vol. 142, No. 6, pp. 615–631.

Cameron K.S., Quinn R.E. (2003). *Kultura organizacyjna – diagnoza i zmiana. Model wartości konkurencyjnych*. Kraków: Oficyna Ekonomiczna.

Chatman J.A. and Jehn K.A. (1994). Assessing the relationship between industry characteristics and organizational culture: How different can you be? *Academy of Management Journal*, No. 37, pp. 522–553.

Deutsch M. (2006). Cooperation and competition. In: M. Deutsch, P.T. Coleman, E.C. Marcus (eds.). *The Handbook of Conflict Resolution: Theory and practise*. San Francisco: Jossey-Bass, pp. 23–42.

Giberson T.R., Resick Ch.J., Dickson M.W., Mitchelson J.K., Randall K.R., Clark M.A. (2009). Leadership and organizational culture: Linking CEO characteristics to culture values. *Journal of Bussiness Psychology*, No. 24, pp. 123–137.

Gilovich T., Keltner D., Nisbett R.E. (2006). *Social psychology*. W.W. Norton. p. 60.

Leiter M., Jackson N.J., Shaughnessy K. (2009). Contrasting burnout, turnover intention, control, value congruence and knowledge sharing between Baby Boomers and Generation X. *Journal of Nursing Management*, No. 17, pp. 100–109.

O'Reilly C.A., Chatman J.A. and Caldwell D.F. (1991). People and organizational culture: A profile comparison approach to assessing person-organization fit. *Academy of Management Journal*, No. 34, pp. 487–516.

Ros M., Schwartz S.H., Surkiss S. (1999). Basic individual values, work values, and the meaning of work. *Applied Psychology: An International Review*, Vol. 48, No. 1, pp. 49–71.

Sagiv L., Sverdlik N., Schwartz N. (2011). To compete or to cooperate? Values' impact on perception and action in social dilemma games. *European Journal of Social Psychology*, No. 41, pp. 64–77.

Schwartz S.H. (1992). Universals in the content and structure of values: Theory and empirical tests in 20 countries. In: M. Zanna (ed.). *Advances in Experimental Social Psychology*, Vol. 25. New York: Academic Press, pp. 1–65.

Schwartz S.H. (1999). A theory of culture values and some implications for work. *Applied Psychology: An International Review*, Vol. 48, No. 1, pp. 23–47.

Sheridan J.E. (1992). Organizational culture and employee retention. *Academy of Management Journal*, No. 35, pp. 1036–1056.

Vandenberghe Ch. (1999). Organizational culture, person-culture fit, and turnover: a replication in the health care industry. *Journal of Organizational Behavior*, No. 20, pp. 175–184.

Westerman J.W., Cyr L.A. (2004). An integrative analysis of person-organization fit theories. *International Journal of Selection and Assessment*, Vol. 12, No. 3, pp. 252–261.

ZOFIA ŁĄCAŁA
Jagiellonian University
Institute of Economics and Management
Chair of Social and Economical Analysis

THE GLASS CEILING PHENOMENON AS A BARRIER TO COMPETITIVENESS IN THE PROMOTION OF WOMEN IN THE UNIVERSITY ENVIRONMENT

INTRODUCTION

The main aim of the study presented here is an attempt to verify the problem of the competitiveness of women in the sphere of academic promotion (in the sense of acquiring ever higher academic titles and holding management positions within the university hierarchy). This topic is especially interesting because in the world literature there are few studies regarding his subject in the university environment. It is equally important to assess the scale of the glass ceiling phenomenon, and also to understand its individual and organizational conditions. This study will allow us both to introduce changes into the management of universities, and also to become aware of the need for a change in the attitudes of women towards a more effective form of competitiveness for academic promotion.

1. AN OVERVIEW OF THEORY AND RESEARCH

The concept of the glass ceiling appeared in print in the 1980s, and has been described as a nearly imperceptible transparent barrier which makes it impossible for women and minorities to rise to the highest levels in the management hierarchy [Hymowitz and Schellhardt 1986; Morrison, Von

Glinow 1990]. Other authors have called this phenomenon the "concrete wall" or the "sticky floor" [Bell and Nkomo 2001; Betters-Reed and Moore 1995], associating it with racism and sexism with regard to women and women of color. Nowadays, it is more common to speak of a labyrinth in order to characterize the "uneven path" of development and promotion which women encounter in organizations [Eagly and Carli 2007]. Sanchez-Hucles and Davis [2010, p. 172], have aptly described this process: "This trajectory involves diverse challenges, indirect forays, and ventures into foreign territory rather than following a straight line to the top."

The seriousness of this problem can be confirmed by the statement that even if women reach high positions in top management, the barriers continue to exist. In studies on a group of senior leaders [Haslam and Ryan 2008], it appears that women must continually prove their worth, especially in high risk environments, in order not to lose their positions. Female managers often feel isolated and unsupported by their mentors and coworkers in challenging situations, which Hewlett et al. [2008] have called the "glass cliff".

The problem of the glass ceiling was identified in statistics mainly concerning the percentage of women in higher management positions in corporations (State of Wisconsin, 1993), as well as generally in the USA [The U.S. Bureau of Labor Statistics 2007; Catalyst 2006].

The U.S. Department of Labor [1991, p. 1] defined the glass ceiling as "artificial barriers based on attitudinal or organizational bias that prevent qualified individuals from advancing within their organization and reaching their full potential".

A survey of the literature shows that the glass ceiling phenomenon can be analyzed with regard to three paradigms [Riger, Galligan 1980].

One theoretical approach supported by psychologists explains women's low professional status by citing individual differences. Traits, behavior, attitudes and upbringing are said to make women fearful of success and unwilling to take risks.

Research has been carried out aimed at verifying the appearance of differences among managers based on sex. This research has shown that men and women in management positions have more in common than they have visible differences in terms of personality, aptitudes, and motivation [Howard, Bray 1988]. In addition, they are characterized by similar aspirations and values, as well as behaviors and skills related to their professional lives [Eagly, Karau and Makhijani 1995; Morrison and Von Glinow 1990; Powell 1988; Noe 1988; Dipboye 1987; Dobbins and Platz 1986; Ritche and Moses 1983; Riger, Galligan 1980].

The second group favors an explanation of the phenomenon which is based on attitudes held by groups or individuals within the organization.

This school of thought proposes, among others, a bias which results from factors in the work environment, the so-called "contextual circumstances"

[Larwood et al. 1984, 1988a]. Discriminatory practices regarding the careers of women and ethnic minorities apply only when they are approved and condoned by relevant stakeholders.

Many authors explain the process of discrimination based on historically entrenched and still current negative stereotypes, according to which it is men who are predisposed to management roles [Powell 1988; Thomas and Alderfer 1989]. Differences in pay between men and women can be attributed to these stereotypes, and not to assessment of their effectiveness on the job.

The third approach is called structural discrimination, as it explains the phenomenon with reference to the balance of power or influence within specific groups within an organization.

The intergroup theory [Thomas and Alderfer 1989] differentiates two types of groups; identity groups, defined with reference for example to sex, age or race, and organization groups, defined with reference to the types of tasks carried out or positions held by members within the hierarchy of the organization. The status of the identity groups mirrors their relations with other groups in society at large.

It seems that an excellent illustration of the functioning of the intergroup theory is analysis of academic leaders [Turner 2002]. Women of color in management positions feel greater pressure to adapt and a lower tolerance for mistakes, they feel isolated and feel difficulty in convincing their cowork-ers of their reliability, and have limited influence and authority. In general, women of color are convinced that the academic world sees them through stereotypes. The situation for white women who identify with the dominant group is substantially different – they are among others supported in their rise to high level positions.

Economists, in turn, explain the phenomenon of discrimination by means of a dual labor market, in which jobs are divided into better and worse cat-egories, which are then addressed to different social groups. The groups associated with the second category of work, women and minorities, have limited employment opportunities and job mobility, and discrimination against them is justified with resort to economic effectiveness [Larwood and Gattiker 1987].

Based on psychological theories, structural barriers in discrimination against women result from the domination of men within the group which runs the organization. Men exaggerate gender differences in accordance with stereotypes regarding the lesser suitability of women to management roles, which in turn undoubtedly influences women's assessment of their own po-tential and chances for promotion [Riger and Galligan 1980; Kanter 1977]. An essential factor in breaking through these stereotypes is an increase in the proportion of women at different levels of management, and it has been estimated that if this proportion is more than 25%, the women are accepted as managers [Gardiner and Tiggemann 1999; Jamieson 1995; Kephart and Schumacher 2005; Van der Boon 2003].

In the context of research on the glass ceiling phenomenon, the role of the superior and his attitude towards the promotion of his subordinates regardless of their sex seems to be an important issue.

A vital role is played by the mentor, who assists individuals with their promotions in the organization, but also influences the personnel policy of the organization. The necessity and effectiveness of mentoring can be confirmed by research [Scandura 1991] which indicates that 72% of women in high management positions at executive level at one time had a mentor.

In analyzing the scale of the glass ceiling phenomenon, Morrison and Van Glinow [1990] pointed out the need to take organizational culture into account in order to assess the influence of structures and organizational systems in limiting job mobility within the hierarchy of authority as one of their important conclusions.

Cheung and Halpern [2010] have introduced the concept of a culture gender in their proposed model of leadership, referring to expectations with regard to women and men. The authors believe that an understanding of the careers of women requires an understanding of different cultural contexts, which are a supplement to the paradigms of individual traits, processes, and the influence of the environment.

In the context of comprehending the mechanism by which the glass ceiling phenomenon functions, one of the fundamental questions concerns the ability of women to reconcile the demands of two worlds, the professional world and that of the family. In other words, it must be determined whether having a family and children creates a significant barrier to promotion. In connection with this, studies of management careers focused on the fulfilment of the role of mother by women.

Numerous studies of the careers of female managers have proved that responsibility for the family, home, and other societal obligations, continue to represent an additional source of stress [Dipboye 1987; Morrison et al. 1987, Powell 1988].

In the USA, half of women holding top executive positions with an income of more than $100,000 annually do not have children [Dye 2005, Hewlett 2002].

The situation is similar for female academics [Mason and Goulden 2004] who have reached the highest ranks at universities. Only one third of them are mothers, and 12 years after completing their doctorate twice as many women as men remain single. The authors explain that in the academic environment there is a double standard regarding the sex of the employee. With men, having children is regarded as a sign of stability and responsibility that positively affects their work, whereas with women the perceived effect is the opposite.

Interpersonal competence significantly influences achievement in the workplace [Holland 1985] and promotion [Snyder 1987], as it is associated with self-monitoring (SM) which in turn conditions the appropriacy of social interactions. According to the definition given by Gangestead and Snyder [2000, p. 390] "At the core of the SM construct are individual differences in the propensity for impression management involving the construction of positive social appearances."

Day et al. [2002] have carried out a meta-analysis on the results of 136 studies carried out with the participation of 23 191 individuals on self-monitoring of personality in an organizational context. The results achieved by men in the area of SM can to a certain extent explain the disproportion in their numbers at top level positions within organizations, which partly explains the glass ceiling phenomenon [Glass Ceiling Commission 1995]. It appears that men, in comparison to women, show better understanding of important organizational aspects concerning, among other things, leadership and the attitudes and behaviors associated with it. Although self-monitoring is not the only cause of professional success, it becomes apparent from the studies that a high level of SM has a direct impact on assessment of work and the way that leadership qualities are seen at all levels of the organization. The results indicate that the holding a high position within the organization goes hand in hand with a high level of SM.

Eagly and Carli [2007] believe that women's promotion is dependent on their creation of social capital, which requires blending of assertive behaviors with friendliness and helpfulness, the maintenance of positive relations with coworkers, cooperation with men and support on the part of the mentor.

2. RESULTS OF THE STUDIES – A POLISH CASE STUDY

RESEARCH PROBLEM AND HYPOTHESES

In studying the phenomenon of the glass ceiling at universities two areas must be considered. The first concerns academic promotion and the acquisition of subsequent ranks, and the second concerns the holding of management positions at various levels of the organizational structure of the university.

For this reason two main research hypotheses have been formulated:

Hypothesis 1: Women at universities are discriminated against in academic promotion.

Hypothesis 2: Women at universities are discriminated against in their management careers within the university hierarchy.

The aim if the research was first of all to assess whether the practice of discrimination against women takes place at Polish universities, and secondly the sex of the respondents was taken into to account to compare the opinions of men and women on that topic.

The respondents were separated into two groups due to the probability that their experiences and perception of many aspects of the workplace, including the glass ceiling problem, are different [Gutek, Searle, Klepa 1991; Heilman 1995; Larwood and Gattiker 1987; Morrison 1992; Powell and Mainiero 1992]. This can be confirmed by studies and theories regarding the functioning of stereotypes on the differing attributes of women and men [Heilman 1983; Ruble, Cohen, Ruble 1984].

RESEARCH SAMPLE

Two hundred academic employees, including 100 women and 100 men, from five Cracovian universities, the Jagiellonian University, the Cracow University of Economics, the Agricultural University of Cracow, the Academy of Mining and Metallurgy, and the Cracow University of Technology, took part in the study.

The biographical data collected was intentionally incomplete, especially that which in the opinion of the respondents would allow them to be identified or compromise their anonymity.

The age of the respondents figured within a range of 30 to 65 years old, with the largest groups representing the range from 32 to 42 (35% of the respondents) and from 49 to 60 (42% of the respondents).

The majority of those studied had a doctoral degree (65%), and the remainder (35%) were tenured. From this incomplete data it can be seen that the majority (62%) were adjuncts, the next largest group were lecturers (12%) and persons holding the title of professor (19%). The marital status of the respondents indicates that 57% of the men were married, while only 31% of the women were.

Only 23% of the respondents declared the management duties that they carried out, including 15% who occupy positions such as dean, associate dean, director of the institute, vice-director of the institute, director of the faculty, and director of the department.

Although from this description the research sample may seem to be random, from the point of view of our research the range of ages and academic titles are highly representative regarding acquired experience in academic promotion practices.

MEASURE

The questionnaire used in the study consisted of two parts and included 35 questions. The first part concerned academic promotion, and the second contained items related to promotion in university management. In addition, the respondents had the possibility to add their own commentary to each question.

In the first part of the questionnaire there were 16 items:
- the content of two of them was generally speaking "discriminatory practices against women at universities" and "equal treatment of men and women;"
- a further six items concerned specific aspects of university work, such as "the need to continually prove one's worth and demonstrate ability in academic work in order to be promoted among women," "respect for women's opinions", "the influence of sex on access to financing for research", "the type and complexity of academic assignments", "variety in assessment of academic activity and level of pay dependent on sex;"
- one question concerned the topic "the percentage of women in progressively higher academic ranks;"
- two questions on the issue of whether "having a family creates difficulties in progressing in an academic career" and "delay of acquiring subsequent academic titles caused by starting a family;"
- four questions on the topic of determinant factors in development and academic promotion, such as "the influence of intelligence and creativity," "the level and value of academic work," "the influence of desire for achievement and ambition," and "the influence of random factors;"
- two questions concerned the relationship between "relations with important individuals in the university hierarchy" and "the role of the superior in professional development."

The second part of the questionnaire included 19 items covering the following areas:
- two questions concerned the general assessment of the competence of the management at the university;
- the content of the next seven questions concerned academic promotion practices at the university, such as "equal opportunity for women in occupying management roles at the university at all levels of orga-

nization," "the percentage of women in progressively higher ranking management positions at the university," "uniform predispositions for carrying out management roles," "decisiveness of women in self-promotion regarding their ability to fill management roles," "interest in this type of career among academic workers at the university with respect to sex." Preferences regarding the sex of the superior," "level of care given to academic development and promotion with respect to sex."

– ten further questions concerned the reasons for lesser representation of women among university authorities, such as "men usually promote men," "lack of support from the superior," "lesser flexibility of women", "promotion fixing," "the conviction that women do not make good managers," "bias against women," "women's distaste for these types of positions," "women's fear of taking on such roles," "the lack of management traits among women," and "stereotypical assignment of management roles to men."

In the questionnaire a five-point answer scale was used, in which specific points were related to the content of the questions, in order to capture the variety of experience regarding different aspects and practices of academic promotion of women at universities.

PRESENTATION OF THE RESULTS OF THE RESEARCH

The first part of the analysis concerns the verification of the hypothesis that women at universities are discriminated against in the area of academic promotion. The sex of the respondents has been taken into account in the presentation of their opinions.

Male respondents express a more decisive opinion on the topic of the lack of sex bias in academic promotion at universities, with 66% of them answering that this practice "doesn't often take place," and 16.2% answering "never takes place." In the case of women, almost a half of the respondents (46.9%) feel that such practices do not often take place, but 12.2% responded that such situations "often take place" and 34.7% that such situations "take place sporadically." The difference in answers among men and women are confirmed by the results of a significance test ($\chi^2 = 22.07$; $p = 0.001$).

Among those respondents who observed the phenomenon of discrimination at the university, the majority of women feel that such practices affect them directly (76%), whereas men feel that the problem affects both men and women equally.

In the case of the next question concerning the equal treatment of men and women in their professional lives at universities, there is a noticeable difference in the answers received based on sex (χ^2 = 12.82; p = 0.002). The answer that the "decision to follow an academic career by a woman is treated with equal seriousness as that decision made by a man" was given by 64% of the men but only 32% of the women. As many as 22% of the female respondents feel that their aspirations and plans are treated rather sceptically due to traditional gender roles assigned to them. The influence of the individual's situation on the answer given can be seen in the frequency of answers such as "sometimes" (46% of women and 32% of men). One of the arguments used was "the influence of the immediate supervisor."

Several specific aspects of the equal treatment of men and women at universities were verified, such as the necessity of proving one's worth and demonstrating one's possibilities in academic and professional work in order to achieve academic promotion, and respect for women's opinions, the influence of sex on access to funding for research projects, the type and complexity of assigned tasks, differences in assessment of academic and research work, and pay levels dependent on sex.

Regarding the greater necessity for women to prove their own worth, opinions of the respondents were significantly different dependent on sex (χ^2 = 35.65; p = 0.001). In the opinion of men (range of answers from "rather not" 52%, and "definitely not" 40%), there is no such pattern that women must continually prove themselves in order to be promoted academically. Women have a very different opinion, as 56% of them feel that their academic career is dependent on how far they are able to prove their usefulness in academic and research work.

Similar patterns are observed in questions concerning the remaining areas of activity at the university (χ^2 = 30.97; p = 0.001), in which as many as 62.5% of women feel that in order to be promoted academically they must work harder than men and prove their professional worth. The opposite opinion is held by 85.3% of the men surveyed.

Half of the women surveyed feel that they rather do have the possibility of stating their own views and winning respect for their opinions. There is a noticeable group, however, that feel differently (30%). In turn, men do not see this problem, as many as 81.6 % feel that women are taken into account and respected by the general scientific community. Tests of significance confirmed the dependence of the answers given on the sex of the respondent (χ^2 = 21.22; p = 0.001).

In the next area surveyed as many as 84% of the total number of respondents feel that everyone has equal access to funding for their own research. A breakdown by sex reveals that 96% of men and 72% of women feel this way. However, the comments provided by those who answered thus in the survey complement the sense of the question, stating for example "the fact that everyone has equal access to funding does not mean that everyone receives it, because other factors are decisive," or "everyone has equal access to funding apart from the group of academic workers excluded by the university authorities." The mechanism for awarding funding is illustrated by the opinion of 20% of the women, who feel that men have easier access to funding if only because of "friendly relations with management." It is women who underscore the influence of the university authorities and the superior on the sharing of financial resources.

Our research on the equality of women and men also included assessment of the relationship between sex and the type of academic tasks assigned at universities. Significance tests do not indicate a sex-determined difference in answers (χ^2 = 5.84; p = 0.12) between male and female respondents, as most of the respondents feel that sex plays no significant role in the assignment of tasks. There is, however, a certain number of respondents (24% of the women and 14% of the men) who answered "I don't know."

In the context of the complexity of tasks carried out by both male and female academic workers in similar positions, there seems to be a justification for searching for an answer to the question about the relationship between sex and pay. It appears that as many as 78% of the men surveyed and only 36% of the women feel that pay is the same for the same work at the same level. In the opinion of a part of the group studied, men are "much better paid" (16% of the women and 6% of the men) and "slightly better paid" (20% of the women and 6% of the men). In turn 28% of the women and 10% of the men answered "I don't know" to this question. Significance tests confirm the dependence of the assessment of pay levels and sex in equivalent positions (χ^2 = 20.60; p = 0.001). Summing up, about one third of the women feel that men are better paid compared to women carrying out the same work.

One more very important area of study is the question of the assessment of academic and research work. Although the majority of academic workers feel that sex does not have an influence on assessment, there is a clear qualitative difference in the firmness of the opinions formulated. In contrast to women, among men the conviction dominates that assessment "definitely does not depend" on the sex of the worker (43% of men and 22% of women) and "rather doesn't depend" on the sex of the worker (39% of men and 54% of women). It must be remembered though that in the opinion of 20% of the women sex has an influence on assessment. An insignificant number of respondents answered "I don't know." Variation in the answers given by men and women was confirmed by a significance test (χ^2 = 26.31; p = 0.001).

In the context of the analysis carried out, one very important question concerns the percentage of women at progressively higher academic ranks, including at the professorial level. In the opinion of 58% of the women surveyed and 38% of the men, there is a difference based on sex. However, 26% of the total of respondents (18% of the women and 34% of the men) "does not see such a pattern at their university." About a quarter of the respondents of both sexes stated that they do not know what the figures are at their university regarding this issue.

In light of the results of the study, an assessment of the influence of the non-work sphere on academic promotion is important. The issue of the influence of having a family on success in an academic career is often raised in the literature, especially in regard to women.

Among the academic workers surveyed, 54% of the women and 42% of the men feel that having a family "to a certain extent creates difficulties in achieving success in an academic career." Only about a quarter of the women as well as men feel that it is possible to "reconcile family and professional responsibilities." There is also a group of women (14%) and men (6%) who feel that having a family seriously interferes with the realization of an academic career, and that the professional sphere should take priority and the family life should be in second place. Summing up, the majority of women (68%) express the opinion that having a family creates a barrier in pursuing an academic career. Men also (48%) recognize this problem. The discrepancy observed in opinions expressed based on sex (χ^2 = 12.05; p = 0.034) can be explained by the fact that having a family is a direct burden on women due to natural and also cultural divisions of roles in the family. Male academics also recognize the problem that having a family means an additional burden for them.

The pattern noted has been additionally confirmed with respect to the answers to the question regarding "postponement of an academic title, including the title of professor, due to the establishment of a family." That this is mainly a problem for women can be seen from the percentage of positive answers (38%) in comparison with 74% of men, for whom establishing a family did not interfere with the achievement of higher academic titles.

It seems to be a justified conclusion that the advancement to higher ranks of academic titles is related to creativity and intellectual traits as well as the value of academic and research work, as objective indicators of a professional career. In the opinion of 58.6% of the respondents, higher academic titles are gained only by those who are creative and intelligent, although only 10.1% of those surveyed state this categorically, while the remainder feel that "intelligence and creativity facilitate academic promotion, but do not guarantee it." A considerable number of women (38%) and far fewer men (26.5%) feel that "academic promotion often does not go hand in hand with intellectual traits." It needs to be further noted that 14.3% of men claim that "the acquisition of further academic ranks and the title of professor do not depend on intelligence and creativity."

Academic promotion is associated with a high level and value of research by 50.5% of the total of respondents (including 62% of women and 79.1% of men). The influence of non-substantive factors in academic promotion at universities can be felt in the number of respondents, 24% of women and 18.4% of men, who answered that they "rather don't" or "definitely don't" see a connection between the value of a person's academic work and academic promotion. In addition, 11.1% of those surveyed (14.2% of women and 8.2% of men) claim that academic promotion depends on "acquaintances and arrangements", and on other factors "not necessarily related to a high level of knowledge and value of research."

In the case of both questions, regarding the relationship of academic promotion to intellectual traits ($\chi^2 = 5.82$; $p = 0.12$) and with academic achievement ($\chi^2 = 4.73$; $p = 0.316$), a considerable overlap in the manner of answering the questions can be seen among workers of both sexes.

In the undertaken study the influence of motivation and career ambition was also assessed. The manner of answering the question was related to the sex of the respondent ($\chi^2 = 4.31$; $p = 0.05$). According to the majority of women (62%), high levels of ambition do not positively influence academic career development, whereas 58% of men feel that it does.

Differences in the perception of determining factors in an academic career also appeared in the case of assessment of the influence of random factors such as luck, to which as many as 36% of the women attribute a significant meaning, in contrast with 80% of the men who do not believe in an accidental course of events ($\chi^2 = 3.17$; $p = 0.075$).

Analyzing the conditions for academic career development, we have taken into account "connections with the right people" and the support of the superior. In as much as the first factor might hold negative connotations, the role of the superior in promoting subordinates is rather positive.

The results of the study show that although the majority of respondents (58%) feel that relations with important people in the university hierarchy do not have an influence on one's career, it must be added that as many as 46% of the women and 38% of the men have the opposite opinion. Undoubtedly, the academic promotion mechanism in each institution should be transparent, and based on the highest standards of objective criteria.

In the case of the role of the superior in career development, as many as 63% of the respondents (including 68% of the women and 58% of the men) are convinced of the vital importance of the support of the superior in academic promotion.

The second part of the analysis concerns the verification of the hypothesis that women at universities are discriminated against in holding of management positions within the university hierarchy. A comparison of opinions was carried out with respect to the sexes of the respondents.

In the real university environment, there is the possibility of promotion in the sense of holding higher positions and carrying out management functions. Depending on norms and organizational culture, holding of management positions is often associated with academic promotion, that is, the holding of the title of professor with *habilitation* and the status of independent researcher. Combing these two criteria may result not from the additive character of an individual's predisposition, but rather from the rules of functioning of a hierarchical organization and respect for decision made by those holding the title of professor. It is well-known of course, basing on the theory of J. Holland [1985], that typically managerial predispositions and scientific ability do not necessarily go hand in hand, and in fact are opposites in the hexagonal model of the typology of professional personality types.

For this reason, the study of the phenomenon of discrimination against women in the holding of management positions at universities was preceded by the assessment of the opinion of employees on the topic of the competence and readiness to manage in individuals carrying out management duties. It appears that in the opinion of the majority of respondents (75.8%), including 80% of the women and 74.1% of the men, individuals carrying out management roles at their universities are insufficiently prepared to manage. Also, in the opinion of the majority of respondents (61.1% of the total, including 56% of the women and 76.3% of the men) individuals carrying out management roles "are not more scientists than managers," which may mean that to a certain extent they stand out in the typical academic environment due to their display of managerial traits. However, in this context, as a complement to the developing picture of the "scientist-manager," 34% of the women and 42.9% of the men feel that individuals in management positions at universities "have many shortcomings as managers."

In order to verify our hypothesis, the participants in the study were asked to answer the question "Do women have equal chances in working in management roles at universities at higher level positions?" the answers given were dependent of the sex of the respondent ($\chi^2 = 27.53$; $p = 0.001$). The majority of men (65.3%) feel that women have the same chances as men, whereas 46% of the women had the opposite opinion. Moreover, similar groups of respondents (12% of the women and 14.3% of the men) chose to answer that women have equal chances in relation to "only certain management functions," with the exception of rector (in the men's answers).

The assessment of equal chances of men and women in academic promotion was complemented by the results of the answers to the question regarding the percentage of women at higher levels and ranks of management functions in the university hierarchy. Significance tests confirmed that the answers given were dependent on the sex of the respondent ($\chi^2 = 18.22$; $p = 0.001$). The majority of women (78%) feel that in the case of higher management positions there are significantly fewer women, and this opinion was shared by a significant number of men (40%). Only 6% of the women and 38% of the men saw no such pattern at their university.

As in the world literature on gender-dependent managerial predispositions, it seemed interesting to assess the opinion on this subject in very specific academic environment (assessment of the managerial staff has been described earlier).

The majority of women (60%) and 44% of the men feel that both women and men have the same managerial predispositions. It must be noted though, that 26% of the women and 38% of the men feel that men are better suited to management roles. Significance tests indicate a fairly similar manner of answering the question among men and women (χ^2 = 7.70; p = 0.103).

In this study women attributed the following traits to female managers; hard-working, organizational ability, meticulousness and precision, integrity, reliability, and emotionality. Men on the other hand see female managers as hard-working, meticulous and precise, and particularly emphasize their ambition, which may be a decisive factor in the women's decision to pursue such a career.

In the case of male managers, both groups named the same traits most frequently; decisiveness, organizational ability, ambition, and confidence. Moreover, women added competence and availability, as well as the negative trait of lack of self-criticism.

As getting a managerial position in the university hierarchy requires self-promotion in the university environment, the subsequent questions aimed to assess this sort of behavior with respect to sex. In the opinion of 68% of the female respondents and 40% of the male respondents, women display less decisiveness than men in self-promotion regarding their suitability for management positions. On the other hand, 34% of the men and 20% of the women expressed the opinion that this is rather not the case, and 7% of the respondents of both sexes that this is definitely not the case. In summary, it can be said that lack of active pursuing a management career and passivity in self-promotion may be one of the important causes of the disproportion among men and women with regard to promotion in ranks of the university.

One important issue is the assessment of the level of interest in this type of career among university workers with regard to sex. Significance tests show that there are similar preferences among men and women (χ^2 = 1.16; p = 0.884). The comments of those studied suggest that, if they were to receive such an offer, 40% of the women and 36% of the men would agree to take on a management position, and listed such positions as dean, director of the institute, department head, team leader, and even rector. In each group compared there is a subgroup of 34% undecided (who answered "I don't know"). A career of this would not be interesting for 28% of the respondents (who answered "rather not" or "no"). This group listed as reasons for this attitude the lack of managerial predisposition, lack of this type of ambition, dedication to a strictly scientific career, and also family duties (mentioned by the women). Summing up, it can be said that the majority of those studied are equally interested in promotion and a career within the management structure of the university.

The comments of the respondents regarding their preferences for the sex of their superior also seem significant. It appears that for the majority of both women (60%) and men (54%), the sex of the person carrying out a management role is irrelevant . It must be noted though, that as many as 32% of women and 38% of men would prefer a male superior. Significance tests confirmed the similar type of answers from men and women ($\chi^2 = 3.08$; $p = 0.379$).

The opinion of the respondents on the amount of care given to academic development and promotion depending on the sex of the superior was also assessed. The majority of the women (63.8%) feel that women in management positions show greater care for the professional development of all their subordinates. A significant group of men (33.3%) and only 14.9% of the women are convinced that "they focus most of their attention on their own professional career." A substantial part of those surveyed (22.8%) had no opinion about this, or indicated that it depended on the individual leader. Significant discrepancies in the answers given were confirmed by tests of significance ($\chi^2 = 17.44$; $p = 0.002$).

In order to explain the lower number of women in university leadership, the following causes were examined:
- Men usually promote men ($\chi^2 = 2.67$; $p = 0.102$);
- Lack of support form the superior ($\chi^2 = 8.30$; $p = 0.004$);
- Lesser availability of women ($\chi^2 = 0.16$; $p = 0.689$);
- Phenomenon of "fixed" promotions ($\chi^2 = 5.26$; $p = 0.022$);
- Conviction that women are not suitable for such positions ($\chi^2 = 0.23$; $p = 0.629$);
- Gender bias ($\chi^2 = 8.30$; $p = 0.004$);
- Unwillingness of women to take such positions ($\chi^2 = 2.76$; $p = 0.096$);
- Fear of women to take such positions ($\chi^2 = 0.832$; $p = 0.362$);
- Lack of managerial traits among women ($\chi^2 = 1.08$; $p = 0.298$);
- Stereotypical assignment of roles to men ($\chi^2 = 5.65$; $p = 0.017$).

An analysis of those aspects in which there was a significant discrepancy between he assessments of respondents of different sexes indicates that women to a greater degree are convinced that the phenomenon of their lesser representation amongst university authorities is influenced by a lack of support from the superior (24% of the women and 4% of the men), by the unofficial system of "fixing" promotions (28% of the women and 10%

of the men), by gender bias (24% of the women and 4% of the men), and by stereotypes concerning the assignment of managerial predispositions and roles to men.

Men, on the other hand, differ from the women in their assessment of the unwillingness of women to take management positions in the university hierarchy (30% of the men and 16% of the women).

Respondents of both sexes agree regarding causes such as the lesser availability of women (46% of women and 50% of men), the conviction that women are not suitable for such positions (24% of women and 20% of men), the fear of women to take this type of position (30% of women and 22% of men), and the lack of typical managerial traits among women (14% of women and 22% of men).

Among other causes for the lesser representation of women in university management positions, the following were mentioned; the lesser percentage of women among independent researchers (with habilitation), greater interest in family life than in the university and promotion to higher positions (the opinion of both men and women), the unwillingness of women themselves to take such positions (the opinion of men).

DISCUSSION OF THE RESULTS

This research was carried out first and foremost to assess whether academic workers see a problem of discrimination and barriers to advancement for women at universities.

In organizations, the problem of the glass ceiling is often marginalized or completely unnoticed despite the results of research which clearly confirms the existence of this phenomenon [Crosby, Clayton, Alksnis, Hemker 1986; Twiss Tabb, Crosby 1989]. In this context, it explains the fact that the women studied, in contrast to the men, see the problem of discrimination regarding promotion and acquisition of further academic titles, as well as their unequal treatment in basic areas of work at the university. This is probably caused by two factors, firstly that men do not experience the phenomenon to a great extent, and secondly that the barriers themselves are difficult to detect because of their informal character. In the work environment, there are formal and informal interactions in which sex may be one of the significant determinants conditioning perception and expectations of employees both with regard to the leadership as well as with regard to the process of their individual and social identity [Lord and Brown 2004; Lord, Brown and Freiberg 1999].

In our studies, the results suggest that in the academic environment there is skepticism regarding the plans and aspirations of women due to traditionally assigned roles. Because of this clear "role conflict," women experience postponement of successive achievements in academic promotion. This is confirmed by the pattern that the responsibility of women for the family comprises an additional and significant burden which influences career achievement [Dipboye 1987; Morrison et al. 1987, Powell 1988]. The study shows that women more often interrupt their careers due to burdens associated with the family [Gallese 1985; Lyness and Thompson 1997; Parasuraman and Greenhaus 1993; Powell and Mainiero 1992; Strober 1982].

The necessity for women to constantly prove their being worthy and demonstrate their skills in the workplace and in the academic realm in order to be promoted is caused by the necessity to break stereotypes [Mason and Goulden 2004] and face the challenge of the double standard which applies to women and men [Foschi 1992, 1996, 2000; Lyness and Heilman 2006]. According to Foschi's theory, women who want to advance academically must considerably exceed the standards set for men, especially in roles identified as typically male. In the opinion of the women studied, the multifaceted support of the superior is exceptionally important, both as a mentor and as an intermediary allowing women access to funding for their independent research. It is women, in fact, who highlight the role of the university authorities and the superior in the distribution of funding.

The observations and feelings of the women studied regarding assessment of their own academic research activity finds justification in studies carried out by Sackett, DuBois, and Noe [1991]. It turned out in that study that if women comprised less than 20% of the workforce, they were assessed worse than men according to different measures of work performance. Sex-based differences in levels of pay can also be explained by the same mechanism.

In the opinion of the respondents, that is the majority of the women and a large number of men, the percentage of women at higher levels of academic rank, including professors, lessens steadily. The assessment of such determinants of academic promotion as academic achievement and individual predisposition (intelligence and creativity specifically), which do not always play the deciding role in acquisition of academic titles, could suggest the influence of contextual factors. From certain statements made by the respondents, we get a picture of outright favoritism of men. Stereotypes regarding women and the barriers described earlier, as well as the arrangement of power between specific groups (for example, the domination of men among university authorities) according to intergroup theory, explain the mechanism of promotion within the academic environment studied.

Promotion at the university also concerns the exercise of power and holding of management positions in the university hierarchy, and so in this study an attempt was made to verify the equal chances of women with regard to men in this area.

The study shows that the majority of men feel that women have the same chances as men for gaining management positions at the university. The problem of discrimination is recognized by the greater part of the women who observe the drastically decreasing numbers of women at higher management levels. Moreover, opinions were given by the whole of the study group suggesting that women have equal chances as men with regard only to "certain management functions" with the exception of rector (the men's comments). This result can be confirmed by a review of the literature, which shows that women most often occupy the lowest rungs of the management hierarchy and are underrepresented at executive levels. Studies have also shown that women are suitable candidates for high-level management positions in the organizational hierarchy [Catalyst 2005; Richardson and Loubier 2008].

The juxtaposition of opinions regarding the representation of women at executive levels in the organization with an assessment of the predispositions seems to be significant. The majority of women studied and a significant group of men feel that both women and men have identical predispositions for management duties. This assessment is in accord with the results of numerous studies which have proved the absence of essential individual differences between men and women in management positions and their similar predispositions in this sphere [Eagly, Karau and Makhijani 1995; Morrison and Von Glinow 1990; Powell 1988; Noe 1988; Dipboye 1987; Dobbins and Platz 1986; Ritche and Moses 1983; Riger, Galligan 1980]. It must be noted though, that about one third of the respondents feel men to be better managers. Such preferences may be explained by the influence of stereotypes, but also by management style and individual traits. Jacobs and McClelland [1994] underscore the differences in the type of power exercised by men and women, though in studies the superiority of one or the other group was not demonstrated [Eagly 2007; Eagly and Carli 2007; Richardson and Loubier 2008].

Women have a tendency to use resourceful power, which involves inspiring, helping, and supporting others. Men are said to use reactive power, involving assertive and aggressive behaviors addressed to other individuals and groups exhibiting power. In these studies, the feminine style of management has a highly administrative character, but also shows care for the professional development of subordinates.

The lower numbers of women at top management levels at universities can be explained not only by barriers such as the glass ceiling, but also by a too infrequent recourse on the part of women to strategies aimed at demonstrating their own capabilities and talents, in contrast to those individuals who occupy high-level management positions [Wickwire and Kruper 1996]. This failure to pursue management positions and passivity with regard to the self-promotion of their predispositions and competences may be one of the significant causes of the disproportion in promotion at universities. As the studies show, the successful realization of such a career demands self-monitoring and an understanding of the importance of self-promotion.

The men studied not only speak of the lack of self-promotion, but also of an outright unwillingness of women to win management positions within the university hierarchy. On the other hand, women are more convinced than men that their lesser representation within the university leadership is influenced by the lack of support from their superiors, by the informal system of fixing promotions, and by a gender bias and stereotypes which assign managerial predispositions and roles to men.

Respondents of both sexes (about half of the total) agrees that the lesser availability of women is a barrier to promotion. About one quarter of those surveyed expressed the conviction that women are not suitable for management positions and do not possess typically managerial traits, and moreover fear promotion to this type of position.

CONCLUSIONS

The most important conclusions of this study are:

- The academic environment is not free of the influence of bias, stereotypes, and barriers characteristic of the glass ceiling as described in the literature.
- Perception of this phenomenon depends on the sex of the workers, and men hardly see the problem at all.
- Awareness of the conditions for professional development and promotion, both on an individual level and within the organization, demands knowledge and cognizance of the patterns illustrated by studies carried out in this area.
- The potential of women enables them to be promoted but demands the use of additional strategies of self-promotion and acquisition of social capital.
- The conflict of roles associated with women's responsibility for the family demands a search for solutions, as it is still a significant barrier to promotion for women.

ACKNOWLEDGMENTS

The authors would like to thank Anna Flaga for the use of parts of research she carried out as part of her master's thesis, written under the guidance of Dr Zofia Łącała.

REFERENCES

Bell E., Nkomo S. (2001). *Our Separate Ways: Black and White Women and the Struggles for Professional Identity*. Boston, MA: Harvard Business School Press.

Betters-Reed B.L., Moore L.L. (1995). Shifting the management development paradigm for women. *Journal of Management Development*, No. 14, pp. 2–24.

Catalyst (2005). *Women "take care," men "take charge": Stereotyping of U.S. business leaders exposed*. Retrieved from http://www.catalyst.org/ publication/94/women-take-care-men-take-charge-stereotyping-of-usbusiness-leaders-exposed

Catalyst (2006). *Connections that count: The informal networks of women of color in the United States*. Retrieved from http://www.catalyst.org/publication/52/connections-that-count-the-informalnetworks-of-women-of-color-in-the-united-states

Cheung F.M., Halpern D.F. (2010). Women at the Top. Powerful Leaders Define Success as Work + Family in a Culture of Gender. *American Psychologist*, April, pp. 182–193.

Crosby E., Clayton S., Alksnis O., Hemker K. (1986). Cognitive biases in the perception of discrimination: The importance of format. *Sex Roles*, No. 14, pp. 637–646.

Day D.V., Schleicher D.J., Unckless A.L., Hiller N.J. (2002). Research Reports. Self-Monitoring Personality at Work: A Meta-Analytic Investigation of Construct Validity. *Journal of Applied Psychology*, Vol. 87, No. 2, pp. 390–401.

Dipboye R.L. (1987). Problem and progress of women in management. In: K.S. Koziara, M.H. Moscow and L.D. Tanner (eds.). *Working Women: Past, Present, Future*. Washington, DC: BNA Books, pp. 118–153.

Dobbins G.H., Platz S.J. (1986). Sex differences in leadership: How real are they? *Academy of Management Review*, No. 11, pp. 118–127.

Dye J.L. (2005). *Fertility of American women: June 2004* (Current Population Reports, P20-555). Retrieved from U.S. Census Bureau website http://www.census.gov/prod/2005pubs/p20-555.pdf

Eagly A.H., Karau S.I., Makhijani M.G. (1995). Gender and the effectiveness of leaders: A meta-analysis. *Psychological Bulletin*, No. 117, pp. 125–145.

Eagly A.H., Carli L.L. (2007). *Through the Labyrinth: The Truth about How Women Become Leaders*. Boston, MA: Harvard Business School Press.

Eagly A.H. (2007). Female leadership advantage and disadvantage: Resolving the contradictions. *Psychology of Women Quarterly*, No. 31, pp. 1–12. http://www3.interscience.wiley.com/doiinfo.html

Foschi M. (1992). Gender and double standards for competence. In: C.L. Ridgeway (ed.). *Gender, Interaction, and Inequality*. New York: Springer-Verlag, pp. 181–207.

Foschi M. (1996). Double standards in the evaluation of men and women. *Social Psychology Quarterly*, No. 59, pp. 237–254.

Foschi M. (2000). Double standards for competence: Theory and research. *Annual Review of Sociology*, No. 26, pp. 21–42.

Gallese L. (1985). *Women Like Us.* New York: Signet.

Gangestad S.W., Snyder M. (2000). Self-monitoring: Appraisal and reappraisal. *Psychological Bulletin*, No. 126, pp. 530–555.

Gardiner M., Tiggemann M. (1999). Gender differences in leadership style, job stress and-mental health in male- and female-dominated industries. *Journal of Occupational and Organizational Psychology*, No. 72, pp. 301–315.

Glass Ceiling Commission (1995). *Good for Business: Making Full Use of the Nation's Human Capital.* Washington, DC: Author.

Gutek B.A., Searle S., Klepa L. (1991). Rational versus gender role explanations for work-family conflict. *Journal of Applied Psychology*, No. 76, pp. 560–568.

Haslam S.A., Ryan M. (2008). The road to the glass cliff: Differences in the perceived suit-ability of men and women for leadership positions in succeeding and failing organiza-tions. *Leadership Quarterly*, No. 19, pp. 530–546.

Heilman M.E. (1983). Sex bias in work settings: The lack of fit model. In: B.M. Staw, L.I. Cummings (eds.). *Research in Organizational Behavior.* Greenwich, T: JAI Press, Vol. 5, pp. 269–298.

Heilman M.E. (1995). Sex stereotypes and their effects in the workplace: What we know and what we don't know. *Journal of Social Behavior and Personality*, No. 10, pp. 3–26.

Hewlett S.A., Luce C.B., Servon L.J., Sherbin L., Shiller P., Sosnovich E., Sumberg K. (2008). *The Athena Factor: Reversing the Brain Drain in Science, Egineering, and Technology.* Boston, MA: Harvard Business Press.

Hewlett S.A. (2002). Executive women and the myth of having it all. *Harvard Business Review*, No. 80, pp. 66–73.

Holland J.L. (1985). *Making Vocational Choices: A Theory of Careers.* Englewood Cliffs, NJ: Prentice Hall.

Howard A., Bray D.W. (1988). *Managerial Lives in Transition.* New York: Guilford.

Hymowitz C., Schellhardt T.C. (1986). The glass ceiling: Why women can't seem to break the invisible barrier that blocks them from the top jobs. *Wall Street Journal*, 24th March, pp. 1, 4.

Jacobs R.L., McClelland D.C. (1994). Moving up the corporate ladder: A longitudinal study of the leadership motive pattern and managerial success in women and men. *Consulting Psychology Journal*, No. 46, pp. 32–41.

Jamieson K.H. (1995). *Beyond the Double Bind: Women and Leadership.* New York, NY: Oxford University Press.

Kanter R. (1977). *Men and Women of the Corporation.* New York: Basic Books.

Kephart P., Schumacher L. (2005). Has the glass ceiling cracked? An exploration of women entrepreneurship. *Journal of Leadership & Organizational Studies*, No. 4, pp. 12–18.

Larwood L., Gutek B., Gattiker U.E. (1984). Perspectives on institutional discrimination an resistance to change. *Group an Organization Studies*, No. 9, pp. 333–352.

Larwood L., Gattiker U.E. (1987). A comparison of the career path used by successful women and men. In: B.A. Gutek, L. Larwood (eds.). *Women's Career Development.* Newbury Park, CA: Sage, pp. 129–136.

Larwood L., Szwajkowski E., Rose S. (1988a). Sex and race discrimination resulting from manager-client relationship. Applying the rational bias theory of managerial discrimination. *Sex Roles*, No. 18, pp. 9–29.

Larwood L., Szwajkowski E., Rose S. (1988b). When discrimination makes "sense" – The rational bias theory discrimination. In: B.A. Gutek, A.H. Stromberg, L. Larwood (eds.). *Women and Work.* Beverly Hills, CA: Sage.

Lord R.G., Brown D.J. (2004). *Leadership Processes and Follower Identity*. Mahwah, NJ: Erlbaum.

Lord R.G., Brown D.J., Freiberg S.J. (1999). Understanding the dynamics of leadership: The role of follower self-concepts in the leader/follower relationship. *Organizational Behavior and Human Decision Processes*, No. 78, pp. 167–203.

Lyness K.S., Thompson D.E. (1997). Above the Glass Ceiling? A Comparison of Matched Samples of Female and Male Executives. *Journal of Applied Psychology*, Vol. 82, No. 3, pp. 359–375.

Lyness K.S., Heilman M.E. (2006).When Fit Is Fundamental: Performance Evaluations and Promotions of Upper-Level Female and Male Managers. *Journal of Applied Psychology*, Vol. 91, No. 4, pp. 777–785.

Mason M.A., Goulden M. (2004). Do babies matter (Part II)?: Closing the baby gap. *Academe*, Vol. 90, No. 6, pp. 10–15. Retrieved from http://ucfamilyedge.berkeley.edu/babies%20matterII.pdf

Morrison A.M., White R.P., Van Velsor E. and the Center for Creative Leadership (1987). *Breaking the Glass Ceiling: Can Women Reach the Top of America's Largest Corporation?* Reading, MA: Addison Wesley.

Morrison A.M., Von Glinow M.A. (1990, February). Women and Minorities in Management. *American Psychologist*, February, pp. 200–208.

Morrison A.M. (1992). *The New Leaders: Guidelines on Leadership Diversity*. San Francisco: Jossey-Bass.

Noe R.A. (1988). Women and mentoring: A review and research agenda. *Academy of Management Review*, No. 13, pp. 65–78.

Parasuraman S., Greenhaus J.H. (1993). Personal portrait: The life-style of the woman manager. In: E.A. Fagenson (ed.), *Women in Management: Trends, Issues and Challenges in Managerial Diversity*. Newbury Park, CA: Sage, Vol. 4, pp. 186–211.

Powell G.N. (1988). *Women and Men in Management*. Newbury Park, CA: Sage.

Powell G.N., Mainiero L.A. (1992). Cross-currents in the river of time: Conceptualizing the complexities of women's careers. *Journal of Management*, No. 18, pp. 215–237.

Richardson A., Loubier C. (2008). Intersectionality and leadership. *International Journal of Leadership Studies*, No. 3, pp. 142–161.

Riger S., Galligan P. (1980). An exploration of competing paradigms. *American Psychologist*, No. 35, pp. 902–910.

Ritchie R.J., Moses J.L. (1983). Assessment Center correlates of women'sadvancement into middle management: A 7-year longitudinal analysis. *Journal of Applied Psychology*, No. 68, pp. 227–231.

Ruble T.L., Cohen R., Ruble D.M. (1984). Sex stereotypes: Occupational barriers forwomen. *American Behavioral Scientist*, No. 27, pp. 339–356.

Sackett P.R., DuBois C.L.Z., Noe A.W. (1991). Tokenism in performance evaluation: The effects of work group representation on male-female and White-Black differences in performance ratings. *Journal of Applied Psychology*, No. 76, pp. 263–267.

Scandura T.A. (1991). *Breaking the Glass Ceiling* (Report funded under Grant E-9-M-0055). Washington, DC: U.S. Department of Labor, Women's Bureau.

Sanchez-Hucles J.V., Davis D.D. (2010). Women and Women of Color in Leadership. Complexity, Identity, and Intersectionality. *American Psychologist*, Vol. 65, No. 3, 171–181.

Snyder M. (1987). *Public Appearances/Private Realities: The Psychology of Self-Monitoring*. New York: Freeman.

State of Wisconsin (1993). *Report of the Governor s Task Force on the Glass Ceiling Initiative*. Madison: Author.

Strober M.H. (1982). The MBA: Same passport to success for women and men? In: P.A. Wallace (ed.). *Women in the Workplace.* Boston: Auburn House, pp. 25–44.

Thomas D.A., Alderfer C.P. (1989). The influence of race on career dynamics: Theory and research on minority career experiences. In: M. Arthur, D. Hall, B. Lawrence (eds.). *Handbook of Career Theory.* Cambridge, England: Cambridge University Press.

Turner C.S.V. (2002). Women of color in academe: Living with multiple marginality. *The Journal of Higher Education,* No. 73, pp. 74–93.

Twiss C., Tabb S., Crosby F. (1989). Affirmative action and aggregate data: The importance of patterns in the perception of discrimination. In: F. Blanchard, F. Crosby (eds.). *Affirmative Action in Perspective.* New York: Springer-Verlag, pp. 159–167.

U.S. Department of Labor (1991). *A Report on the Glass Ceiling Initiative.* Washington, DC: U.S. Government Printing Office.

U.S. Department of Labor, Glass Ceiling Commission (1995). *Good for Business: Making Full Use of the Nation's Human Capital* (Report of the Federal Glass Ceiling Commission). Washington, DC: U.S. Government Printing Office.

U.S. Bureau of Labor Statistics (2007). Employed women by occupation, race, and Hispanic or Latino ethnicity, 2006 annual averages. In: *Women in the Labor Force: A databook.* Washington, DC: U.S. Department of Labor. Retrieved from http://www.bls.gov/cps/wlf-table12-2007.pdf

Van der Boon M. (2003). Women in international management: An international perspective on women's ways of leadership. *Women in Management Review,* No. 18, pp. 132–147.

Wickwire K.S., Kruper J.C. (1996r). The Glass Ceiling Effect. An Approach toAssessment. *Consulting Psychology Journal: Practice and Research,* Vol. 48, No. 1, pp. 32–39.

TECHNICAL EDITOR
Anna Poinc-Chrabąszcz

PROOFREADER
Małgorzata Szul

TYPESETTER
Tomasz Pasteczka

Jagiellonian University Press
Office: ul. Michałowskiego 9/2, 31-126 Kraków
Phone: +48 12-663-23-80, Fax: +48 12-663-23-83